"The Muses Common-Weale"

Essays in Seventeenth-Century Literature, 3

"The Muses Common-Weale"
Poetry and Politics
in the Seventeenth Century

Edited by
Claude J. Summers
and
Ted-Larry Pebworth

University of Missouri Press
Columbia, 1988

Copyright © 1988 by
The Curators of the University of Missouri
University of Missouri Press, Columbia, Missouri 65211
Printed and bound in the United States of America

Library of Congress Cataloging-in-Publication Data

The Muses common-weale : poetry and politics in the seventeenth century /
edited by Claude J. Summers and Ted-Larry Pebworth.
    p. cm. —(Essays in seventeenth-century literature : 3)
    Papers originating at the Seventh Biennial Renaissance Conference held
at the University of Michigan-Dearborn, Oct. 17–18, 1986.
    Includes index.
    ISBN 0-8262-0691-3 (alk. paper)
    1. English poetry—Early modern, 1500–1700—History and criticism—
Congresses. 2. Politics and literature—Great Britain—History—17th century—Congresses. 3. Political poetry, English—History and criticism—
Congresses. I. Summers, Claude J. II. Pebworth, Ted-Larry. III. Renaissance Conference (7th : 1986 : University of Michigan-Dearborn). IV. Title:
Muses commonweale. V. Series.
PR438.P65M8   1988
821'.4'09358—dc19   88-4847
                                                                 CIP

For
Eugene Arden

Contents

Claude J. Summers and Ted-Larry Pebworth

Introduction

Michael Drayton, in his bitterly disillusioned verse epistle written during the Spanish match controversy, "To Master William Jeffreys, Chaplaine to the Lord Ambassadour in Spaine," complains of the strict censorship imposed by King James.[1] Veering self-consciously from violent satire to tender elegy, the poem is most remarkable for the way in which it uses the act of censorship and the occasion of the addressee's mission to Spain as the impetuses for its assertion of the power of poetry. With calculated disingenuity, the poet insists, "In this with State, I hope I doe not deale, / This onely tends the Muses common-weale" (ll. 23–24), and proceeds to bemoan the evil times that have beset England, tacitly blaming the nation's decline on James and Buckingham. For all the fettering of poetry by the state, Drayton remains confident of the muses' ultimate triumph:

> For tis alone the Monuments of wit,
> Above the rage of Tyrants that doe sit,
> And from their strength, not one himselfe can save,
> But they shall tryumph o'r his hated grave.
>
> (ll. 83–86)

Ostensibly submissive to state power and apparently relegating poetry to a position subordinate to the state, the poem actually defies James's authority and aggressively asserts the dominance of poetic power. Drayton's notion of a muses' common-weale is intriguing and instructive, for it creates a binary opposition of poetry and politics that it simultaneously subverts. At the same time that it privileges poetry as transcending politics, it unmistakably implicates the one in the other.

The relationship of poetry and politics in the earlier seventeenth century is complicated, for political poetry includes not merely public poems or topical works that respond to particular political questions. Nor is it limited to works that represent hierarchical relationships or address issues of power and patronage. In a real sense, all poetry—all discourse—is political, for texts inescapably both reflect and reflect on society, constructing imaginary social and political

---

1. James's censorship was intended to restrict public discussion of the Bohemian crisis. Drayton's poem was probably written in 1621 or 1622. The quotations are from *The Works of Michael Drayton,* ed. J. William Hebel, 5 vols. (Oxford: Shakespeare Head Press, 1961), 3:238–41.

1

worlds that bear some relation to actual social and political realities. Hence, politics and poetry exist in a reciprocal cultural relationship in which literature is necessarily politicized and politics unavoidably attempt to co-opt social forms, including literature, in a project of aestheticization and mystification. Although the privileging of poetry in relation to politics is deeply embedded in humanist thought and in Renaissance critical theory from Sidney's *Apology for Poetry* to Jonson's celebration of the poet's ability to "faine a *Common-wealth* [and] governe it with *Counsels,* strengthen it with *Lawes,* correct it with *Judgments,* informe it with *Religion,* and *Morals,* "[2] such privileging is impossible to sustain. The very notion assumes that poetry can be separated from politics, an assumption as disingenuous as Drayton's pretense to create a muses' common-weale removed from the real commonwealth and ostensibly irrelevant to it. As Drayton well knows, the muses' common-weale is itself a mystification of the discursive practices of Renaissance culture.

This volume is a contribution toward a better understanding of the intersections of art and ideology in seventeenth-century England. Focusing on the complex and subtle interplay of artistic technique and social context, and proceeding by means of practical criticism, the essays collected here participate in what is perhaps the most vital enterprise in current Renaissance literary scholarship, the re-contextualizing and re-historicizing of Renaissance literature. They examine the poetry of the seventeenth century in the light of that turbulent age's social and political tensions, recognizing literature as both the product and the expression of the period's discursive ideology. As self-consciously historical and cultural critical endeavors, these essays are implicitly anti-formalist, even as most of them employ traditional formalistic methodologies. That is, they all locate the texts they study in concrete historical realities, which are themselves interpretive constructs. Inevitably, the volume as a whole bears the influence of the revisionist historicism that has recently dominated literary studies of the Renaissance, yet it is by no means a narrowly conceived project of the new historicism, at least not in any programmatic or doctrinaire way.

Less polemical in tone and more firmly rooted in traditional humanist assumptions than is characteristic of the work of the vanguard new historicists and cultural materialists, the essays collected here share many presuppositions with the practitioners of what has been defined as "cultural poetics."[3] Perhaps the most crucial reflections of "cultural poetics" in this volume are the recurrent concerns with issues of power and subversion and the pervasive recognition that *politics* encompasses far more than explicitly political behavior. As history itself has been redefined as a subjective, socially constructed concept, so has politics

---

2. Jonson, *Discoveries* (1035–1037), *Ben Jonson,* ed. C. H. Herford, Percy and Evelyn Simpson, 11 vols. (Oxford: Clarendon Press, 1925–1952), 8:595.

3. The term comes from the introduction to Stephen Greenblatt's *Renaissance Self-Fashioning from More to Shakespeare* (Chicago: University of Chicago Press, 1980), the single most influential work of American new historicism.

been broadened to embrace the interactions and behaviors of individuals and groups in areas far removed from traditionally conceived political action and spheres of power, including the realms of religion, personal relationships, sexuality, self-definition, and even discourse itself. In addition, the contributors to this collection are (like the new historicists) aware that the relationship of poetry and politics is necessarily reflexive: just as politics influences poetry, so poetry affects politics. The production of literature is a cultural phenomenon that helps shape other aspects of culture.

Moreover, most of the essayists represented here are aware that even academic endeavors reflect and participate in (either openly or silently) the politics of social change. They write with an awareness that both literature and literary studies are mired in political and social realities. Nearly all the contributors to this volume would agree with Louis Montrose's formulation that "to speak today of an historical criticism must be to recognize that not only the poet but also the critic exists in history; that the texts of each are inscriptions of history; and that our comprehension, representation, interpretation of the texts of the past always proceeds by a mixture of estrangement and appropriation, as a reciprocal conditioning of the Renaissance text and our text of the Renaissance."[4] Most would probably assent to Oscar Wilde's even more radical proposition that criticism is the only civilized form of autobiography.[5]

The essays collected here can be differentiated from the more polemical exercises in the new historicism largely on the basis of their resistance to the antihumanist doctrines that posit literature as merely a product of a sociocultural system in which individual authorship is dissolved and that impose on literary production various schools of historical determinism and social dogmatism. If the debate between the new and old historicisms centers on the question of *essentialism* (the notion that man possesses a transhistorical essence or core of being) versus *social constructionism* (the notion that human nature is the product exclusively of social forces),[6] a debate that recapitulates in dialectical terms the old questions of the relative importance of heredity and environment and of social determinancy and human autonomy, most of the contributors to this volume would probably describe themselves as essentialists who nevertheless acknowledge the power of society to construct realities. That is, if the litmus test for new historical political correctness is adherence to the doctrine that there is no human essence linking contemporary and Renaissance men and women, then most of the essayists represented here are not new historicists. Rather, they are humanistically oriented critics who acknowledge the enormous power of

4. Montrose, "Renaissance Literary Studies and the Subject of History," *English Literary Renaissance* 16 (1986): 8.

5. See Wilde, "The Critic as Artist," *Complete Works of Oscar Wilde*, intro. by Vyvyan Holland (London: Collins, 1948), 1027.

6. On this debate, see Jean E. Howard, "The New Historicism in Renaissance Studies," *English Literary Renaissance* 16 (1986): 20–24.

social and historical forces and ideologies to shape individual lives and to affect individual and collective enterprises, including literary production. Some of the contributors would argue that culture largely determines the possibility of textuality, while others would stress the individual's power over the materials of his or her culture.

But it is a mistake to think of either the new historicists or the contributors to this volume (some of whom would define themselves as new historicists, others of whom would fiercely—and justifiably—resist such labeling) as monolithic. In fact, many of the critics whose work has been repeatedly described and self-consciously conceived as "new historical" successfully resist the anti-humanism on which the new historicist movement (if it can even be described as anything so organized as a *movement*) theoretically rests. As Jean Howard remarks of the group of scholars most prominently associated with the "new history," they "employ quite different methodological and theoretical perspectives."[7] Certainly, that statement is true of the contributors to this volume, which is designed not to articulate or illustrate any particular theory or methodology of historical scholarship but to illuminate through various approaches and vantage points the relationship of poetry and politics in the earlier seventeenth century.

The original, abbreviated versions of all of the essays included here were presented at the seventh biennial Renaissance conference at the University of Michigan–Dearborn, 17–18 October 1986.[8] The final versions printed here have benefited from the stimulating exchanges and responses afforded by the conference, and they intersect, reinforce, and challenge each other in significant ways. But the essays were written independently and without consultation among the authors. No topics or approaches were suggested or assigned, and none were proscribed. All the essays are historically grounded and critically focused, but they vary widely in their historical and critical presuppositions. The authors bring to bear on their topics a number of critical and scholarly techniques, from broadly based cultural criticism to formalist analysis and source study; while some are interested in new interpretations of familiar works, others attempt new syntheses of broad categories of material. Nearly all

7. Ibid., 14.

8. Selected papers from the first six Dearborn conferences have been published: those from the 1974 conference as *"Trust to Good Verses": Herrick Tercentenary Essays,* ed. Roger B. Rollin and J. Max Patrick (Pittsburgh: University of Pittsburgh Press, 1978); those from the 1976 conference on seventeenth-century prose as a special issue of *Studies in the Literary Imagination* 10, no. 2 (1977), ed. William A. Sessions and James S. Tillman; those from the 1978 conference as *"Too Rich to Clothe the Sunne": Essays on George Herbert,* ed. Claude J. Summers and Ted-Larry Pebworth (Pittsburgh: University of Pittsburgh Press, 1980); those from the 1980 conference as *Classic and Cavalier: Essays on Jonson and the Sons of Ben,* ed. Claude J. Summers and Ted-Larry Pebworth (Pittsburgh: University of Pittsburgh Press, 1982); those from the 1982 conference as *The Eagle and the Dove: Reassessing John Donne,* ed. Claude J. Summers and Ted-Larry Pebworth (Columbia: University of Missouri Press, 1986); and those from the 1984 conference as *"Bright Shootes of Everlastingnesse": The Seventeenth-Century Religious Lyric,* ed. Claude J. Summers and Ted-Larry Pebworth (Columbia: University of Missouri Press, 1987).

employ to some extent the classic "close reading" techniques of the so-called New Criticism, but with important qualifications: none views the works under consideration as autonomous entities or attempts to relate each part of a work internally to all the other parts in a closed system with no relationship to the external world or even the author. Rather, all the essays attempt to relate the works that they engage to the external social and political realities that necessarily impinge on the creation of poetry. Some of the essays explore connections between the work of several poets, while most examine the achievement of a single author or even a single work. Nearly all bring to bear on their subjects a fresh awareness of historical and political contexts, discovering by means of this juxtaposition the reciprocal nature of poetry and politics in earlier seventeenth-century England. The only criterion for selection has been that each essay contribute to the understanding and informed appreciation of the interaction of artistic technique and political context in the period.

Perhaps the most ideologically self-conscious of the essays presented here is Annabel Patterson's discussion of the political tensions and cruxes in Milton's early poems, especially *Comus* and the deceptively innocent "L'Allegro." Noting that Milton's poetry exhibits strain and disruption at precisely those moments when ideological issues—including the mystification of labor and the relationship between personal ethics and social structure—come nearest the surface, Patterson explores both the poetry and the critical responses these moments of dissonance and contradiction have occasioned. Describing Milton as "*both* a radical who wrestled all his life against hierarchy and authority *and* an elitist who believed in a meritocracy for which there were no defining categories other than those of rank and class," she urges that the search for a coherent and consistent account of Milton's political thought and behavior be abandoned. Instead of accepting uncritically Milton's masterful authorial self-construction, we should—Patterson argues—accept Milton as himself intelligently and creatively confused.

Meg Lota Brown, in an attentive reading of Donne's "The Sunne Rising," shows how Donne's opposition to social and cultural restraints on love leads to a poetic inversion of his society's power structure. Parodying practical theology as it more than half-seriously invokes casuistical principles, the poem forges a new social order by empowering love with political legitimacy. The work wittily and extravagantly compliments the speaker's lady, but it also places in perspective assumptions about power and authority. "The Sunne Rising," Brown demonstrates, both redefines the political in terms of the personal and vice versa.

Three essays are devoted to the poetry and politics of Ben Jonson. Robert Wiltenburg examines Jonson's complex relationship with Robert Cecil, earl of Salisbury, the most skilled and successful politician of his age. Examining Jonson's *Entertainment of the King and Queen at Theobalds* and some key epigrams, Wiltenburg concludes that in Jonson's view the politician and the poet are mutually dependent, but that the politician finally stands in most need of the poet and what he can provide. Similarly grounded in thorough scholarship, the essay by Robert C. Evans also focuses on the question of Jonson's poetic freedom. Evans uses the texts and contexts of epigrams to Sir Henry Neville, Sir Edward Coke, and Bishop John Williams to explore the nature of Jonson's poetic independence. The essay admirably demonstrates how an awareness of the tangled social and political life of Jonson's time can lead to an appreciation of the multivalent textures of the work and to an understanding of the ambiguities inherent in Jonson's claim to rigid independence. The poet's ambiguous relationship to the social hierarchy and patronage system of his age is also explored in the contribution by Michael Schoenfeldt. Reading two of Jonson's most accomplished and best-known poems in the context of Renaissance manners, Schoenfeldt demonstrates how the poet in "To Penshurst" and "Inviting a Friend to Supper" at once creates a place for himself in the hierarchical society and discloses its hostility to poetry. In these poems, Schoenfeldt concludes, Jonson turns "dependence into victory, subordination into authority, praise into poetry, and poetry into power."

Thomas Carew and Sir William Davenant are the subjects of the essays by Diana Benet and Michael Parker. Reading Carew's poems to or about fellow authors in the context of the writings and speeches of Kings James and Charles, Benet explores how Carew transfers his monarchs' absolutist principles into the domain of letters. The poems reflect the royal anxiety that the public voice might usurp rightful authority. But Carew's appropriation of the kings' rhetoric actually facilitates his subversion of their absolutism by positing his own muses' common-weale, an alternate order of authority governed by poets. In an informative account of Davenant's mock-epic "Jeffereidos" and the incident that occasioned it, the capture of the dwarf Jeffery Hudson by Dunkirk privateers in 1630, Michael Parker places the poem in its social and political context. Arguing that the work is a critique of Caroline foreign policy and that Hudson is a surrogate for his royal master, the essay offers a fascinating meditation on the significance of court dwarfs in the seventeenth century. Advocating a foreign policy urged by Queen Henrietta Maria but resisted by Charles, Davenant's bold burlesque is also important as a reminder of the latitude allowed to dissident voices at the Caroline court.

The contributions of Sidney Gottlieb and Donald Friedman illuminate in strikingly different ways the political meaning of Herbert's *The Temple* and Milton's *Comus* respectively. Gottlieb helps recontextualize *The Temple* by interpreting it in light of its originating circumstances. Pointing to Herbert's deep involvement in public issues and worldly affairs, Gottlieb argues that the poet's characteristic literary gesture was neither submissive retreat nor inaction. Gottlieb's approach allows him to broaden the interpretive frame of Herbert's allegorical references, to demonstrate how many of the poems are embedded in concrete social and political reality, and to reveal Herbert as a poet of greater breadth and topical relevance than is usually recognized. In contrast, Friedman concentrates on text rather than context. He begins by noting the unusual number of neologisms in *Comus* and proceeds to read the masque as an educative work that challenges the audience's ability to hear, see, and know correctly. Calling on its auditors to listen and to hear truthfully, and to open the self to the divine word by surrendering the mediations of "premeditated" structures, the masque decenters the monarch both materially and figuratively. By paying careful attention to the poem's emphasis on the importance of accurate perception, Friedman discerns in *Comus* the emergent shape of Milton's later radical Protestantism.

In their studies of Herrick and Crashaw, Achsah Guibbory and Paul Parrish reveal the political dimensions and poetic expressions of the religious controversies of the period. Guibbory demonstrates that a surprising number of the poems of *Hesperides* are concerned with issues that were the subject of intense Anglican-Puritan religious controversy. Herrick's anti-Puritanism and extreme royalism are by now well known, but what has been less apparent is the way his poetry reaffirms and re-presents a Laudian ideal of worship. During the period of the civil wars, when parliament had forbidden the use of the Anglican liturgy, Herrick, ousted from his parish by the Puritans, continued his priestly role in the "Temple" of *Hesperides*. Like Herrick, Crashaw has also traditionally been considered an apolitical poet far removed from the turmoil of his age. But Parrish points out that Crashaw's life and poetry were more complex than such a generalization admits. By reconsidering the poet's life and art in terms of commitment to private and public virtues—particularly those values conventionally aligned with gender roles—Parrish demonstrates how Crashaw's divided allegiances are mirrored in his poetry. In ways that are subtle and transforming, the poems reveal a deep commitment to feminine virtues, and their tendency to feminize power frequently results in a "cultural androgyny" that challenges received ideas as to the masculine and the feminine.

In his "new historical" analysis of Caroline panegyric, Michael Donnelly sketches the literary accommodations that emerged after the Civil War decisively disrupted the royalist semiotics of hierarchy and power. Proceeding from the premise that this semiotics represented a deeply felt belief-system, Donnelly demonstrates how the profound psychological impact of the royalist defeat is mirrored in the poetry of the period. He analyzes poems by Vaughan, Cleveland, Lovelace, and Cowley to illustrate the transformation of the attitudes that supported Stuart power.

The final two essays consider works of Andrew Marvell. Stella Revard argues that the model for "The First Anniversary" was Pindar's Pythia 1. She illuminates Marvell's poetical design and the complexity of his political statement by viewing "The First Anniversary" as a political pindaric: "a poem of celebration that does not shrink from grappling with hard issues, that looks at Cromwell, wart and all, and, while praising him as a man of destiny, acknowledges that he walks, like all human beings, in mortal flesh." Marshall Grossman, in a tightly argued essay, locates "Upon Appleton House" in a transitional moment of history, when the rentier oligarchy had not been fully displaced by an emergent bourgeois class. The poet, like his subject, may have felt himself suspended between a dying past and an inchoate future. Examining the organizing tropes of "Upon Appleton House," Grossman demonstrates how Marvell represents "an inward division of the self as a discontinuity in the relationship of individual action to providential design, choice to destiny, during a period of material historical change."

The volume concludes with excerpts from a panel discussion on "Historicism, New and Old," chaired and organized by Richard Strier and featuring Leah Marcus, Richard Helgerson, and James Turner. The panelists focus on the strengths and weaknesses—the potentials and the problems—of both the traditional and the revisionist historicisms and call for an end to the unseemly combativeness that has characterized the debate between adherents of the rival methodologies.

In their varied approaches, these essays illustrate the richness of seventeenth-century poetry and its susceptibility to a number of critical techniques. Illuminating important authors and significant texts, and revealing concretely the interaction of art and ideology in seventeenth-century literature, the essays collected here contribute to a fuller and more precise understanding of the complex relationship between text and context in the period. They focus on the cultural dynamics of literary production and offer a wealth of insights into individual works. In so doing, they help elucidate the muses' common-weale as a necessary fiction that mystifies poetry and politics alike.

✻   ✻   ✻

This book and the scholarly meeting from which it originated have profited from the great effort, wide learning, and scholarly generosity of the conference steering committee. Judith Scherer Herz, Robert B. Hinman, Leah S. Marcus, John R. Roberts, John T. Shawcross, and Gary A. Stringer helped referee the submissions to the conference and offered valuable suggestions for revision. Their contributions have been extensive, and we join the authors of the essays in expressing gratitude for their insights and devotion. It is also our happy duty to acknowledge the support of the Horace H. Rackham Graduate School of the University of Michigan and the Campus Grants Committee of the University of Michigan–Dearborn. We are particularly grateful for the support of John H. D'Arms, Dean, Rackham Graduate School, and of the following administrators at the University of Michigan–Dearborn: Sheryl Pearson, Interim Chair, Department of Humanities; Manuel A. Esteban, Interim Dean, College of Arts, Sciences, and Letters; and Eugene Arden, Vice Chancellor for Academic Affairs and Provost.

Annabel Patterson

1. "Forc'd fingers": Milton's Early Poems and Ideological Constraint

There is a reputation to be made by the scholar-critic who solves the riddle of Milton's ideology in the poems, early and late. I do not aim so high. Here, instead, is merely an introduction to the problem by way of some of the early poems whose scale makes it possible to isolate certain features, to make tests and comparisons without seeming irresponsibly selective. Although a consideration of the full enigma must include the great late poems (Is *Paradise Lost* anti- or merely post-revolutionary, is *Samson Agonistes* apolitical or subversive of the Restoration?), I shall only gesture toward those in closing. The preparatory work, I believe, should be done on the conflicting postulates about social and political relations that are manifest in Milton's canon up to and including the two-volume *Poems of Mr. John Milton* of 1645. That there *is* conflict here is witnessed to by the critical tradition, which consistently shows signs of stress or interest in the same textual locations. My focus on these is motivated, I hope, not by any sense of superior objectivity but rather by a respect for the intransigence of the problems Milton's poetry poses in an extreme and admonitory form.

These problems include at least the following questions. How do we recognize the presence in any text of concepts or sentiments for which "ideology" is an appropriate or even a necessary category, using ideology in its more restricted sense as a set of beliefs or practices that relate specifically to political or socioeconomic experience? To what extent does poetry constitute a text with its own rules, or can we assume that such recognition may legitimately be triggered by analogies with other types of discourse, such as the controversial prose pamphlets of Milton and his contemporaries? What does it mean when we have difficulty assigning an ideological component of a poem to the profile that we have drawn for its writer, whether in terms of his "intellectual growth," the biographical record of his stated "positions" and allegiances, or what we would *expect* him to think on certain issues, given what he apparently thought on related ones? What does it mean when, within a single poem, Milton seems to contradict himself, if we judge by the standards of ideological consistency? Finally, what can we learn from the gyrations performed by individual critics in an effort to produce coherence in the face of seeming contradiction?

9

I start with a tough case, *L'Allegro,* because the poem seems so innocent. Yet, in *L'Allegro,* Milton presents a view of country life that is not innocent of ideology, provided that we recognize the language of social consciousness or of its avoidance. The poem's perspective on the countryside is one that would in the eighteenth century be characterized as picturesque, that John Barrell has identified as a dark strategy in eighteenth-century landscape painting,[1] and that today we might call aestheticizing. "Streit mine eye hath caught new pleasures," l'Allegro states, "Whilst the Lantskip round it *measures.* "[2] In that verb are implicated the acts of both framing and metricalization, two related operations by which phenomena may be contained and rendered pleasurable. Further, the speaker's pleasure in rusticity is accomplished by erasing all realistic signs of agricultural labor. Not only is l'Allegro himself clearly a man of leisure, but his pleasure depends on the assumption that the rural work that his prospect includes is enjoyable to those who do it. He takes his morning walk

> While the Plowman neer at hand,
> Whistles ore the Furrow'd Land,
> And the Milkmaid singeth blithe,
> And the Mower whets his sithe,
> And every Shepherd tells his tale
> Under the Hawthorn in the dale.
> (ll. 63–68)

As he does so, the poem subtly shifts from the visual to the aural, introducing the theme of rustic musicality and tale-telling. The theme of recreation is thus transferred to the rural inhabitants of this landscape, permitting the two audiences, those inside and outside the poem, to experience rustic work as social harmony.

Another way of describing this accomplishment is to say that *L'Allegro* transmutes georgic back into the pastoral from which, at least in the Virgilian model of poetic thinking, it arose. The farmhands are individualized by names derived exclusively from Virgil's *Eclogues*—Corydon, Thyrsis, Phyllis, and especially Thestylis. I doubt that this is a neutral convention. Corydon and Thestylis both belong to Virgil's second eclogue, from which Milton would shortly choose an epigraph under which to publish his Ludlow masque. But in the original they stand for different principles *within* the pastoral matrix, Corydon for a lovelorn passivity and social uselessness, Thestylis for a silent but ironic critique of Corydon. Thestylis pounds thyme and garlic for the heat-exhausted reapers, and it

1. *The Dark Side of the Landscape: The Rural Poor in English Painting 1730–1840* (Cambridge: Cambridge University Press, 1980).

2. All citations of the early poems are from *Works of John Milton,* ed. F. A. Patterson et al., 18 vols. (New York: Columbia University Press, 1931–1942), vol. 1, pt. 1 (1931). Citations of the prose are from *Complete Prose Works,* ed. D. M. Wolfe et al., 8 vols. (New Haven: Yale University Press, 1953–1980).

is only by her appearance that rural labor can be brought to consciousness; yet for Corydon she has no more significance than the green lizards hunting for shelter from the heat. Milton remembers the "dinner . . . of Hearbs," which his Phillis dresses for his Corydon and Thyrsis; but he also presents Phillis as leaving "in haste," eager to join "With Thestylis to bind the Sheaves." The heat of the fields, so dominant in Virgil's poem, is nowhere present in Milton's. The poem continues its unlikely emphasis on rustic nonwork, with the entire village community seen primarily at recreation:

> When the merry Bells ring round,
> And the jocond rebecks sound
> To many a youth, and many a maid,
> Dancing in the Chequer'd shade;
> And young and old com forth to play
> On a Sunshine Holyday,
> Till the live-long day-light fail,
> Then to the Spicy Nut-Brown Ale.
> (ll. 93–100)

Allusions to other poems are, of course, one of the many structural features of poetry that can make it so resistant to sure solution. When allusions are *apparently* selected so as to exclude features of the pre-text that would unsettle the poetic effect *apparently* striven for, we may reasonably infer that either intentional or unintentional repression has taken place. Milton's response to Virgil is one of the signs that *L'Allegro* does indeed belong in that very large group of texts, both poetic and nonpoetic, that in some way speak to the ideology of labor. And *L'Allegro* contains other textual signs that there is a sensitive social issue here. Even the landscape is made to participate in the fiction of a naturally short workweek, including mountains "on whose barren brest / The *labouring clouds do* often rest" (ll. 73–74; italics added). Indeed, the poem itself admits to the interdependence of fiction and recreation. The transitional stage between rural life and literature, between l'Allegro's vision of the country and his midnight reading of "mask, and antique Pageantry," of Jonson and Shakespeare, is his account of the folktales that succeed the "Sunshine Holyday." The most telling of the tales told around the fireside is of

> . . . how the drudging *Goblin* swet,
> To ern his Cream-bowle duly set,
> When in one night, ere glimps of morn,
> His shadowy Flale hath thresh'd the Corn,
> That ten day-labourers could not end.
> (ll. 105–9)

Wishful thinking could hardly be clearer. The painful physical labor that Milton's rustics cannot be allowed to perform within the aesthetic frame of the poem is accomplished magically, overnight, by a friendly spirit; but even then the forbidden word *earn*, which brings to mind the specter of economics, is softened by its completion in the "Cream-bowle duly set," a symbol of a purer if archaic system of exchange. The "shadowy Flale," however, tells the secret of what imaginative alchemy is brewing here, turning base metals back into cream. Like Milton's Death in *Paradise Lost*, the idea of work, otherwise inconceivable in poetry, has been rendered "shadowy," a shape of the imagination, "if shape it might be called that shape had none."[3] This section of the poem resonates with Milton's later self-injunctions or self-reproaches, as when, in the autobiographical section of *The Reason of Church Government*, he tells himself that "ease and leisure was given thee for thy retired thoughts out of the sweat of other men" (3:232), or, still more tellingly, in the sonnet on the parable of the talents, inquires of himself whether God exacts "day-labour" of the blind. In both *L'Allegro* and the sonnet, the specific references to day labor acknowledge the long and slow but inarguably revolutionary transformation of English agrarian practice from villeinage to a wage structure; in both poems one can sense the same compressed instinct, to translate the language of the market, with its implicitly leveling forebodings, back into the language of a moral economy.

L'Allegro, then, manifests the same social attitudes that Raymond Williams, James Turner, and Anthony Low have repeatedly shown to be characteristic of the Jacobean and Caroline court and gentlemen poets. Williams speaks of the "mystification" or "mediation" by Jonson and Carew, in "To Penshurst" and "To Saxham," of the complex social relations of landownership and land use and of the "magical extraction of the curse of labour . . . achieved by a simple extraction of the existence of labourers."[4] Turner develops his suggestions into a more sharply articulated and coordinated cultural conspiracy of the landed class, designed to persuade at least themselves that their economic exploitation of the landless was natural, generous, and aesthetically pleasing. He notes the element of social control implicit and sometimes explicit in accounts of rural holidays, quoting John Taylor on "the merry Gambolls, dances and friscolls, [with] which the toyling Plowswaine, and Labourer, *once a year* were wont to be recreated, and their spirits and hopes reviv'd for a whole 12 month"[5] (italics added). Low, still more exhaustively, charts the relationship between social class and pro- or anti-georgic writing and discovers a firm connection between a sympathy for georgic values and social or religious reformism.[6]

But (and here is the first of the critical contradictions that will lead us to posit contradictions or conflicts in Milton himself) none of these critics was apparently prepared to see in *L'Allegro* what they saw elsewhere. Williams never men-

3. The absence of actual work in *L'Allegro* was first noted by Cleanth Brooks, *The Well Wrought Urn* (New York: Harcourt Brace, 1947), 61–63.

4. *The Country and the City* (1973; rpt. New York: Oxford University Press, 1975), 32.

5. *The Politics of Landscape: Rural Scenery & Society in English Poetry, 1630–1660* (Cambridge: Harvard University Press, 1979), 145–47.

6. *The Georgic Revolution* (Princeton: Princeton University Press, 1985).

tions the poem. Turner cites it only as an example of landscape composition (although he notes that its landscape is "an assembly of topographical metaphors for social class" since "'russet' and 'gray' were associated with peasant clothing, barren mountains with great men and meadows with the 'labouring' poor" [p. 38]). Low, bent on his thesis that Milton was committed to the georgic ideal all his life, a commitment that would culminate in his modeling the four-book structure of *Paradise Regained* on the *Georgics*, perceives the theme of work in *L'Allegro* as benign: "Even when Milton celebrates leisure, play, and pastoral beauty in his early poetry, he finds a place for georgic elements that most of his contemporaries would have found jarring . . . his is an imaginative and sympathetic tact for the common worker that is rare outside of satire and radical invective" (p. 307). Thus the fictional sweat of the "drudging Goblin" is cited as proof of Milton's georgic sympathies; and the remark in *Reason of Church Government* "has more to do with Christian dedication than with aristocratic pride" (p. 299).

Low, apparently, was so concerned that Milton be perceived as humane, on the right side of the social dialectic Low himself had so persuasively documented, that he could not penetrate Milton's personal system of self-justification, his use of georgic metaphor to defend the privileged position of an intellectual. No one would deny that Milton was one of the hardest workers in literary history; but it is worth noting that the author of *L'Allegro*, though well into his twenties, was not even a white-collar worker. And the poetic strategies I have just outlined are sufficiently consistent, both with each other and with aristocratic poetry of the same period, to induce in today's reader a certain creative suspicion. One might also take note of Fredric Jameson's attack on contemporary efforts to create "a labor theory of poetic value" by a misappropriation of Marxist terminology. "Writing and thinking are not alienated labor," Jameson remarks with admirable self-consciousness, and it is "fatuous for intellectuals to seek to glamorize their tasks . . . by assimilating them to . . . genuine manual labor."[7]

For Williams and Turner, themselves committed to a Marxist perspective, it would, we might guess, be essential to retain Milton's reputation as a great revolutionary thinker untarnished. Hence their silence on *L'Allegro*. Had they applied to that poem the same critical standards as were used to interpret Jonson's estate poems and those of the Caroline poets, the only conclusion would have been that *L'Allegro* (whether knowingly or unknowingly) articulated Milton's instinctive upward mobility, his desire to associate himself with a gentlemanly world of rural leisure to which his father's occupation and Horton estate had given him access. Of course, the dating of *L'Allegro* and *Il Penseroso* remains hypothetical, the two most frequent guesses being Milton's period of self-enforced post-secondary education at Horton and the still earlier period at

7. *The Political Unconscious* (Ithaca: Cornell University Press, 1985), 45.

Cambridge, proposed by Tillyard and implicitly endorsed by Christopher Hill, when the poems can be relegated to the biographically insignificant context of "academic disputation."[8]

We cannot overlook the fact that the paired poems are formally structured as dialectic. But to recognize that their debating aspect must be taken account of does not resolve the problem of their ideological content and its relation to Milton's putative views. Suppose it were argued that *L'Allegro satirizes* the social and aesthetic stances of the Caroline courtier poets, the same crew that has been thought to lie behind those irresponsible "others" rebuked in *Lycidas,* who have no better grasp of the "Shepherds trade" than to "sport with Amaryllis in the shade."[9] We would then expect, by virtue of the choice-of-life structure that the paired poems present, to find in *Il Penseroso* signs of an alternative ideology, more compatible perhaps with a notion of Milton as already noble of mind and intellectually independent. But this solution is not available. To begin with, the poems do not relate to each other as sociopolitical thesis and antithesis. If the focus of *L'Allegro* is the ideology of work and recreation in their relation to imaginative activity, the focus of *Il Penseroso* is the relation between serious mental work and a religious vocation. More disturbingly, that very seriousness is represented in language and images that would, probably in the mid-1630s and certainly in 1645, when the poem was published, have cried aloud its affinities with Laudianism. Melancholy is a "pensive Nun," her dress not only black like Spenser's Una but significantly "decent"; the "studious Cloysters" are as much clerical as academic; the "storied Windows" belong unmistakably to the controversy over images.

Is Il Penseroso, then, an aspect of Milton's younger self, whose latitudinarianism belongs to the period before religious ideology was polarized? Or could his position, like l'Allegro's, also be constructed ironically? S. R. Gardiner, who endorses the first hypothesis, *also* records that in 1633 the Star Chamber heard a significant case, in which Laud and Bishop Neile were the hardliners, condemning Henry Sherfield, member of parliament for Salisbury, for having three years earlier conscientiously destroyed the painted windows in his local parish church.[10] Had Milton heard of this case, as well he might, on which side would he and his poetry have aligned themselves? It is clear that we may not rescue Milton from the company of the Caroline poets and the high churchmen by formal recourse to debate and dialectic, unless we sever the poems entirely from their author's beliefs, desires, and habits of self-expression.

Uncertainty about Milton's own position only increases when we move, by our imputed chronology, from *L'Allegro* and *Il Penseroso* to Milton's own encounter with l'Allegro's "mask, and antique Pageantry." The *Masque at Lud-*

---

8. Hill, *Milton and the English Revolution* (New York: Viking Press, 1977), 37.
9. Compare J. W. Saunders, "Milton, Diomede and Amaryllis," *ELH* 22 (1955): 254–86.
10. *The Personal Government of Charles I,* 2 vols. (London, 1887) 1:302–4.

low, which I shall from here on refer to as *Comus,* enormously complicates even the framing of ideological questions, let alone their answers. We have, first, the fragmentation of the poetic persona or narrator into dramatic parts, known to be written for real persons with personalities and social roles of their own; yet a strong case can be made that the same lines that served for Lady Alice Egerton were equally or more appropriate to the Lady of Christ's. Second, for no other poem in Milton's canon is there so much evidence of, and historical significance accruing to, the date of composition, producing a surplus of contextual information. Yet the historical context can be made to point in diametrically opposite directions. The Castlehaven sexual scandal of 1631, the controversy over Charles's reissue of his father's *Book of Sports,* the publication of William Prynne's *Histriomastix* and his subsequent trial for treason, the revival of Fletcher's *Faithful Shepherdess* for Henrietta Maria, all in 1633, might argue that Milton had agreed to take on the multifarious social, political, and cultural project of defending the morals of the aristocracy, of representing as acceptable both aristocratic and rustic pastimes, of asserting, in defiance of Prynne, the ethical efficacy of theater, and of endorsing the queen's taste for both pastoral drama and chastity plays. Yet the same facts have been inducted into the task of proving that Milton wrote in *Comus* not a court masque but a Puritan, reformist one, a generic contradiction in terms. As Christopher Hill puts it, "a masque appears at first sight rather a surprising thing for a Puritan to write—if we can properly call Milton a Puritan at this time" (p. 45).

But beyond the expectations created by genre lie layer upon layer of conflicting textual detail. It is easy to agree, for instance, with Mary Ann McGuire that Comus and his revelers are represented as court masquers, or rather as masquers and antimasquers simultaneously, their "glistering" costumes contradicting the moral meaning of their animal heads. It is important to know that Comus's claim, "We that are of purer fire / Imitate the Starry Quire" (ll. 111–12), is an echo and hence a parody of Carew's *Coelum Britannicum,* where Jove was supposed to be "tem'ring purer fire," as Charles I was supposed to be reforming the court;[11] yet if Milton was also alluding to Jonson's *Pleasure reconciled to Virtue* the imitation cannot so easily be resolved into irony, and we may have to settle for competition. But competition of what kind? Leah Marcus, in the most persuasive and subtle argument for the revisionist theory, has asserted that the Bridgewater context of performance implied a project distinguishable from both court aesthetics and official Caroline policy on "public mirth" and that the masque was intended to encourage the earl in his resistance to Laud on matters of ecclesiastical jurisdiction that went far beyond the recreation controversy.[12] Yet even Marcus notes how resistant the text of *Comus* is to simple resolution

11. *Milton's Puritan Masque* (Athens: University of Georgia Press, 1983), 41–42.
12. *The Politics of Mirth: Jonson, Herrick, Milton, Marvell, and the Defense of Old Holiday Pastimes* (Chicago: University of Chicago Press, 1986), 169–212.

along the fault lines of the "rigidly polarized positions which fueled the *Book of Sports* controversy in 1634" (p. 190). Her response to the ideological ambiguity that results from a close examination of the court/country antithesis, or its not quite matching corollary, the choice between pleasure and virtue, is to posit Milton in the position of mediator between unacceptable extremes: "Milton's portrayal of the confrontation between the Lady and the enchanter shows considerable sympathy for a Puritan dilemma in the face of Laudian power—the plight of those who were locked into rigid rejection of all arts and pastimes because those which were most culturally conspicuous seemed tainted with political and sexual corruption. . . . Milton was interested in freeing the Lady and freeing the Puritan party more generally from such a limiting stance" (pp. 198–99). In Marcus's view of the masque, the key symbols of this mediation are the herb hæmony and the spirit Sabrina, both associated with ritual and festival.

But there are aspects of contradiction in *Comus* that remain unmediated by even this attractive hypothesis and that relate directly to the issues raised, however asymmetrically, by the dialectic of *L'Allegro* and *Il Penseroso*. Several years ago I argued that the ethical meaning of *Comus* depended on its logical relationship to the (presumably) earlier pair of poems.[13] Thus Comus and his revelers are sinister incarnations of L'Allegro, whose "jest and youthful Jollity" become in the masque "Tipsie dance and jollity" (l. 104). So too l'Allegro's invitation to "Come, and trip it as ye go / On the light fantastic toe" is transformed into Comus's "Com, knit hands, and beat the ground, / In a light fantastick round" (ll. 143–44). Comus, then, logically represents the negative view of mirth and pastime that is banished at the opening of *Il Penseroso*, while similar echoes bind together the Lady of the masque and *Il Penseroso*'s personified Melancholy.

I see now that these examples of intertextuality have to be locked into the larger historical argument as to what forms of recreation Milton allowed his masque to recommend; but at the same time this principle of self-quotation extends to the ideology of work (versus play), and hence to the issues of class and economics that intersect with the recreation controversy. There are, for example, distinct resonances of class prejudice in the Lady's response to hearing Comus's revels in the distance, as the "sound / Of riot, and ill manag'd Merriment."

> Such as the jocund Flute, or gamesom Pipe
> Stirs up among the loose unletter'd Hinds,
> When for their teeming Flocks, and granges full
> In wanton dance they praise the bounteous Pan,
> And thank the gods amiss.

> (ll. 172–76)

13. In "*L'Allegro, Il Penseroso, Comus:* The Logic of Recombination," *Milton Quarterly* 9 (1975): 75–79.

"I should be loath," she adds, "To meet the rudeness, and swill'd insolence / Of such late Wassailers" (ll. 176–78). Yet, as the audience and the Lady will shortly discover, this "ill manag'd Merriment" is not the consequence of giving rustic laborers a little free time but the ambience of the consummate courtier Comus. If this was Milton's strategy for squeezing into his poem a version of the Puritan objection to the *Book of Sports,* one should wonder why it is introduced as the Lady's *misunderstanding* of the evidence. But if we argue, as does Marcus, that this very misunderstanding points to Milton's revisionist purpose, we are still stuck with that contemptuous reference to "loose unletter'd Hinds," which prevents the formation of an anti-court argument. This phrase has provoked considerable unease in critics who have invested in Milton's early radicalism. For David Norbrook, the "opposition between literacy and traditional cultural forms is a characteristic Puritan emphasis," and the "Lady's anxieties reflect the concern amongst Welsh Puritans that the Laudian regime was defending idolatrous sports at the same time as it was placing restrictions on the preaching of the word."[14] For Hill, it is impossible to avoid the conclusion that there is "a certain class-consciousness in *Comus,*" but he draws comfort from the fact that "the Lady's aristocratic assumptions . . . are rebuked by the subsequent action" (p. 47).

It is true that the Lady quickly learns that her theory of the revelers' social class was wildly inverted and that she has fallen instead into the clutches of a court whose debaucheries confirm the darkest of Puritan hypotheses. It is true, as Hill says (p. 47), that she is led to articulate the "Country" or pastoral commonplace that courtesy "oft is sooner found in lowly sheds / With smoky rafters, then in tapstry Halls, and Courts of Princes" (ll. 322–24). But this principle is itself invoked as the result of a *second* mistake by the Lady, this time accepting the pastoral disguise of Comus for the real thing. One could argue that Comus's disguise implies a critique of the pastoral pretense of Henrietta Maria's theatricals, were it not that Milton's own theater features another pretended shepherd, who is really the Attendant Spirit, who is really Henry Lawes. Any attempt to argue that the Lady articulates Milton's views on the Caroline ideology of recreation, which in turn implies his own ideology of class, runs up against these mistakes, this instability of social apprehension and definition.

So too with the masque's allusions to the ideology of work. Anthony Low notes (p. 307), as if it were good news, that Comus himself contributes some georgic details, a glimpse of how "the labour'd Oxe / In his loose traces from the furrow came / And the swink't hedger at his Supper sate" (ll. 290–92). But this view of the charm of rustic work, when we know it will continue but need not actually observe it, is that of l'Allegro. It is consistent with Comus's happy notion that silk is produced by Nature, who "set to work millions of spinning

14. *Poetry and Politics in the English Renaissance* (London: Routledge and Kegan Paul, 1984), 254.

Worms / That in their green shops weave the smooth-hair'd silk" (ll. 714–15), a fallacy of production that matches l'Allegro's enjoyment of the fiction of the "shadowy Flail" that magically replaces ten day-laborers. It is no accident that the naturalization of labor in *Comus* focuses on the manufacture of cloth, simultaneously a reference to England's primary industry (one since the 1620s in serious economic crisis) and an allusion to a form of luxury associated with the masque as a court entertainment, since expensive theatrical costumes, or "Apparel glistering," were one of the most conspicuous forms of consumption. Yet the Lady's attack on "lewdly-pampered Luxury" is unconscious of the industrial subtext of Comus's brilliant oxymoron "green shops," his pastoralizing of a threatened class of human spinners and weavers; her refutation, no less than what she refutes, is based on the fiction that Nature is the great impersonal provider.

Most telling, perhaps, as Comus and the Lady debate the relationship between personal ethics and the social structure, is the Lady's proffer, much welcomed by Hill, of what looks like an argument for the redistribution of goods, however naturally produced:

> If every just man that now pines with want
> Had but a moderate and beseeming share
> Of that which lewdly-pamper'd Luxury
> Now heaps upon som few with vast excess,
> Nature's full blessings would be well dispenc't
> In unsuperfluous even proportion.
>
> (ll. 767–72)

But we cannot overlook the textual fact that the category of the underprivileged is restricted to "every just man," an inevitably small group, and significant to the intentionalist problematic we are pursuing in that it resembles that other Miltonic selectivity, the "wise and few."

And it cannot be disputed (although Milton's critics tend to avert their eyes at this point) that the masque ends by reinstating the class distinction of the Lady's first mistake. "Back Shepherds, back," enjoins the Attendant Spirit, "anough your play"

> Till next Sun-shine holiday,
> Here be without duck or nod,
> Other trippings to be trod
> Of lighter toes, and such Court guise
> As Mercury did first devise.
>
> (ll. 957–64)

That this echoes *L'Allegro*'s "Young and old come forth to play / On a Sunshine Holiday," only underlines the stratification built into the very form of the masque, while the echo itself permits us to notice the *differential* between the seemingly endless holiday of *L'Allegro* and the admission of *Comus* that the occasions for rustic pastimes are strictly limited. In the 1637 printed version the roughness of this social doctrine is obscured by the restoration to its original position of the Spirit's account of Elizium; perhaps, as Norbrook suggests (p. 263), because Milton had begun to feel awkward about the "conventional" ending of the Bridgewater version, or perhaps because the transcendentalized conclusion obscured from Milton himself the ideological perplexities into which he had stumbled, and which were not to be solved by making internal adjustments to a form of social discourse designed to deny the need for change.

One could extend this kind of analysis also to *Lycidas*, not least because its notorious headnote is the one discordant note in the 1645 *Poems of Mr. John Milton*. This, as Louis Martz has persuasively argued, was presented as a volume (or rather two volumes) of Cavalier poetry, under the auspices of Lawes, now identified as in charge of "his Majesties Private Musick," and associated by Moseley with Waller, in exile for his royalist plot against the Long Parliament.[15] The headnote, *retrospectively* claiming *Lycidas* as a prophecy of Laud's defeat, asserts that this John Milton was one and the same as the author of the antiprelatical pamphlets; the sociopolitical presentation of the *Poems* appears to argue the contrary. The poem itself, when read without its author's wisdom of hindsight, contains nothing that could not have been found in anticlerical satire or pastoral of the early reformation and indeed presents St. Peter's "Miter'd locks" (l. 112) as an image of reverend authority, whereas in *The Reason of Church Government* (1642) the miter had become for Milton "the badge of schisme, or the stampe of his cloven foot whom they serve . . . according to their hierarchies acuminating . . . in a cone of prelaty" (1:790). In the 1645 *Poems*, then, was Milton in search of cultural respectability, distinguishing himself from "licentious low-class antinomianism" so that he might better proceed with reform?[16] Or was he in temporary realignment with the royalist court, reacting against the Presbyterians in the Long Parliament whose restrictions had the previous year provoked the *Areopagitica*? Why, when he wrote the headnote to *Lycidas*, did he not notice, or choose to ignore, the change that had occurred in his own poetic and ecclesiastical semiotics?

Although the answers to this question seem unlikely to be forthcoming except as the expression of critical desire, one small piece of evidence, usually overlooked, bears on Milton's social feelings, his political stance on the revolution, and his retroactive view of his early poems. It is not much remarked that the period between the 1645 *Poems* and the regicide pamphlets of 1648 and following is inexplicably vacant. That is, Milton interrupted the activities of his left hand for four years, after the divorce pamphlets and *Areopagitica*. He published his poems as so far accumulated; but he wrote scarcely any others. The only

15. *Poet of Exile: A Study of Milton's Poetry* (New Haven: Yale University Press, 1980), 34.

16. Compare Thomas M. Corns, "Milton's Quest for Respectability," *Modern Language Review* 77 (1982): 769–79.

explanations given by his biographers for this lacuna in his productivity are either that he was at work on the *History of Britain* or that he was distracted by family problems, with the return of his wife and the arrival, after the fall of Oxford, of all her family.

But he did write one poem. On 23 January 1647 he sent to John Rouse, the librarian of Oxford University, a Latin ode whose subject is the 1645 *Poems*. Someone had stolen the Bodleian's copy of Milton's book, and Rouse had requested a replacement. The gesture itself is significant, given the symbolic importance of Oxford in Royalist thought and strategy during the civil war; and the poem is indistinguishable in its sentiments from those of Royalist poets who lamented the effect of the war on English culture and represented their opponents as the enemies of art and intellect. Milton wrote to Rouse:

> What god or what god-begotten man will take pity on the ancient character of our race—if we have sufficiently atoned for our earlier offenses and the degenerate idleness of our effeminate luxury—and will sweep away these accursed tumults among the citizens? What deity will summon our fostering studies home and recall the Muses who have been left with hardly a retreat anywhere in all the confines of England? Who will use the arrows of Apollo to transfix the foul birds whose claws menace us.[17]

While a trace of social criticism lingers in the attack on luxury and idleness, one cannot avoid concluding that the harpies who menace the poets of 1647 are those whose organized opposition to idleness and luxury had become a radical attack on the sociopolitical structures underwriting them. Where Milton himself stood in January 1647 was unmistakable. He sent to Rouse the new copy of the 1645 *Poems* with a message to his book that clearly applies as much to himself: "I bid you look forward to quiet rest, after you have outlived envy, in the blessed retreats provided by kind Hermes, where the insolent noise of the crowd never shall enter and the vulgar mob of readers shall forever be excluded."

To state "where Milton stood" is, of course, to beg most of the procedural cautions with which I began. The ode tempts one in this direction because its form provides no protection from the sound of its author's beliefs and desires. Given that its subject is Milton's construction of his own poetic oeuvre, his desire for its physical preservation and just estimation in a future literary history, there could scarcely be a more authorial utterance. It is precisely this concept of authorship that postmodernist criticism has outlawed; and it is a central predicament of Milton scholarship that Miltonists continue to credit the existence, and interest, of Milton as author, as the organizing principle of an oeuvre. They owe this less to their own theoretical backwardness than to Milton's supreme success in constructing an authorial ego so powerful that it has resisted all theoretical attacks and may well survive long after Roland Barthes and Michel

---

17. The translation is cited from *Complete Poems and Major Prose*, ed. M. Y. Hughes (New York: Odyssey Press, 1957), 147.

Foucault have become absorbed into the history of French intellectualism. It may be said of Milton that he invented the author-function; we are all familiar with his interposition of a self, of self-regard and self-defense, into texts purportedly designed to serve impersonal causes. There are aspects of his autobiography that deserve a richer investigation, in terms of the new psychological work on mnemonics; like his retroactive rationalization of motives (the *Second Defence* of the divorce pamphlets), Milton's habit of self-quotation implies his capacity to create an orderly self, developing in time, with clear goals and without confusions.

It is this masterly construction, I suggest, that proves the major obstacle to discerning the ideological components in Milton's poetry. We suffer from the belief (one in large part controlled by Milton himself) that anything he wrote can somehow be brought into coherent relation with everything else he wrote, that his oeuvre forms, could we but see it, a world view that is compatible with the apparent shape of his life and his career. Beyond that, a critic who embarks on ideological analysis must suffer from the disability of personal investment in the results. The presence of ideology in the text, once it becomes visible, produces an ideological reaction in the reader. Because each of us *needs* Milton to behave in every instance in accordance with our largest account of him, which in turn will have been constructed in accordance with some principle of *self*-accounting, critics who deal in ideology are often reduced to explaining things away.

It is time, perhaps, that the search for a coherent, cover-all-eventualities explanation of Milton's thought and behavior be abandoned, as an unacknowledged relic not so much of historical or biographical criticism but of the New Critical doctrines of unity and coherence. In its place, we might tentatively posit something resembling the theory of literature sketched by Pierre Macherey.[18] The most fruitful aspects of Macherey's theory have been his insistence that literature bears a special relationship to ideology, conceived in the Marxist sense as a social construct or set of beliefs that fictionalizes or mystifies socioeconomic relations; that since ideology itself represents a conflict between the fictional and the real, any text that commits itself to representing ideology will exhibit dissonances, gaps, and contradictions, symptoms of the social stresses and strains that ideology represses and that literature makes visible. It is therefore the business of criticism, Macherey believes, not to smooth out or normalize contradictions in the interest of coherence but to focus on the symptoms of a repressed sociopolitical anxiety, much as the Freudian analyst will work with the language and imagery of dreams to determine the underlying complex.

As others are beginning to perceive, there are many contradictions in Mache-

---

18. *A Theory of Literary Production,* trans. Geoffrey Wall (London: Routledge and Kegan Paul, 1978).

rey's theory, not least in its attempt to fuse a materialist and hence impersonalist theory of production with a psychoanalytic theory of interpretation, albeit one that Macherey reduces to a metaphor. Nor is it clear from Macherey's elliptical pronouncements how one distinguishes texts deliberately addressed to ideological issues, such as Balzac's novels, from those that unwittingly express them; the notion that it is the defining function of literature to give formal representation to ideology and so to create an aesthetic distance from it is simultaneously too broad to stand up to close inspection and curiously reminiscent of the New Critical dogma of disinterestedness. Lastly, as Terry Eagleton remarks, "it is not invariably true that a text is thrown into grievous internal disarray by its relation to ideology, or that such a relation consists simply in the text's forcing ideology up against the history it denies."[19]

But it does seem to be true that, to repersonalize the discourse, *Milton's* poetry exhibits the formal signs of internal strain and disruption at precisely those points where the ideas we tend to call ideology come almost to the surface. If we were to permit the concept of repression in Macherey's theory to have more than metaphorical force, though without limiting it to Freudian preoccupations, it might very well serve for Milton. For Milton was, as the struggles of his readers surely testify, *both* a radical who wrestled all his life against hierarchy and authority *and* an elitist who believed in a meritocracy for which there were no defining categories other than those of rank and class. Elitist radical, the last contradiction that this essay will articulate: despite its seeming reductiveness, it offers us a chance to move beyond apologetics to an acceptance of Milton as himself intelligently, instructively, confused.[20] What freedom might it give us in tackling the elusive political sympathies of *Paradise Lost,* including its sexual politics? As for *Samson Agonistes,* its analysis might begin anew with the language of its first stage direction, which may now, in its condensed allusion to the ideologies of work and recreation, sound more interesting than it did when we began:

> Samson made Captive, Blind, and now in the Prison at Gaza, there to labour as in a common work-house, on a Festival day, in the general cessation from labour, comes forth . . . to sit a while and bemoan his condition.

19. *Criticism and Ideology: A Study in Marxist Literary Theory* (London: NLB, 1976), 93.

20. Since this essay was completed, Michael Wilding's *The Dragon's Teeth* (Oxford: Clarendon, 1987), 7–27, has made a new attempt to disprove the argument of Cleanth Brooks with respect to the erasure of work in *L'Allegro* and to reestablish Christopher Hill's claim for Milton's early radicalism. The strain of the exercise speaks for itself.

Meg Lota Brown

2. "In that the world's contracted thus": Casuistical Politics in Donne's "The Sunne Rising"

In 1608, Donne wrote to Sir Henry Goodyer that the highest titles and distinctions are meaningless unless those who hold them "be so incorporated into the body of the world, that they contribute something to the sustentation of the whole."[1] Donne himself sought such an incorporation into the body of the world, particularly the political world of power and position for which he was groomed at university, at the Inns of Court, under the military command of men who were themselves placed near the vortex of power, and as secretary to Sir Thomas Egerton, a central figure in Elizabethan and Jacobean government. For fourteen years after his secret marriage to Ann More, however, Donne's efforts to secure employment and to take an active part in political life were unavailing. "I would fain do something," he confided to Goodyer; "to this hour I am nothing, or so little, that I am scarce subject and argument good enough for one of my own letters."[2]

Assimilation into society was not simply a financial necessity for Donne. He believed that those who do not participate in the political community violate both social and divine order: "idle and unprofitable persons; persons of no use to the . . . State," he preached in 1626, disrupt "the order that God hath established in this world."[3] After his marriage, Donne was well aware that his being "of no use to the . . . State" was not the only way in which he violated "the order that God hath established in this world." By seventeenth-century standards, his elopement was both politically and socially disruptive. Ilona Bell points out that marrying a minor without her father's consent challenged "the patriarchal social structure on which all the country's laws were founded."[4] That Donne was a

1. John Donne, *Letters to Severall Persons of Honour,* ed. Charles Edmund Merrill (New York: Sturgis and Walton, 1910), 44. For their generous and helpful criticism of this essay, I would like to thank Joel Altman, Michael Schoenfeldt, and Jack Teagarden.

2. Ibid.

3. John Donne, *Sermons,* ed. George R. Potter and Evelyn Simpson (Berkeley: University of California Press, 1953–1962), 7:149.

4. "'Under Ye Rage of A Hott Sonn & Yr Eyes': John Donne's Love Letters to Ann More," in *The Eagle and the Dove: Reassessing John Donne,* ed. Claude J. Summers and Ted-Larry Pebworth (Columbia: University of Missouri Press, 1986), 44. Although the dating of many of the *Songs and Sonets* is problematic, I have inferred that "The Sunne Rising" was written after

member of the middle class, while Ann was of the gentry, further undermined "the hierarchical norms of the time."[5]

Donne's opposition to cultural constraints on love, along with his political ambition to "contribute something to the sustentation of the whole," resonates in "The Sunne Rising." The poem establishes a new order that places love at the center of the generative power from which Donne was excluded. Elevating love above sociopolitical demands, "The Sunne Rising" playfully enacts the defiance of authority that Donne's marriage expressed, and it invests the lover's motives with a legitimacy that they were never accorded in fact. The poem justifies love in terms of the same political order and structures of power that Donne's elopement was seen to subvert. His persona wittily challenges the value of social status and power only to appropriate them and to claim the crowning position in the political hierarchy. One of the ways in which he effects such an appropriation is by parodying the principles and methods of casuistry or practical theology.

Because casuistry offers a means of adjudicating the conflicting claims of self and law, it is a useful vehicle for the speaker's assertion that conventional laws of behavior—arising at daybreak and pursuing distinction in worldly activities—do not apply to lovers. Casuistry is a system of defining, interpreting, and applying ethics according to specific cases. It attempts to mitigate tensions that arise from political or moral antinomies. Above all, it teaches that no authority (whether the Pope, the king, or, in Donne's case, the sun) is so absolute that it can exercise legitimate power in disregard of circumstances.[6] When public policy unduly restricts private action, casuistry affords equitable sanctions that protect the integrity of the individual. William Perkins acknowledged the political utility of casuistry when he termed its practitioners "Embassadours of reconciliation."[7] While recognizing the need for collective order and shared standards of conduct, casuists accommodate legal and ethical judgments to the exception. In "The Sunne Rising," Donne's persona comically exploits this accommodation; he argues for a new definition of authority, claiming that his exceptional love constitutes the standard against which political structures and social values should be measured.

Donne's marriage to Ann in 1601. A number of critics, the most recent of whom is Arthur F. Marotti in *John Donne: Coterie Poet* (Madison: University of Wisconsin Press, 1986), 156–57, have argued that line 7 ("Goe tell court-huntsmen that the king will ride") alludes to James and his well-known penchant for the hunt.

5. William Zunder, *The Poetry of John Donne: Literature and Culture in the Elizabethan and Jacobean Period* (Sussex: Harvester Press, 1982), 42.

6. Two primary tenets of casuistry are that no precept should be abstracted from experience and that circumstances determine the ethical and legal status of any act. Donne advocates both tenets in several of his works. *Biathanatos* insists on the relativity of natural and scriptural laws. *Pseudo-Martyr* asserts the relativity of canon law and papal authority; and Donne's sermon on Esther 4:16 makes the same argument in terms of positive law and monarchical control.

7. *The Whole Treatise of Cases of Conscience,* ed. Thomas Merrill (Nieuwkoop: B. De Graaf, 1966), 83.

Although the political reversal in "The Sunne Rising" proceeds from the speaker's abuse of casuistry, challenging authority is common among practical theologians. Casuistical deliberation is predicated on the assumption that legislators are fallible and that laws or conventions exert contradictory demands. Fundamental to casuistical deliberation is the belief that conclusions drawn in conscience have greater legitimacy than institutionally mediated truths; as a result, the judgments of practical theologians often controvert the claims of established authority.[8] Donne recognized the potential for subversion in such beliefs, and his "Sunne Rising" is a playful realization of that potential. As Pascal's *Provincial Letters* makes clear, Donne was not alone in using casuistical principles to undermine conventional authority. Nevertheless, in the early 1600s, practical theology was most often the resource of conservatives and moderates. It provided the individual with an invaluable means of measuring his obligations and governing his actions when confronted with the political controversies of the period.

Indeed, the ability of casuistry to address the political and religious perplexities that beset seventeenth-century England accounts for the proliferation of published cases of conscience during Donne's lifetime and the thirty years that followed.[9] Responding to the conflicting claims of authority advanced by Catholics, Anglicans, Puritans, Pope and monarch, foreign and domestic governments, casuists frequently assessed the extent of an individual's duty to civil and ecclesiastical powers. During the Armada threat, for example, a casuistical tract entitled "Whether catholics in England might take up arms to defend the queen and country against the Spaniards?" argued that Philip's motive for attacking was political gain and not defense of the Faith. The author of the tract, a priest named Wright, reasoned that since Christians owe political allegiance to the State and spiritual allegiance to the Church, and since Spain's chief objective was not religious, English Catholics were bound in conscience to resist the foreign aggressor. Similarly, Donne's *Pseudo-Martyr* examines why Catholic subjects should take the Oath of Allegiance to their Anglican king, and Bishop Sanderson's "Case of the Engagement" tries to reconcile a Royalist's conscience with the 1649 oath of loyalty to parliament. In a period when competing powers warned that obedience to another could imperil one's life and livelihood, cases of conscience were often concerned with political and physical survival.

The speaker of "The Sunne Rising" is also concerned with problems of allegiance, although his account of political and physical well-being is hardly that of Wright or Sanderson. Parodying the methods with which Renaissance casu-

---

8. More specifically, the primacy of conscience directed by Scripture, reason, and faith is a tenet of Protestant casuistry. Catholic casuists are more authoritarian and usually advise the individual to submit to the judgments of Church officials. See, for example, Martin Azpilcueta's *Enchiridion sive Manuale Confessariorum et Poenitentium* (Antwerp, 1566).

9. A. E. Malloch, "John Donne and the Casuists," *Studies in English Literature* 2 (1962): 58, notes, "More than six hundred [cases of conscience] appeared between the years 1564 and 1660."

ists decided among conflicting demands, he constructs a mock case of conscience that pits worldly obligations against the claims of love. Since neither sentiment nor appetite warrants the casuistical dispensation that he needs in order to stay in bed, he pretends to be caught in a moral dilemma of conflicting duties. Casuists define such a dilemma as "perplexity," and they maintain that it can be resolved only by determining which claim has greater force.[10] According to the directives of practical theology, the speaker must compare the purpose and repercussions of each conflicting obligation, and he must define the lovers' circumstances in order to determine how they constitute an exception to general laws of conduct. His manipulation of casuistical sanctions transforms the futile enterprise of commanding the sun into a sophistic coup. Arguing that his beloved is "all States," Donne's persona can become "incorporated into the body of the world" as he is incorporated into her body politic. He "proves" not only that the lovers may remain in bed with impunity but also that their doing so enriches the sublunary world with new criteria of value. The intensely private love that left Donne politically dispossessed becomes in "The Sunne Rising" a touchstone for public power and prestige.

Because the sun is both an agent of quantification—demarcating hours, seasons, and climates—and instigator of the day's pursuits, the speaker personifies it as the legislator of conventional laws of activity and measurement. Against the sun's summons to arise, the speaker poses love's obligations. "All alike," love and its laws of behavior conflict with the sun's laws of change and difference. The distinctions that the world seeks in its diverse activities are already realized in the lovers; consequently, their duty is to remain together and cultivate the value that proximity enables. In the course of the poem, Donne's persona contracts the sun's province from public summoner to private sanctioner, just as casuists contract the focus of general law to the individual.

Opening with a malediction forbidding morning, the speaker reproves the sun for violating its jurisdiction.

> Busie old foole, unruly Sunne,
>   Why dost thou thus,
> Through windowes, and through curtaines call on us?
> Must to thy motions lovers seasons run?
>   Sawcy pedantique wretch . . .
>
> (ll. 1–5)[11]

Differentiation is the sun's domain. Its motion measures change, and it regulates a society whose hierarchies of title, vocation, and age ("Schoole boyes," "prentices," "Court-huntsmen," and "the king") depend on the same laws of differ-

---

10. For Donne's familiarity with the technical terms that casuists use to distinguish moral problems, see his *Letters*, p. 74; and *Sermons*, 5:222.

11. *The Complete Poetry of John Donne*, ed. John T. Shawcross (Garden City, N.Y.: Anchor, 1967), 93. All citations of Donne's verse are to this edition.

entiation that the sun occasions. But love's law, the speaker remonstrates, is unification; the constancy of the speaker and his lover exempts them from the activities that time regulates. Consequently, the sun exceeds its authority when it enjoins them to arise at daybreak. It ignores the casuistical precept that legislators must accommodate laws to exceptional circumstances. In its narrow-minded insistence on convention, the "pedantique" sun is remiss, not the lovers.

Paradoxically, the pedantic sun is also unruly. It is "sawcy" in both Renaissance uses of the term: lewd, and insolent to superiors. An unruly voyeur, it spies on the lovers through their bed curtains. Since the speaker later argues that love exerts a greater claim in his case of perplexity, the sun is also unruly for infringing on a higher law. In calling the sun impertinent, the first line of the poem anticipates the speaker's casuistical strategy: his objective is not only to establish that lovers are exempt from the convention of arising at daybreak but also to prove that their remaining in bed is of greater merit, and therefore a higher obligation, than are the world's matutinal activities.

To defend love's superiority, Donne's persona depicts as insignificant the activities that the sun instigates. In a list of those over whom the sun does have jurisdiction, the speaker trivializes society's pursuit of wisdom, wealth, title, and authority by reducing its practitioners to dilatory schoolchildren, recalcitrant apprentices, gossiping courtiers, and an idle king.

> . . . goe chide
> Late Schoole boyes, and sowre prentices,
> Goe tell Court-huntsmen that the king will ride . . .
>
> (ll. 5–7)

The list of characters progresses hierarchically from schoolboys to king before culminating in the bathetic line, "Call countrey ants to harvest offices." Juxtaposing the king to insects deflates the dignity of rank, and the reference to harvest offices of ants recalls and further diminishes the offices that society "harvests." As the Puritan casuist William Perkins states, "The necessitie of the lawe ariseth out of the necessitie of the good end thereof."[12] Minimizing the moral force of the sun's demands, Donne's persona calls into question the "good end," and therefore the "necessitie," of the activities to which the world attaches value.

Thus, the first stanza initiates a reversal in the status of private love and public authority. In Donne's world, the poet's unruly marriage resulted in his exclusion from power and prestige, but in the world of the poem it is the lover who excludes, discredits, and commands representatives of authority. A political outsider, Donne could only watch from a distance the privileges and privileged at court, but in his poem, the sun is the outsider, a voyeur of the privileged lovers. The reversal is particularly striking when one considers that the sun was a Re-

---

12. *A Discourse of Conscience,* ed. Thomas Merrill (Nieuwkoop: B. De Graaf, 1966), 34.

naissance emblem of sovereignty. "In the reign of James I, the image was used to promote the absolutist pretensions of the monarchy."[13] The speaker's efforts to undermine the sun's authority, then, appear to be an assault on absolutism. William Zunder remarks that Donne's poem shatters the idea of sovereignty "and with it the principle of social hierarchy."[14] I would argue, however, that in the speaker's fantasy of power, the political structures remain intact; the difference is that they derive their authority from the lovers rather than from the sun. In the remaining stanzas, Donne's persona appropriates rather than subverts monarchical control. His objection is not to absolutism; instead, it is to the subordination of his absolutist love to the lesser claims of a "Busie old foole."

"The Sunne Rising" is not the only one of Donne's lyrics that privileges love in political terms. In an elaborate and witty comparison of lovemaking to warfare, the speaker of "Elegie: Loves Warre" describes intercourse as a civic act of heroism; those who beget soldiers, he argues, perform a "More glorious service" to the state than any other patriots. Like "The Sunne Rising," the elegy playfully grants political legitimacy to lovers who remain in bed. Less jocular, but claiming an even greater entitlement, is the speaker of "The Anniversarie." Donne's persona celebrates the ennobling power of love, perhaps in response to objections about the disparity between Donne's own social status and Ann's.[15] Regardless of their worldly rank, the lovers are "Prince enough in one another." Indeed, the speaker insists that they are sovereign even over the forces of time, change, and decay;[16] and he repeatedly describes their union—"our raigne"—in monarchical terms. "Here upon earth, we'are Kings, and none but wee / Can be such Kings, nor of such subjects bee." Even the slight qualification, "Here upon earth," disturbs the absolutist speaker. He seems to regret that in heaven they will no longer be peerless: "And then wee shall be throughly blest, / But wee no more, then all the rest." As in "The Sunne Rising," Donne's persona attempts to privilege love above "all the rest," in part by appropriating monarchical authority.

Donne's creation of "affairs of state" reaches its wittiest climax in stanzas 2 and 3 of "The Sunne Rising." Having repudiated the world's endeavors and its criteria of value in the opening lines, his speaker attempts to prove love's greater worth in stanza 2. He begins by belittling the sun's power, thus playing on his own casuistical claim to a "stronger" law.

> Thy beames, so reverend and strong,
> Why shouldst thou thinke?
> I could eclipse and cloud them with a winke. . . .
>
> (ll. 11–13)

13. Zunder, *Poetry of John Donne*, 39.
14. Ibid., 41.
15. Bell, "'Under Ye Rage,'" 46, suggests that Donne wrote "The Anniversarie" for Ann before their marriage.
16. The speaker's protestations of permanence, however, are interwoven with references to destruction, decay, graves, corpses, death, tears, divorce, treason, and "True and false feares."

The separation of love and the world begun in stanza 1 is now a veritable divorce. To emphasize his autonomy from the mundane conventions that the sun enforces, Donne's persona reifies the metaphor of the lovers' microcosm and likens himself to a separate world with the power to eclipse the sun. Further, his suggestion in line 15 that his lover's eyes might blind "thine" is more than a Petrarchan tribute; it implies that the beloved is a stronger sun, one that has the jurisdiction (unlike the speaker's "unruly" interlocutor) to compel him to "rise" to love's activities. But the speaker's claim of exemption from sublunary rules comes perilously close to solipsism when he threatens simply to shut his eyes; eclipsing the sun may dramatize his claims to a greater law, but refusing to acknowledge the sun's demand would only stultify his defense. If the speaker were truly able to disregard social and political obligations, he would never have felt the need to vindicate his position.

Significantly, Donne's persona does not carry out his boast, explaining, "I would not lose her sight so long." If he denies the sun by "winking," he will literally lose sight of his lover; more importantly, if he denies the standards of differentiation that the sun personifies, he will deprive himself of any evaluative means of championing love's greater claims. He can measure love only in terms of the political distinctions that he has disparaged throughout the first half of the poem. Consequently, the volta at the end of line 14 signals a reversal in the speaker's argument: the second half of the poem restores the value of social distinctions. Once trivialized, kings and the world's "harvest" (now promoted to a harvest of "spice and Myne") are expressive of love's properties. Once "all alike," love is now defined in terms of divisions: geographical ("both th'Indias"), chronological (all that the sun sees between "to morrow late" and "yesterday"), and hierarchical ("those kings whom thou saw'st"). But while the speaker has altered the terms of his exceptional status, he has not rendered his case any less exceptional. On the contrary, love is greater than the sum of its newly acknowledged parts; it synthesizes the power, wealth, and luxury of all the rulers, gold, and spices that are dissipated throughout the earth.

> Looke, and to morrow late, tell mee,
> Whether both th'Indias of spice and Myne
> Be where thou leftst them, or lie here with mee.
> Aske for those Kings whom thou saw'st yesterday,
> And thou shalt heare, All here in one bed lay.
> (ll. 16-20)

While Donne's persona asserts in stanza 1 that he and his lover are exempt from the convention of arising at daybreak and cultivating worldly values, by stanza 3 he argues that they are the locus of value itself. All that society profits by and esteems is embedded in the bedded lovers ("All here in one bed lay"). Since the world's benefits are only simulacra of love's paradigm, conventional criteria of value must be amended: the speaker and his beloved become society's gauge of distinction, and not vice versa. "Princes doe but play us; compar'd to this, / All honor's mimique; All wealth alchimie." A model for kings, these lovers are not the "idle and unprofitable persons; persons of no use to the . . . State" that Donne admonishes against in his 1626 sermon. Together, the lovers hypostatize the Ideal; consequently, they have a greater obligation to remain in bed than to arise and pursue the counterfeit distinctions of wealth and honor. Their pretended case of perplexity is thus resolved: love's law exerts a greater claim than does the unruly sun. With a witty reversal of Donne's own experience, love becomes the means whereby they are "so incorporated into the body of the world, that they contribute something to the sustentation of the whole." As exemplars, they benefit the princes who play them and the society that emulates them.

But clearly Donne's resolution is sophistically achieved. His persona pushes to an extreme the casuistical accommodation of exceptional circumstances in order to argue for an ontological reversal that makes love the standard for a dimly analogous world. Moreover, he reasons speciously from adjunct to subject—from "love constitutes all the world's value" to "love constitutes all the world"—in order to transform the reified microcosm of lines 11–13 into the macrocosm that the sun orbits. The new ontology allows the sun the same retirement that the speaker is allowed: the sun must illuminate the world, but since love constitutes a superior world, the sun can fulfill its responsibility simply by shining on the lovers. Like them, it can combine duty and pleasure by remaining in the bedroom.[17]

> Thou sunne art halfe as happy'as wee,
> In that the world's contracted thus;
> Thine age askes ease, and since thy duties bee
> To warme the world, that's done in warming us.
> Shine here to us, and thou art every where;
> This bed thy center is, these walls, thy spheare.
>
> (ll. 25–30)

Of course the sun *does* illuminate them. It has done so throughout the poem. But its originally censorious beams are now invested with new significance. Casuists allow immunity from the law as long as one can prove "the undoubted tolerance by authority of [the law's] neglect."[18] By "obeying" the speaker's command to "Shine here to us," the sun not only tolerates the lovers' neglect of conventional activities but also ratifies love's claim to a stronger law. According to the speaker's terms, the sun's shining is a tacit endorsement of love's new ontology. With the submission of authority to his commands, Donne's persona completes his political inversion and appropriation of power.

---

17. Line 25 has the only overt mention of pleasure in the poem. Since casuists insist that intention is crucial to establishing the ethical status of an act, Donne's speaker avoids the obvious issue of sensual gratification and defends remaining in bed as a moral duty.

18. Kenneth E. Kirk, *Conscience and Its Problems* (London: Longmans, Green, 1927), 270.

But the authority that submits to the speaker's conclusions is as bogus as the logic from which the conclusions are deduced. Much of the speaker's sophistic wit results from his personification of the sun as "lex loquens." Throughout the poem, he appeals to the sun as his judge, attributing to it the faculties for weighing evidence ("Looke, and . . . tell mee"; "Aske for . . . and thou shalt heare") and the casuistical ability to determine exceptional circumstances. Although every one of his imperatives directs the sun to do exactly what it always does, the speaker treats its natural shining as a rational response. His arguing with and pretending to "persuade" an insentient object dramatize one of the many characteristics of casuistry that is vulnerable to abuse: the practical theologian must be his own objective judge. Cases of conscience are private deliberations in which the individual must argue both sides of a dilemma, even if he is predisposed to one.

It is appropriate that the speaker addresses a Ptolemaic sun. Donne was well aware of "the new philosophy," and his self-conscious sophistry is all the more apparent in that it assumes a cosmology that has been called into doubt. (Once again, the speaker's "judge" is as false as his arguments.) More importantly, the orbital hub of the Ptolemaic sun is earth, and contracting the sun's center from all of humanity to only the lovers is emblematic of casuistry's contracting a general law to the necessities of the individual. The same contraction of public to private is evident in the speaker's imagery. In stanza 2, for example, kings and kingdoms, gold and spices crowd into the lovers' bed. Vast distances ("both Th'indias") are telescoped into one room. Even when Donne's persona dispatches the sun to compare the public and private worlds, his repetition of "here" redirects its focus to the lovers: "lie here with me"; "Shine here to us"; "And thou shalt heare, All here in one bed lay." The Ptolemaic sun must orbit the lovers because "the world's contracted" to them. Arguing that even the laws of astronomy must be amended in his case, the speaker burlesques casuists who redirect the focus of general law to particular circumstances.

Indeed, the casuistical terms in which the speaker casts his argument are false from the start. By pretending to be caught in a case of perplexity, he can exploit the equitable sanctions of casuistry and at the same time posture as one who is concerned not with defending sensuality but with submitting to a higher law. Part of the humor of "The Sunne Rising" is that its elaborate and complex argument is simply a disguise for the speaker's motive of pleasure. His comic maneuvering of casuistical principles enables him to legislate his own gratification, to feign moral and political legitimacy for staying in bed.

But the speaker's wittiest distortion of casuistry is in forcing its principles of compromise to support his absolute claims. His efforts to make love a permanent and universal standard far exceed the province of practical theology. Donne's persona embraces casuistical assumptions about the relativity of right action because they afford him the opportunity to challenge convention; but he then endows love with the absolute authority that casuists insist only Scripture possesses. As in "A Valediction: of the booke" and "Twicknam Garden," the speaker argues that his love is both a model of instruction and a standard for judgment. The speaker of the latter poem asserts that, unlike women's tears, his are genuinely expressive of love, so he offers them as touchstones for others.

> Hither with christall vyals, lovers come,
>   And take my teares, which are loves wine,
>   And try your mistresse Teares at home,
> For all are false, that tast not just like mine.
>   (ll. 19–22)

The hyperbolic speaker portrays himself as a standard of judgment that will benefit mankind, if not womankind. Similarly, "A Valediction: of the booke" maintains that in the lovers' "Annals" will be "Rule and example found" for posterity; the chronicle of their relationship will provide an authoritative model for "all whom loves subliming fire invades." "The Canonization," too, presents its lovers as "a patterne" that "all shall approve." As in "The Sunne Rising," Donne's persona credits his love with the unconditional authority that casuists attribute solely to God's Word.

The speaker of "The Sunne Rising," then, invokes the methods and assumptions of practical theology in order to defend a position that casuistry finally cannot accommodate. Practical theologians attempt to mitigate the conflict between general law and anomalous situations without violating the integrity of either. But Donne's persona tries to dispel all conflict by becoming the law itself, like the kings to whom his attention returns in every stanza. With wit that dazzles the sun, he appropriates that monarchical figure's power, constructing his own "Monarchy of wit." Moreover, while casuistry proceeds by qualification, the speaker insists on absolutes: "all States, and all Princes"; "All honor's mimique; All wealth alchemie"; "All here in one bed lay." The insistent "all" recalls the equally insistent "nothingness" of Donne's self-description in his letters,[19] just as the speaker's opening banishment of the sun recalls Donne's own exclusion from the court. If not in fact, then in fiction, the poet achieves an authoritative status that legitimates his love in social and political terms, an achievement that depends in part on his playful abuse of practical theology.

To observe that Donne distorts casuistical principles, however, is not to say that casuistry does not inform his arguments. Like any parody, "The Sunne Rising" reflects its casuistical model clearly enough to play upon the contrast. Donne poses a mock case of conscience, but his premises are rooted in legitimate assumptions of practical theology: general laws are not always applicable to idiosyncratic experience; moral precepts are not always consonant, and when they conflict, the lesser obligation ceases to bind; ignoring a law is justified when authority tolerates its neglect. Despite their misapplication, casuistical formulas are central to the speaker's argument.

19. See Marotti, *John Donne: Coterie Poet*, 156.

Donne's parody of casuistical procedures ends by inverting even the customary objective of casuists: the final achievement of a case of conscience is that it enables action, but the final achievement of "The Sunne Rising" is that it enables inaction. Neither the lovers nor the sun should rise. Ironically, the speaker's exploitation of practical theology and his ontological transformation simply confirm, in effect, the status quo. The action at the end of the poem is exactly what it was at the beginning. The sun still shines, the lovers remain in bed, and society still awakens to its quotidian endeavors. But the speaker has invested each of these circumstances with new significance by manipulating casuistical sanctions. He has forged a new political order in which lovers govern rather than obey society's laws. He has empowered love with political legitimacy and, in the process, has delivered an extravagant compliment to his own lover.

Robert Wiltenburg

3. "What need hast thou of me? or of my *Muse?*": Jonson and Cecil, Politician and Poet

For many readers of early seventeenth-century poetry, now as then, there may be something faintly offensive in the conjoining of "poetry" with "politics." Anyone who accepts, as Ben Jonson did, Sidney's idea of the high calling of the poet to deliver to us a golden world transcending our own brassy one of nature, experience, and history,[1] and who is accustomed to using *policy* and *politician* as terms of suspicion or abuse,[2] may well feel some irreconcilability. What should poets have to do with politicians? With most members of the governing elites Jonson can readily make his peace and fulfill his self-imposed cultural purpose: academics may be praised for their learning and industry, soldiers for their steadfast courage, magistrates for their wisdom and probity, noblewomen for their "high huswifery," the landed gentry for fulfilling their traditional obligations, patrons for their generous and disinterested love of the muses, and the king and his court as the patterns of all the rest. Not that Jonson can be entirely complacent about these transactions: inevitably, there will be some disproportion between his golden praises and their brassy objects; as he playfully "confesses" to his friend Selden:

> (As every Muse hath err'd,
> And mine not least) I have too oft preferr'd
> Men past their termes, and prais'd some names too much,
> But 'twas with purpose to have made them such.
> Since, being deceiv'd, I turne a sharper eye
> Upon my selfe, and aske to whom? and why?

---

1. Sir Philip Sidney, *An Apology for Poetry,* in G. Gregory Smith, *Elizabethan Critical Essays* (Oxford: Clarendon Press, 1904), 1:156. On the relation of Jonson's practice to Sidney's idea of poetry, see Jonathan Z. Kamholtz, "Ben Jonson's *Epigrammes* and Poetic Occasions," *Studies in English Literature* 23 (1983): 94; Harris Friedberg, "Ben Jonson's Poetry: Pastoral, Georgic, Epigram," *English Literary Renaissance* 4 (1974): 112, 117; Richard C. Newton, "'Ben./Jonson': The Poet in the Poems," in *Two Renaissance Mythmakers: Christopher Marlowe and Ben Jonson,* ed. Alvin Kernan (Baltimore: Johns Hopkins University Press, 1977), 85.

2. The *OED* notices *policy* in a pejorative sense as early as 1587; *politician,* 1628. But as Mario Praz has observed in *The Flaming Heart* (Gloucester, Mass.: Peter Smith, 1966), "by the middle of the sixteenth century *policy* is a synonym to 'sleight, trick'" (p. 104); "*politician* is already found with a bad connotation in Nashe" (p. 108); and "*politic . . .* came to be an equivalent of *Machiavellian*" (p. 99).

And what I write? and vexe it many dayes
Before men get a verse: much lesse a Praise;
So that my Reader is assur'd, I now
Meane what I speake: and still will keepe that Vow.³

These are the venial sins of the poetry of praise and do not seriously threaten the public poet's function of praising the great in order to encourage them to be good. Indeed, the quoted passage, while focusing on a real problem, comically exaggerates; Jonson is here having some rare fun with his rare friends. But what can he make of the politician, the "professional" statesman who pursues no recognized profession or calling, who maintains no hereditary dignities or responsibilities, who is concerned not to serve some clear moral imperative but to serve the state—often through intrigue, rumor, spies, and the deliberate manipulation of patronage, friendship, truth, and even justice itself? The mere pretenders to such "statecraft" can be simply laughed off: Sir Politic Would-Be, with his *"ragion del stato,"* or the "ripe" young statesmen growing "in every street" of "The New Crie" who

talke reserv'd, lock'd up, and full of feare,
Nay, aske you, how the day goes, in your eare.
Keepe a *starre*-chamber sentence close, twelve days:
And whisper what a Proclamation sayes.
(*Epig.* XCII, 17–20)

Others, like the spies of Epigram LIX, who "are lights in state, but of base stuffe," burn themselves down, "Stinke, and are throwne away." Still others, like the Pooly and Parrot of "Inviting a Friend to Supper" (*Epig.* CI), must be deliberately excluded before the wise and the good may enjoy their "innocent" "mirth" and "liberty." Such politasters do not seriously test Jonson's attitude toward politics. For this, we may turn to his relationship with and poems concerning Sir Robert Cecil, the first earl of Salisbury, the most skilled and powerful politician of his time. The case is important not only because of Cecil's prominence and complexity but also because Jonson chose to place him at a critical point, near the center of his *Epigrammes.*

I

The outline of Robert Cecil's biography is well known.⁴ He was the second son of William Cecil, Lord Burghley, Elizabeth's Lord Treasurer and principal

---

3. *Underwoods* XIV, 19–28. All quotations of Jonson are from the edition of C. H. Herford and Percy and Evelyn Simpson, *Ben Jonson,* 11 vols. (Oxford: Clarendon Press, 1925–1952), hereafter abbreviated as H&S; I have modernized the use of i/j and u/v. *Epigrammes* will be abbreviated as *Epig.*

4. A full modern life is wanting; but see Lord David Cecil, *The Cecils of Hatfield House: An English Ruling Family* (Boston: Houghton Mifflin, 1973), 91–161; Algernon Cecil, *A Life of Robert Cecil, First Earl of Salisbury* (London: John Murray, 1915); P. M. Handover, *The Second Cecil* (London: Eyre & Spottiswoode, 1959); and Lawrence Stone, *Family and Fortune: Studies in Aristocratic Finance in the Sixteenth and Seventeenth Centuries* (Oxford: Clarendon Press, 1973), 3–114.

adviser for much of her reign. Burghley managed to place him on the Privy Council at the age of twenty-eight in 1591, where he served first unofficially and later officially as Principal Secretary. When he also became Lord Treasurer in 1608, he held the two most important administrative offices in the country. Cecil was instrumental in putting down the "rebellion" of his cousin Essex, in assuring the smooth succession of James (with whom he had been in secret correspondence), in making an unpopular but profitable peace with Spain, in the disgrace and imprisonment of his sometime ally Ralegh, in detecting and defeating the Gunpowder Plot, and in countless other affairs of state. He maintained an efficient network of spies throughout Europe, manipulating information as he saw fit. His influence and authority were such that one historian has described a "regnum Cecilianum" (albeit with considerable falling off after 1610) between the last years of Elizabeth and Cecil's death in 1612.[5] As a contemporary observed: "He, more than a president, was alpha and omega in council, he solely managed all foreign affairs, especially Ireland, he directed parliament, he managed all the revenue and greatest affairs of the king, queen, prince, and Duke of York."[6]

On his character and motives there has been, both then and now, more complex agreement. He was articulate, energetic, accurate in his judgment of men and affairs, devoted to his sovereign, to his duty, and to his vision of a strong, peaceful, and prosperous England.[7] Thomas Sackville, the Earl of Dorset, Cecil's immediate predecessor as Lord Treasurer, praised him not only for "dexterity, sincerity, and judgment . . . divine virtues . . . incessantly exercised and employed for the good of the public," but even for having "so sweet a nature, so full of mildness, courtesy, honest mirth, bounty, kindness, gratitude, and good discourse."[8] This seems, however, to have been a minority view, for he was early nicknamed *Robertus Diabolus* and seen as cool, friendless, the perfect Machiavel who would readily sacrifice any personal consideration if his "allegiance" hung in the balance and who "to attain his ends . . . ignored the moral distinction between good and evil."[9] Even a sympathetic modern biographer concedes, "He did not fit in with any accepted pattern of character. His complex nature, glinting forth through his mask of apparent gentleness, baffled people and made them feel uneasy; all the more because events showed it to be combined with such a formidable capacity quietly to eliminate his opponents."[10] In the

---

5. Robert Ashton, *Reformation and Revolution, 1558–1660* (London: Granada, 1984), 185ff. The consensus on the decline of Salisbury's influence after the failure of the Great Contract has been challenged by Eric N. Lindquist, "The Last Years of the First Earl of Salisbury, 1610–1612," *Albion* 18 (1986): 23–41.

6. "Journal of Sir Roger Wilbraham," *Camden Miscellany X*, 106, as cited by Florence M. Grier Evans, *The Principal Secretary of State* (Manchester: University Press, 1923), 62.

7. See G. R. Elton, *England Under the Tudors*, 2d ed. (London: Methuen, 1974), 470n.

8. Algernon Cecil, *A Life*, 375.

9. Handover, *Second Cecil*, 1.

10. Lord David Cecil, *The Cecils*, 118.

sonorous judgment of *The Dictionary of National Biography:* "Life was to him a game which he was playing for high stakes, and men and women were only pieces upon the board, set there to be swept off by one side or the other or allowed to stand so long only as the risk of letting them remain there was not too great."[11]

Yet this was the man who quietly governed England and, by most accounts, governed it well. He guarded against the king's foreign and domestic enemies, restrained, as best he could, the king's own excesses, and proposed, in the Great Contract of 1610, his one major attempt at constructive, long-range policy, a restructuring of the relations between king and parliament that might not only have secured the king's finances but also have altered, or even avoided, the course of conflict ending three decades later in the Civil War.

Jonson's experiences with Cecil were as extensive (though not so intensive) as with any of the "great names" in the *Epigrammes.* Jonson would have come to Cecil's attention as early as 1597 for his role in *The Isle of Dogs,* for which he was imprisoned.[12] When he was later imprisoned for *Eastward Ho* in 1605, Jonson specifically solicited Cecil's favor; later in the same year, he offered to help ferret out information on the Powder Plot. About this time Jonson apparently wrote his first two epigrams to Cecil (XLIII and LXIII), and in the following two years he was commissioned to provide entertainments at Cecil's estate Theobalds (July 1606 and May 1607). In May 1608, when Cecil was named Lord Treasurer, Jonson again provided an entertainment,[13] and evidently wrote the third epigram on Cecil (LXIV) and another on his father, Burghley, which Jonson later placed in the *Underwoods* (XXX). In April 1609, Jonson was again called on for the entertainment at the naming of Cecil's latest project, Britain's Burse (later the New Exchange).

Against these indications of a comfortable understanding between poet and patron must be set Drummond's reports that Jonson had once felt himself slighted at Salisbury's table and Jonson's judgment that "Salisbury never cared for any man longer nor he could make use of him."[14] What can be made of such contradictions: the high praises in the epigrams and the dissatisfaction reported by Drummond? Did Jonson flatter Cecil while reserving his true opinion? Or think well of him initially only to be disenchanted? I think the evidence suggests

11. *The Dictionary of National Biography,* ed. Sir Leslie Stephen and Sir Sidney Lee (London: Oxford University Press, 1917-), 3:1311. See also Stone, *Family and Fortune,* 57.

12. In 1599, Jonson was one of several who contributed commendatory verses to Thomas Palmer's *The Sprite of Trees and Herbes,* dedicated to Cecil (H&S, 11:124-25). B. N. De Luna, *Jonson's Romish Plot: A Study of* Catiline *and Its Historical Context* (Oxford: Clarendon Press, 1967), evidently relying on an error in Palmer, claims that Jonson "stood in a poet-patron relationship" to Cecil from "about 1603" (p. 122). It may be so.

13. Given at Salisbury House. The texts of this and of the entertainment at Britain's Burse are not preserved. For what is known of them, see Scott McMillin, "Jonson's Early Entertainments: New Information from Hatfield House," *Renaissance Drama* n.s. 1 (1968): 153-66.

14. *Conversations with Drummond,* ll. 317-21, 353-54 (H&S, 1:141, 142).

that the poet took a consistently complicated view of this complicated man and of the moral phenomenon—the politician—that he presented.

Such a view is apparent even in a minor piece like *The Entertainment of the King and Queen at Theobalds,* performed in May 1607, "when the house was delivered up" to them.[15] James had on previous occasions admired the house and enjoyed its hunting, and he had offered to trade several properties, including Hatfield, for it. Cecil had agreed to the exchange and was by this time engaged in the planning and construction of Hatfield House, a project scarcely completed at his death five years later.[16] Jonson invests this ceremonial transfer with remarkable seriousness, casting it as a dialogue between the disconsolate Genius of the house on the one hand and Mercurie and the fates on the other. The piece opens with the "sad" Genius in gloomy obscurity puzzling over the rumored necessity of "changing" his "loved lord" who now purposes "in the twy-light of sere age" to

> Begin to seeke a habitation new;
> And all his fortunes, and himselfe engage
> Unto a seat, his fathers never knew.
>
> (ll. 17–19)

We are, I think, meant to take this tragic scenario as exaggerated (Cecil was only forty-four at the time), but for Jonson, the homeless celebrator of "housekeeping" at Penshurst and elsewhere, this deliberate desertion of one's home demands examination. The immediate response comes from Mercurie, at the sound of whose voice the scene changes to "a glorious place, figuring the *Lararium,* or seat of the household-gods," in whose presence the ensuing debate takes place. Mercurie now appears, accompanied by Good Event (who hovers over the proceedings) and the Parcae, who are required to instruct Genius in the house's "fate," that he may know it for a "grace, beyond his hopes." Genius is not easily persuaded:

> But is my Patron with this lot content,
>   So to forsake his fathers moniment?
> Or, is it gaine, or else necessitie,
>   Or will to raise a house of better frame,
> That makes him shut forth his posteritie
>   Out of his patrimonie, with his name?
>
> (ll. 74–79)

These questions come uncomfortably near the nerve: why *is* this exchange being made? Greed? Constraint? Ambition? Are these motives powerful enough to make Cecil not only lose his own piety toward the paternal but also deny his son his rightful inheritance, and the rooted identity, the "name," it would support? We seem a long way from Penshurst here.

15. H&S, 7:151–58; see also their comments, 10:402–3.
16. See Stone, *Family and Fortune,* 40–42, 62–91.

These unworthy motives Mercurie briefly denies ("Nor gaine, nor need"), and he jokes that Cecil has lately had quite enough to do "with mortar" to want to "build" any "higher." These denials only prompt further questions from Genius:

> Doe men take joy in labors, not t'enjoy?
>   Or doth their businesse all their likings spend?
> Have they more pleasure in a tedious way,
>   Then to repose them at their journeys end?
>   (ll. 86–89)

For Cecil, whose life was all but consumed in his political labors, this has special point. But here, Mercurie's patience (and the poet's license) have expired, and Mercurie peremptorily commands

> GENIUS, obey, and not expostulate;
>   It is your vertue: and such powers as you,
> Should make religion of offending fate,
>   Whose doomes are just, and whose designes are true.
>   (ll. 91–94)

There follow the fates' praises of the king and queen, and Genius's joyful submission. The entertainment concludes with a song, the choral "burdens" of which are "So, little sparkes become great fires, / And high rewards crowne low desires" (ll. 134–35) and "So, gentle winds breed happie springs, / And dutie thrives by breath of Kings" (ll. 140–41). The final lines of each couplet may be read as either positive or negative judgments. Genius has been reduced to obedience and professes himself glad, but his questions have not been persuasively answered, and their echoes linger. Are we, in the end, quite sure that the "low" desires so well rewarded are "humble" rather than "base"; or that we should be glad to see "dutie" thriving under this king, or be uneasy that it seems to require the sacrifice of piety and is supported by nothing more substantial than the king's "breath"?

This is not to suggest that Jonson has cleverly cheated his patron (or his king), insulting his motives while taking his money. Rather, the piece presents an acute, sympathetic consideration of Cecil's complex situation, of the sacrifice he is making, its necessity, its potential moral or spiritual danger, and, so we are assured, the good that will flow from it. The statesman puts himself and his soul at risk for the common good. As Cecil himself wrote in a letter of 1603 to Sir John Harington: "'Tis a great task to prove one's honesty, and yet not spoil one's fortune. . . . I am pushed from the shore of comfort and know not where the winds and waves of a Court will bear me. I know it bringeth little comfort on earth; and he is, I reckon, no wise man that looketh this way to Heaven."[17] The

---

17. Algernon Cecil, A Life, 197.

complexity of the moral challenge posed by the idea of the politician, and by Cecil himself, is yet more sharply examined in the "ripest" of Jonson's studies, the *Epigrammes*.

II

Placed between the plays and the masques in the carefully arranged *Workes* of 1616, the *Epigrammes* should be central to our understanding of Jonson. As Douglas Bush has said, "Jonson the playwright and even Jonson the lyrist may be said to see and think and feel in terms of the epigram."[18] As do the plays, the *Epigrammes* present alchemists, bawds, whores, gamesters (reformed and otherwise), lechers, surly captains, shifty lieutenants, spies, effete courtiers, corrupt lawyers, preening poetasters, ignorant critics and self-important would-be statesmen—all the "wise world" as Mosca in *Volpone* calls it, of "Parasites, or Sub-Parasites" (3.1.12–13). But the *Epigrammes* share also in the higher world of the masques: here too are the king and his true courtiers, wise judges, brave soldiers and men of affairs, generous patrons and patronesses; and, beyond the politically and socially prominent, Jonson's own teacher Camden, friends, fellow actors, poets, and scholars, children—and Jonson himself, whose presence and personality dominate the collection. We have here a portrait of Jonson's whole world, literary and practical, a common ground on which all the elements of his experience are juxtaposed and interact in a way unique in his works.

The speaker, the "Jonson" who holds this disparate collection together, is characterized by two recurring patterns of action: first, he continually makes and fulfills contracts and obligations—with reader, bookseller, king, critics, friends, children, even God; second, he continually judges what he observes and embodies those judgments in definitive acts of naming. As Edward Partridge and others have remarked, naming is the habitual activity of the poet, by which he creates a named circle of the "good and great," a circle of admiration, sympathy, obligation, and common effort, while excluding a nameless horde of beasts and frauds.[19] But I would suggest that Jonsonian naming goes beyond separating the named from the nameless, beyond sorting objects into categories to discover, test, and describe the categories themselves. Like the "name-giver" of Plato's *Cratylus* (388–90), and like contemporary physicists, whose increasing vocabulary of *mus, pi-mesons, quarks,* and so on does not so much "describe" reality as *constitute* a kind of reality as a field for investigation and understanding, the Jonsonian epigrammatist (poet, not herald) is concerned not simply to separate

18. *English Literature in the Earlier Seventeenth Century,* 2d ed. (Oxford: Clarendon Press, 1962), 109. On the poems as links between the masques and the drama, see Stephen Orgel, *The Jonsonian Masque* (Cambridge: Harvard University Press, 1965), 190–94.

19. Edward Partridge, "Jonson's *Epigrammes:* The Named and the Nameless," *Studies in the Literary Imagination* 6 (1973): 153–98. See also Claude J. Summers and Ted-Larry Pebworth, *Ben Jonson* (Boston: Twayne, 1979), 138–57.

the moral from the immoral but also to stimulate our consideration of what we mean by the names we think with: such names as "virtue" and "vice," and particularly the two most frequent names in the book, "good" and "great."[20] What content and connection do these have? should they have? can they have? To the extent that the poet succeeds in this sort of "naming" he shows us not only how to act but also how to think and feel about moral categories.

This is in some sense a heroic enterprise—and Jonson, in his two addresses to the dedicatee, Pembroke, gives us two heroic metaphors for the collection as a whole. In the epigram to Pembroke we hear of "this strife / Of vice, and vertue: wherein all great life / Almost is exercis'd" (CII, 5–7). In the dedication, the combatants are characterized as the vicious, who will not "remit any thing of their riot, their pride, their self-love, and other inherent graces" (that is, original sins), and the virtuous, the "many good, and great names" that are to be led forth "to their remembrance with posteritie." Thus the book presents itself as both a battle and a procession, a struggle for and a celebration of the values of the whole society or commonwealth. Yet it is very much a seesaw battle, in which we may see a masquelike shift (antimasque to masque) in the preponderance of forces but no clear victory.

The first half of the book is dominated by the satirized self-lovers whose poems exhibit a teasing quality, of things irritatingly half-formed and half-related, of mocking juxtapositions, inversions, direct and ironic half-parallels and half-references—that is, of a subworld of actions and agents inextricably bound to each other, yet incoherent. Thus, the "great art" pretended by alchemists, the illusory alchemical "marriage" of the elements, follows the true marriage of realms arranged by King James. The "Hot-house" that follows next glances ironically at both the "marriage" and the glass retorts, or, as we might say, forcing beds, of the alchemists. These poems are juxtaposed in such a way that they seem, like those they describe, opportunistic and parasitical; they mirror, in their imperfect relatedness, men's imperfect awareness of themselves and of the implications of their actions. The hope and example of virtue are kept alive in the first half primarily by the speaker himself, who maintains minimal order by adequately judging and placing the grotesques that he meets, and is in turn supported by his own connections to things and purposes larger than himself. Thus he is the devoted "son" of Camden, preserving what is deepest and best of the past, but also a father, like Aeneas, laboring for his children, aiding and aided by his friends and companions.

The second half of the collection starts to trace the beginning of a new "city," a society of the virtuous contrasting with the promiscuous nonsociety of the

20. See Michael James Preston, "A Verse Concordance to the Non-dramatic Poetry of Ben Jonson" (Ph.D. diss., University of Colorado, 1975), 1620–24. "Great" appears forty-five times; "good," twenty-nine. On Jonson's familiarity with the *Cratylus,* and on the significance of "naming" throughout his work, see Anne Barton, *Ben Jonson: Dramatist* (Cambridge: Cambridge University Press, 1984), 170–93.

first half. But before the city can be built, "Jonson," as both poet and man, must pass a crisis as sharp, if not so extended, as Aeneas's journey to the underworld. He must return to the source of poetic authority, must "seek out his ancient mother"—his muse. "To My Muse" (LXV) occurs very near the midpoint of the book, where the dominant mood shifts from satire to encomium; where the virtuous begin to outnumber (though never quite extinguish) the vicious;[21] where those praised will have primarily social, professional, and political, rather than personal, connections with Jonson. Jonson has so arranged the poems that this crisis of transitional self-examination is provoked by the epigrams to Cecil.[22]

They must be among the prickliest poems of praise on record. The first (XLIII) was written when Cecil was at the height of his power in the aftermath of the Gunpowder Plot, a time in which, according to the Venetian ambassador, "All envy of him . . . is now dead; no one seeks ought but to win his favour; it is thought that his power will last for it is based not so much on the grace of his Majesty's as on an excellent prudence and ability which secure for him the universal opinion that he is worthy of his great authority and good fortune."[23] In the poem, we find the poet painfully self-conscious:

> What need hast thou of me? or of my *Muse*?
> Whose actions so themselves doe celebrate;
> Which should thy countries love to speake refuse,
> Her foes enough would fame thee, in their hate.
> 'Tofore, great men were glad of *Poets:* Now,
> I, not the worst, am covetous of thee.
> Yet dare not, to my thought, lest hope allow
> Of adding to thy fame; thine may to me,
> When, in my booke, men reade but CECILL's name,
> And what I write thereof find farre, and free
> From servile flatterie (common *Poets* shame)
> As thou stand'st cleere of the necessitie.

Is this praise at all? Jonson often mixes subtle admonition with encomium; but here the lines are so roughly broken, so full of suppressed violence (*refuse, foes, hate, covetous, servile, shame*), the praise so negatively and grudgingly expressed, the poet so much more concerned with his own motives and situation than with Cecil's virtues, that one feels the thrust of the poem lies almost entirely in the first line: "What need hast thou of me, or of my *Muse?*"

Cecil the politician raises a special challenge to Jonson's whole cultural project

---

21. Partridge, "Named and Nameless," 171.

22. See Robert C. Evans, "Frozen Maneuvers: Ben Jonson's Epigrams to Robert Cecil," *Texas Studies in Literature and Language* 29 (1987): 115–40.

23. *Calendar of State Papers and Manuscripts Existing in the Archives and Collections of Venice, 1603–7* (London, 1907), 10:354, as quoted in C. Northcote Parkinson, *Gunpowder, Treason and Plot* (London: Weidenfeld & Nicolson, 1976), 120–21.

in the *Epigrammes*. One has no qualms in praising the virtues of a Camden, or a Lucy, Countess of Bedford, who is "Of greatest bloud, and yet more good then great" (*Epig.* LXXVI, 6); nor in reprehending a Don Surly, a Fine Grand, or a Sir Voluptuous Beast. But what to do with Cecil, who is great but not good, a powerful man who does both good and ill: good for the state, ill to individual men and women? What to do with a man who cares for others only insofar as they can be used to his own ends, and by whose efforts, according to Bacon, "able men were by design and of purpose suppressed"?[24] Like the satirist who punishes the vice but leaves the man, Jonson the encomiast must here find a way to praise the work but leave the man. Thus the second epigram to Cecil (LXIII), after briefly considering Cecil's active "vertue" (for which we might well read Machiavelli's *virtù*), his lonely strength of character and the king's "judgement" in using him, concludes:

> [Who] can to these be silent, *Salisburie,*
> Without his, thine, and all times injurie?
> Curst be his *Muse,* that could lye dumbe, or hid
> To so true worth, though thou thy selfe forbid.

Attention is again deflected to the poet and his responsibilities, which must be fulfilled even, if necessary, against the secretive Cecil himself.[25]

The third epigram, which immediately follows and precedes "To My Muse," is yet subtler in its strategy. The first eight lines emphatically detail the reasons for which he is *not* writing ("Not glad . . . nor glad . . . nor glad . . . nor . . . nor"); the next six rather pointedly praise the happy time of King James (*not* Cecil), "Where merit is not sepulcher'd alive"; Cecil himself appears almost as a graceful afterthought:

> These (noblest CECIL) labour'd in my thought,
> Wherein what wonder see thy name hath wrought?
> That whil'st I meant but thine to gratulate,
> I'have sung the greater fortunes of our state.

This seems exactly right: the compliment to Cecil's power, particularly the power of his name—in his case, this is no mere poetic conceit—is precise, and to subsume the power and effect, the "art" of the politician, morally dubious as it often is, to the "greater fortunes of our state" is perhaps the best accommodation of this anomaly that can be expected. Cecil, the complete statesman, has indeed submerged his own "fortunes," practical and spiritual, within those of the state, his great work: with it they rise and fall, on *its* success or failure depends our judgment of his goodness or greatness.

24. In a letter of 1616, quoted by H&S, 1:167. As a frequent antagonist of the Cecils, both father and son, Bacon is, of course, hardly a disinterested judge.

25. De Luna, *Romish Plot*, 67–68, reads the poem as an indication of Jonson's determination to celebrate Cecil's role in the Powder Plot. This specific application of the poem seems to me unpersuasive.

Jonson seems to have successfully negotiated Scylla and Charybdis, praising Cecil for what he contributes to the public good without committing himself to Cecil morally. He has not flattered him; nor has he avoided the imputation of flattery by the easy (and dangerous) device of some subterranean or contextual irony at Cecil's expense. So much the more surprising then is the radical self-doubt of "To My Muse":

> Away, and leave me, thou thing most abhord,
> That hast betray'd me to a worthlesse lord;
> Made me commit most fierce idolatrie
> To a great image through thy luxurie.
> Be thy next masters more unluckie *Muse,*
> And, as thou'hast mine, his houres, and youth abuse.
> Get him the times long grudge, the courts ill will;
> And, reconcil'd, keepe him suspected still.
> Make him loose all his friends; and, which is worse,
> Almost all wayes, to any better course.
> With me thou leav'st an happier *Muse* then thee,
> And which thou brought'st me, welcome povertie.
> Shee shall instruct my after-thoughts to write
> Things manly, and not smelling parasite.
> But I repent me: Stay. Who e're is rais'd,
> For worth he has not, He is tax'd, not prais'd.

In context, the association of "worthlesse lord" and "great image" with Cecil seems inescapable.[26] Yet how can it be so, when we have seen Jonson so jealously and skillfully struggling to maintain his integrity while fulfilling his social purpose in a radically imperfect world?

Here it seems that a lesser victory has led to a larger challenge: having survived the crisis of the moral categories, the inability of "good and great," "vice and virtue" to encompass fully the phenomenon of a Cecil, Jonson now faces the crisis of poetry itself. What claims of special authority does the poet have? Although he may adopt the mask of the satirist and encomiast, the *magister* and *arbiter,* he is, after all, no poetic or platonic demiurge, but a man who must live within, not merely observe and comment on, human life. How can he be sure that he is not, at times, only a more refined "Parasite or Sub-Parasite?" It is a crucial question for Jonson, who was, among poets, probably the most successful gatherer of patronage of his day—and he has been conscious of it from the beginning, remarking defensively in the dedication, "If I have praysed, unfortunately, any one, that doth not deserve; or, if all answere not, in all numbers, the pictures I have made of them: I hope it will be forgiven me, that they are no ill

---

26. Richard Dutton, *Ben Jonson: To the First Folio* (Cambridge: Cambridge University Press, 1983), suggests rather arbitrarily that Epigrams LVIII–LXV form a "sequence" in which "by implication and inference" Jonson makes "accusations . . . of guilt and unworthiness" against Salisbury and Mounteagle (p. 145). The argument is unconvincing as presented.

pieces, though they be not like the persons." How can the poet legitimately aspire to his heroic naming? How can he be trusted if he cannot trust his muse, or himself? Is the book finally no more than a tissue of flattery or self-importance? All those praised are in some degree imperfect; Cecil is only the most conspicuous and intransigent example of the impossibility of adequate "naming."

Jonson, like any good logician, when faced with this difficulty makes a distinction. He will have a second muse. If the first was high and luxurious and easily deceived by appearances, she will be corrected by a second who will be low, poor, given to "after-thoughts," like the one with which "To My Muse" ends. Thus the technique of the epigram, exposition and judgment, is turned upon the epigrammatist himself, and in the most thorough and intimate way: he confesses the difficulty and submits to judgment. As the personal inadequacies of the politician are transcended in his "art," so now must those of the poet be. For the poet and the politician are in Jonson's conception similar in the complexity and dynamics of their situation and character.

What Puttenham asserted of the earliest poets, that "they were the first lawmakers to the people, and the first polititiens, devising all expedient meanes for th'establish-ment of Common wealth,"[27] remains true for Jonson, who wrote in the *Discoveries:* "I coulde never thinke the study of *Wisdome* confin'd only to the Philosopher: or of *Piety* to the *Divine:* or of *State* to the *Politicke.* But that he which can faine a *Common-wealth* (which is the *Poet*) can governe it with *Counsels,* strengthen it with *Lawes,* correct it with *Judgements,* informe it with *Religion,* and *Morals;* is all these."[28] Jacob Burckhardt showed long ago that the first thing to notice about the Renaissance is its discovery of "The State as a Work of Art."[29] Though based in natural needs and, ideally, shaped and guided according to religious precept, the state or commonwealth is understood to be neither natural nor divine but the work of human hands. This is equally true of the intellectual or spiritual "commonwealths" of learning, of manners, of whatever "goodness and greatness" men and women can attain. The primary concern of both poet and politician, whether establishing the commonwealth of England or that of the *Epigrammes,* must be effective "faining"—for all commonwealths must be feigned, deliberately created in the pursuit of some ideal that they only imperfectly realize. And the art that seeks to create them must be incremental, occasional, open-ended, "imperfect," adapting itself with the greatest flexibility to all the circumstances, high and low, that fortune and the shifting interests of men present. Those who would "faine" a commonwealth must, like Cecil and like the speaker of *Epigrammes,* be willing to get their hands (if not their souls)

27. *The Arte of English Poesie,* I.iii, in G. Gregory Smith, ed., *Elizabethan Critical Essays* (Oxford: Clarendon Press, 1904), 2:7–8.

28. H&S, 8:595.

29. *The Civilization of the Renaissance in Italy,* trans. S. G. C. Middlemore (Vienna: Phaidon Press, 1937), pt. 1.

dirty. As Joseph Anthony Mazzeo notes with regard to Machiavelli: "Freedom, reason, glory, law, ability are embedded in force, fraud, desire, change, natural and cultural necessity. . . . Life presents us with the opportunities for the realization of order and value, what Machiavelli calls 'occasions,' and we must learn to grasp them before they lapse back into the chaos from which they emerged. . . . the degree to which a man is aware of and able to take advantage of the occasion is a function of his *virtù.*"[30] The speaker of the *Epigrammes* sets himself just such a test of his intellectual and moral *virtù:* can he, Mosca-like, be "present to all occasions" changing as his objects change and yet retain his honesty?

"To My Muse" acknowledges that this purpose, however heroically pursued, is beyond even Jonson's capacity to perfect. This admission of his own inadequacy does not invalidate the enterprise; rather, it entitles the poet to praise an ideal he can only imperfectly fit to experience and to actual men and women. The good the poet can pronounce absolutely; *who* is good only partially and provisionally. But in this limitation the poet discovers a powerful resource, unavailable to the politician in the construction of his commonwealth: the subject and the reader (often the same) must live up to the names they have been given; life must correct and complete the inevitable "imperfections" of art—or stand exposed by that art. Having passed this validating crisis—a crisis brought on by his attempt to "name" the politician—and having achieved an essential clarification of his own role and purpose, the poet's heroic yet also modest effort to build, through myriad exemplary "occasions" of observation and judgment, a society of the "good and great" can begin in earnest. His authority has been restored (and increased) by acknowledgment of its limits: the poet who seeks authoritatively to "name the good" will, given the radical imperfection of his objects and instrument, always fall short, as will the hero who would found a golden or an eternal city. The "Jonson" of the *Epigrammes* now begins to construct, poem by poem, at least a better commonwealth—one in which goodness, warily allied with greatness, can predominate, even if it cannot triumph.

III

"What need hast thou of me, or of my *Muse?*" It is Jonson's first question to Cecil and remains fundamental throughout, both in their relations and in Jonson's thinking about the relations of politics to poetry. It is, as we have seen, susceptible of no single or simple answer. Any easy dichotomy between the "facts" of politics and the "fictions" of poetry is immediately subject to attack from both directions: the state is not simply a "fact" but a willed common fiction, a public work of art giving to an idea or system of ideas a local habitation

30. *Renaissance and Seventeenth-Century Studies* (New York: Columbia University Press, 1964), 116, 155.

and a name; a poem or book of poems is not only a "fiction" but also an analysis of the most pressing social and moral realities and a guide to the practical heroism of better seeing, thinking, and acting. "What need hast thou of me?" The answer must depend on time and circumstance and the contrasting fortunes of the commonwealths each artist, the poet and the politician, creates. When the question is first put in 1605, with Cecil at the zenith of his power and Jonson, among other things, soliciting his help in getting out of jail, the politician hardly seems to need the poet. But after the failure of the Great Contract in 1610, after, that is, the king's and the country's rejection of Cecil's vision for the future of the commonwealth, the builder of the moral commonwealth of the *Epigrammes* might well feel his own analogous, perhaps even superior, dignity in imaginatively demonstrating the need for a sense of "contract"—with the past, with the future, with one's fellow men and women—at the heart of civilized life. By Cecil's death in 1612, the original relation is almost completely reversed. Cecil, ten years earlier the cynosure of all eyes, was now widely and violently damned: "Now that he was dead . . . hostility . . . burst out in a torrent of abuse. . . . He was accused of cheating the King, the Church, the Parliament; of oppressing the poor and twisting the law to suit his purpose and to add to his fortune."[31]

It is finally the politician who stands in need of the poet and of what he can provide: a commonwealth of mind and imagination in which even such a complex character as the politician, that most intricate mixture of "vice" and "virtue," can be understood and brought to careful, tempered judgment. A commonwealth in which a vision of the good society more durable than any local, partial, and temporary realization of it not only survives but revives anew in every understanding reader.

31. Lord David Cecil, *The Cecils,* 160.

Robert C. Evans

4. "Games of Fortune, Plaid at Court": Politics and Poetic Freedom in Jonson's Epigrams

"Patronage" and "power," recently popular as scholarly topics, will undoubtedly become passé. Ironically, when this happens one cause may be the various pressures felt within our own academic power structure. Socially oriented criticism may thus fall victim to the very kinds of social influences it seeks to describe. Yet an eclipse of this sort, if it does occur, will only validate more deeply the claims of much recent theory. Power-concerns will always remain crucial to the genesis and reception of texts and other performances, whether "power" itself remains in vogue as a subject of scholarly study.

Few Renaissance poets were more conscious of power relations than Ben Jonson was. His extraordinary success in attracting patronage led to a prominence that was unprecedented, yet for that reason also unstable and uncertain. His role as a courtier poet made him acutely aware both of the need to compete for status and of the hazards such competition entailed. As a professional poet he lacked the separate standing enjoyed by those amateurs for whom writing was merely an attractive sideline to more "serious" and respectable pursuits. His professionalism was at once a key to success and a source of enduring insecurity. Of course, Jonson's dependence on patrons was hardly unique. Patronage was the central social arrangement of his day, and most of the patrons he courted were themselves dependent on influential superiors or peers. Indeed, for most people in his society, power derived so greatly from pleasing others that it could never be wholly or securely *possessed*. It could never be felt as completely real, substantial, or permanent. The experience of power seems to have been largely a hollow and empty one: true independence or autonomy were alluring but impossible ideals.[1]

---

1. I sometimes use *patronage* as an adjective because bulkier phrases are more awkward and simplistic, and because I want to suggest that patronage relations helped condition nearly every facet of the period's thought and behavior. Valuable discussions of Jonson in his social context include: Richard Helgerson, *Self-Crowned Laureates: Spenser, Jonson, Milton and the Literary System* (Berkeley: University of California Press, 1983); Don E. Wayne, *Penshurst: The Semiotics of Place and the Poetics of History* (Madison: University of Wisconsin Press, 1984); David Norbrook, *Poetry and Politics in the English Renaissance* (London: Routledge and Kegan Paul, 1984); Annabel Patterson, *Censorship and Interpretation: The Conditions of Writing and Reading in Early Modern England* (Madison: University of Wisconsin Press, 1985); and Stanley Fish,

Appreciating the gap between lofty ideals and complex realities can help us better appreciate the rich textures of Jonson's poems. It can help us see how he used his works to advertise, assert, defend, and insinuate his power. And it can help us assess more objectively not only those poems in which he openly professes autonomous moral judgment but even more importantly those in which such claims seem compromised. Jonson himself, of course, boasted that "he would not flatter, though he saw Death," and throughout his career he gloried in a reputation for ethical independence and forthright dealings with superiors.[2] There is no need to doubt his sincerity, but there is a need to recognize the tactical, practical advantages such claims entailed.

Three poems in particular—to Sir Henry Neville, Sir Edward Coke, and Bishop John Williams—provide fascinating evidence for exploring the nature of Jonson's poetic independence. All three poems commend figures whom it might seem daring or dangerous to have praised. All three can at first suggest a defiance of authority, an uncompromising personal integrity. All three seem to pose quite sharply the whole problem of poetic freedom, but all three reveal—on closer examination—the real ambiguities this problem involves. Each resonates more richly when examined in a fuller social context, and one benefit of such examination is precisely the distrust it breeds in any simple, univocal assertions about Jonson's independence. Like a number of provocative incidents in his life that also invite simplistic conclusions about his autonomy, these poems profit by being studied with a fuller awareness of their intricate contexts. The influence of patronage pressures and ambitions, the shifting flux of political events, the power of competing factions, the instability of personal fortunes, motives, and alliances—all these made for a complex social and political life. A fuller awareness of such factors can help us better appreciate not only the contours of Jonson's life but also the rich multivalence of his works. And it can help prevent us from judging too harshly those poems that seem to disappoint anachronistic expectations about the kind of independence Renaissance poets should have enjoyed.

With its proud avowal of sturdy self-respect, Jonson's poem to Neville (*Epigrammes* CIX) has often evoked the idealization it so clearly invites. The poem begins by asserting that its Muse is one that "serues nor fame, nor titles; but doth chuse / Where vertue makes them both" (ll. 2–3). Neville himself is praised (in a nice paradox) as one who does not seek "miseries with hope" (l. 5), who does not pretend to serve "the publique, when the end / Is priuate gaine" (ll. 7–8). Instead, he strives "the matter to possesse, / And elements of honor, then the

---

"Authors-Readers: Jonson's Community of the Same," *Representations* 7 (1984): 26–58. My *Ben Jonson and the Poetics of Patronage* (Lewisburg, Pa.: Bucknell University Press, 1988) provides more documentation, especially for claims about Jonson's life, than I have space for here.

2. *Ben Jonson*, edited by C. H. Herford and Percy and Evelyn Simpson, 11 vols. (Oxford: Clarendon Press, 1925–1952), 1:141; see also 1:150. All references to Jonson's works are to this edition, hereafter cited as H&S.

50 · Robert C. Evans

dresse" (ll. 9–10). As in many of Jonson's poems of praise, the qualities he ascribes to his subject are ascribed implicitly to himself. Just as Neville is too scrupulous to make "priuate gaine" his ruling passion (l. 8), so Jonson implies the same thing about his own relations with Neville, while his praise of his patron's selflessness helps promote the self-interests of them both. Although the second line at first seems to dismiss fame and titles as unimportant compared with virtue, the third subtly revises this notion, implying that virtue can ideally lead to worldly power and renown. Indeed, Jonson's poem is partly designed to help ensure that it does. The reference to Neville's "pedigree" (l. 4) is added almost as an afterthought, as if to minimize its importance, but it *is* added, and in a society highly conscious of family heritage and hierarchical ranking, it helps strengthen Jonson's argument on Neville's behalf. In a sense this poem is highly argumentative; it does not passively affirm what everyone acknowledges to be true but rather tries to make a political and persuasive *case* on behalf of a particular individual seeking to attain or maintain power.

Jonson's poems praising patrons can easily be misread if they are seen simply as static or "inert" compliments; the more we know about the political contexts from which they emerged, the better we can appreciate their full rhetorical and political complexity.[3] Thus, although the epigram's third line pays tribute to Neville's merited eminence, part of its unintended irony is that Neville was, for much of his career, dissatisfied with his status and ambitious for advancement. The poem attributes more autonomy and serenity both to Neville and to the poet than either was able to enjoy in fact. Neville supposedly is not one who "Wrestlest with dignities" (the verb cleverly suggesting not only a graceless lack of *sprezzatura* but also an unseemly, impotent desperation that could only further subvert the power of anyone who appeared guilty of it). He is credited with a kind of self-respect that the poem uses tactically to attract respect *for* him.

Just as Jonson collapses the distinction he had initially seemed to pose between fame and titles on the one hand and virtue on the other, so he similarly complicates our understanding of the apparent opposition between "publique" service and "priuate gaine" (ll. 7–8). Although the poem initially seems to contrast the two, in the final analysis it implies that what might *seem* "priuate gaine" can actually lead to profound private loss of all that is really important; the "long guilt" that accompanies "priuate gaine" (l. 8) can refer to a troubled conscience, to eventual public humiliation, and perhaps even to judgment of a more final kind. By the same token, the truest, most ethical kind of "priuate gaine" is actually a crucial prerequisite for genuine public service. Neville's apparent withdrawal from the political fray, his attention first to his "owne state, then the States" (l. 12), actually stands as splendid evidence of his fitness for public trust. Although Jonson's poem can be misread as endorsing a kind of Stoic resigna-

---

3. On the idea that Jonson's complimentary poems often seem "inert," see E. Pearlman's "Ben Jonson: An Anatomy," *English Literary Renaissance* 9 (1979): 378.

tion, it actually constitutes a finely nuanced advertisement for Neville's talents and availability. Jonson implies that a badly motivated concern with "larger" political issues signifies not an expansive mind but a trivial one, whereas self-concern of the right kind inevitably leads to a proper concern for others and to a willingness to serve them. Yet such service is inevitably also self-serving in the narrower sense, and for all of Jonson's praise of Neville's virtue as capable of making his life (with nice equivocation) "good" against the fates (l. 11), we should not ignore the ways in which virtue and (more important) *a reputation for virtue* could serve as potent political weapons against more immediate threats and antagonists.

Here as in other poems, Jonson paradoxically ascribes substantiality to the literally immaterial, speaking of the "matter" and "elements" of honor (ll. 9–10) and praising Neville for letting his soul "giue thy flesh her weight" (l. 14). Such phrasing implies the importance not so much of virtues in the abstract but of their literal embodiment in exemplary public figures. In its final lines, however, the poem skillfully equivocates, making it unclear whether such embodiment alone is sufficient to guarantee Neville's lasting fame, or whether his virtue's additional embodiment *in the poem* is also necessary. Jonson's instruction to Neville to "Goe on, and doubt not, what posteritie, / Now I haue sung thee thus, shall iudge of thee" (ll. 15–16) is a complicated mixture of deference and self-assertion. The abrupt opening phrase, for instance, communicates both the poet's self-confidence and his respect. It can mean either "you may go now, since I have had my say" or "proceed as you have been; continue with what you have been doing and being." Similarly, the phrase "Now I haue sung thee thus" can mean either "now that I have sung about you in this attractive way" or "now that I have sung about you as you really are and have captured the essential *you.*" Jonson's confidence that his song will guarantee Neville's future reputation is complicated, especially in light of the claim that "Thy deedes, vnto thy name, will proue new wombes" (l. 17). The poet expresses pride in the worth of his song, but he also attributes part of its value to Neville's own worthiness, suggesting that it is the latter that makes the song worth singing.

If the penultimate couplet seems mainly to attribute the strength of Neville's future reputation to the poem, the final couplet modestly balances this by attributing it to the deeds themselves; yet the earlier couplet implies that the deeds alone would be insufficient to win Neville a truly lasting and vital fame. Others, after all, "toyle for titles to their tombes" (l. 18)—meaning both that they work throughout their lives to win distinctions and that those distinctions survive merely as decorative inscriptions on their monuments. Jonson's professed confidence in the greater durability of his praise both compliments and intimidates his readers, suggesting that once they understand the truth of his praise they will respond to Neville as he predicts, but also thereby pressuring them to do so. Although the audience he claims to write for is "posteritie" (a glance at the future that balances the earlier reference to Neville's "pedigree"), his and

Neville's most immediate and pressing concerns were probably with the reception the work would receive from their peers, competitors, and patrons.

For, however much the poem tries to distance Neville from the scramble for preferment, it inevitably reflects his involvement in the pursuit of power. Whether intended primarily to console him for some momentary setback, to enhance his competitive standing, or both, it served some purpose in relation to the patronage system in which Neville was inescapably implicated, and which he could not afford to ignore. This reading of the poem—stressing how the epigram serves the mutual patronage interests of both its author and its subject— seems to contradict what Jonson's editors have had to say about Neville's position in the social hierarchy of his time. Ian Donaldson, for instance, follows Herford and the Simpsons in reporting that Neville, an "MP from 1584 to 1614, ambassador to France 1599–1600, had been imprisoned in the Tower and heavily fined for his involvement in Essex's plot; though released in 1603, he remained out of royal favour."4 Similarly, William Hunter, after noting Neville's imprisonment, adds that he "was not in James's favor because of his sympathy with the popular party."5 And from such information Edward Partridge draws the reasonable (and appealing) conclusion that "it could not have been profitable to praise [Neville] since he was apparently as out of favor with James as he had been with Elizabeth." Partridge concludes: "Something about Neville's courage and integrity, and his refusal to knuckle under to either Elizabeth or James may have caught Jonson's admiration; something certainly caught his poetic interest."6 The appeal of this reading is that it confirms the image Jonson presents of both Neville's and his own essential independence. To praise a man so clearly out of favor seems an act of clear and disinterested principle, and Partridge's statement that "it could not have been profitable" to praise Neville can even be taken to imply that Jonson did so at some risk to his own standing.

But Neville's actual place in the Jacobean hierarchy was more complicated and ambiguous than brief notes are able to suggest. His involvement in Essex's plot may have been partly motivated by his ambition to replace Robert Cecil as principal secretary. When the plot failed, he went to the Tower; but after James's accession he was released, and his hopes of becoming secretary revived. Again, however, Cecil stood in his way, and it may have been frustrated ambition as much as anything else that led to his involvement with the so-called popular party. Never, though, did he become a full-fledged opponent of James or "the court" (itself an amorphous institution full of conflicting factions); his power derived, in fact, from his position as a middleman, as someone who could serve

4. Donaldson, ed., *Ben Jonson* (Oxford: Oxford University Press, 1985), 663.
5. Hunter, ed., *The Complete Poetry of Ben Jonson* (New York: Norton, 1963), 53.
6. "Jonson's *Epigrammes:* The Named and the Nameless," *Studies in the Literary Imagination* 6 (1973): 153–98; see 184–85.

as a bridge between court and Commons. But he never quite gave up his aspiration to serve as secretary.[7]

That opportunity seemed to present itself early in 1612, as Cecil's health deteriorated. Months before Cecil actually died, rumors were circulating that Neville might replace him, and although Neville at first publicly denied any interest in the office, with the help of influential allies he spent the next year and more campaigning for it. He proposed plans designed to reconcile the king and parliament while simultaneously advancing the interests of himself and his faction, but despite the friendship or support of such powerful figures as Prince Henry, the earl of Pembroke (Jonson's patron), Rochester (the royal favorite), Sir Thomas Overbury (the favorite's favorite), and the earl of Southampton, James never did appoint Neville.[8] Partly he seems to have resented the extent of solicitation on Neville's behalf, but he seems also to have recognized that Neville could be of more use to him so long as he was kept in a state of constant expectation. Francis Bacon, in fact, in a memo to the King dated 1613, asserted that James had effectively neutralized any potential opposition from such men as Neville by "having kept a princely temper towards them," by choosing "not to persecute or disgrace them, nor yet to use or advance them." For the time being, Bacon felt that the king had little reason to expect much opposition from Neville, because "Nevell hath his hopes."[9]

Thus, although the secretaryship once again eventually slipped from Sir Henry's grasp, at the time when Jonson's *Epigrammes* volume was entered in the Stationers' Register in the spring of 1612,[10] it would not have seemed unprofitable to publish praise of Neville. This is not to say that Jonson's motives in writing the epigram were opportunistic or expedient; the poem was almost certainly written well before its publication in the 1616 Folio.[11] It is only to argue

7. On Neville's life, see Clayton Roberts and Owen Duncan, "The Parliamentary Undertaking of 1614," *English Historical Review* 93 (1978): 481–98, esp. 494; Owen Duncan's "The Political Career of Sir Henry Neville: An Elizabethan Gentleman at the Court of James I" (Ph.D. diss., Ohio State University, 1974); and the first chapter of Clayton Roberts's *Schemes & Undertakings: A Study of English Politics in the Seventeenth Century* (Columbus: Ohio State University Press, 1985).

8. Linda Levy Peck notes that the secretaryship "provided the holder with constant access to the king and made him privy to his every decision. Writing to Rochester, Northampton made clear Southampton's purpose (and his own) in pursuing the office: 'his end in making his dear Damon [Neville] Secretary [was] that by him he might have understood which way to set his compass at all times.'" See *Northampton: Patronage and Policy at the Court of James I* (London: George Allen and Unwin, 1982), 31. David Riggs's forthcoming biography of Jonson stresses the importance of his connections with the Pembroke faction. Neville's hopes were doomed when Rochester, the favorite, married into the Howard family, leaders of an opposing group.

9. Francis Bacon, *The Works of Francis Bacon,* ed. James Spedding et al., 14 vols. (London: Longmans, 1862–1901), 11:365.

10. See H&S 8:16, 11:356.

11. Neville died in July 1615. In 1614, rumors (perhaps circulated by the Howard faction) alleged his involvement in a self-serving and secret "undertaking" to manage parliament for the king.

that Neville's status—and consequently Jonson's relations with him—were more complicated than either the poem suggests or its modern readers are likely to realize. If Neville was as clearly out of favor as some notes imply, it is unlikely he would have been taken so seriously for so long as a candidate for such a prestigious office. It is worth wondering, too, whether Jonson could have afforded to praise Neville in print if he had really been so utterly disliked by the king.

Similar questions arise concerning Jonson's epigram addressed to Sir Edward Coke. Coke is remembered today mainly for having been a vigorous upholder of traditional common law against the encroaching prerogative of the king. As lord chief justice of the Court of Common Pleas (1606–1613) and then as chief justice of the King's Bench (1613–1616), Coke often had the power to frustrate James's ambitions. Indeed, his "promotion" in 1613 was partly designed by his rival, Sir Francis Bacon, to weaken Coke's power and to enhance his own. For years Bacon had hoped to serve as attorney general, and the king had promised him that he could expect to assume that office when it opened up. In 1613 Bacon proposed his famous scheme to ensure that it would. The plan—which called for elevating Coke to the more prestigious but less powerful and less remunerative chief justiceship of the King's Bench—not only brought Bacon a step closer to realizing his more cherished ambition of becoming lord keeper, but it also dealt a humiliating blow to the man who had been his greatest personal and political competitor for nearly two decades. When both had sought the attorney generalship in 1594, Coke had won it; when both had sought the hand of Lady Elizabeth Hatton, it was Coke who had prevailed. While Bacon's career stagnated, Coke as chief justice of common pleas occupied one of the most powerful positions in the land. His use of that power to restrict the royal prerogative eventually won him the king's disdain, so that when Bacon submitted his memorandum of "Reasons for the Remove of Coke," James was only too willing to read it.[12]

The Letters of John Chamberlain provide an intriguing glimpse into the backstage maneuverings of both sides:

> The choise of a new Lord Cheife Justice hath bred great varietie and much canvassing, but in conclusion yt was once resolved, and so stands still for ought I heare, that

---

Although Neville was eventually cleared of blame, Clayton Roberts notes that "only by prevarication had he survived condemnation"; see *Schemes & Undertakings*, 25–30, esp. 29. Jonson's defense of Neville's integrity was probably composed long before these allegations circulated, but the controversy must have added to the poem's resonance for some readers of the 1616 Folio.

12. On these events, see Catherine Drinker Bowen, *The Lion and the Throne: The Life and Times of Sir Edward Coke* (Boston: Little, Brown, 1956), 336–41. For an excellent overview of Coke's career, see the first chapter of Stephen D. White's *Sir Edward Coke and "The Grievances of the Commonwealth," 1621–1625* (Chapel Hill: University of North Carolina Press, 1979). White emphasizes Coke's practical goals, personal ambitions, and involvement in factional struggles, noting that after Cecil's death in 1612 "Coke had no powerful protector at court and became more vulnerable to the political intrigues both of the Howard faction and of his old rival, Bacon" (6).

the Lord Cooke shold be Cheife Justice, Master Atturny [Sir Henry Hobart] Cheife Justice of the common pleas, and all to make way for Sir Fraunces Bacon to be atturny, whom the King hath promised to advance: these removes were looked for the first day of the terme, but all thinges stand yet *in statu quo prius,* for the Lord Cooke doth so stickle and fence by all the meanes and frends he can make, not to remove, as being loth he sayes to be brought out of a court of law which is his element, and out of his profit, in regard whereof he values not the dignitie, that he hath written very earnestly to his Majestie about yt, and the King is so gracious that he will not force him against his will, but saith yf he will accept yt he shall do yt with as much honor as ever any went to that place, which is a kind of promise of a bar-ounie or counsaillor-ship at the least.[13]

Eventually the plan was enacted: Coke was "promoted," the more pliant Hobart succeeded him in Common Pleas, and Bacon took Hobart's place as attorney general. Chamberlain reported that Coke "parted dolefully from the Common Place, not only weeping himself, but followed with the teares of all that bench and most of the officers of that court."[14] But as the long passage from Chamberlain suggests, James's distrust of Coke should not be exaggerated; apparently he hoped that removing Coke from his troublesome position while simultaneously elevating him would make him more pliable. Thus, at the same time Coke became chief justice of the King's Bench, he was also made a privy councilor—"which honor" (Chamberlain reported) "no man envies him yf he keepe on his right course, and turne not to be atturny again."[15] A short time later Coke was considered by some to be in the running for the treasurership,[16] and as late as February 1615/16 Bacon considered Coke a serious enough rival to succeed Sir Thomas Egerton as lord chancellor that he wrote a memorandum to the king listing possible objections and proposing his own candidacy instead ("For my-selfe, I can only present your Majesty with *gloria in obsequio*").[17] Catherine Drinker Bowen, the biographer of both men, notes that "for the first years" after his elevation to the chief justiceship, Coke did indeed seem to become more compliant; she mentions, for instance, his role in advising James to call a parliament in 1614: "Bacon, Coke, Winwood advised that with proper management, the Commons would give down milk." And she notes that initially, at least, "all was harmonious."[18]

These data are important in evaluating Jonson's intriguing epigram to Coke, written "*when he was Lord chiefe Iustice of* England" (*Underwoods* XLVI). In the poem, Jonson praises Coke as one of the most virtuous of "all rais'd servants of the Crowne" (l. 2) and commends him for having "Stood up thy Nations

---

13. *The Letters of John Chamberlain,* ed. Norman Egbert McClure, 2 vols. (Philadelphia: American Philosophical Society, 1939), 1:479.
14. Ibid., 1:481–82.
15. Ibid., 1:485.
16. Ibid., 1:493.
17. Bacon, *Works,* 12:241–44, esp. 243.
18. *The Lion and the Throne,* 342, 348.

fame, her Crownes defence" (l. 14). The epigram is implicitly presented as the fruit of the same kind of intellectually diligent "search" mentioned in its opening line; its writing is as acute and capable in its own way as Coke's is praised for being (ll. 18–20). Jonson's celebration of Coke's "manly Eloquence" (l. 13) and insightful judgment reflects back upon himself, just as his tribute to Coke's ability at "explat[ing]" the knottie Lawes" helps call attention to his own careful unraveling and explication of the details and stages of Coke's career. Indeed, the poem's logical and reasonable structure—moving from Coke's "beginnings" (l. 5) to his "Processe" (l. 9) to his "stand" (l. 15)—mirrors the very qualities Jonson values in his subject. It thus pays him a subtle compliment while also demonstrating the reasonable workings of the poet's own mind. The use of rhetorically similar units to discuss all three stages of Coke's career cleverly underscores the idea that constant principles animated his conduct throughout his life, that his present "stand" is continuous with his earliest principles.

But the poem's structural and rhetorical skill seems to falter—twice—near its end, when the poet seems lamely to repeat himself and then seems to add an afterthought to the epigram's already completed argument. "Such," he concludes, "is thy All; that (as I sung before) / None Fortune aided lesse, or Vertue more" (ll. 21–22). The repetition might at first seem redundant or clumsy, as if Jonson could think of no new commendations, but in fact he goes out of his way to call attention to the repeated phrase. Repeating it does give the poem a kind of symmetry, but it is symmetry with a difference, for after the poet's detailed explication of Coke's career, we cannot (or should not be able to) read the repeated words in the same way we read them at first. Now—after having read the results of Jonson's "search"—their truth should strike home more forcefully; we should be less likely to regard them as conventional, trite, or hyperbolic. The full impact of the words depends on the ability of the preceding lines to invest them with deeper meaning. What might have seemed dully repetitive helps instead to highlight the effects and effectiveness of Jonson's poem. But what about the final couplet, in which Jonson seems at first to subvert the argument just concluded and concede the possibility that "Chance" *may* have had some part in Coke's ascent? Once again the apparent stumble only helps exhibit the poem's considerable grace, for the concession that Chance *did* lend Coke her blindfolded eyes allows Jonson to allude subtly to another blindfolded goddess—Justice—whose spirit Coke personifies. But whereas the blindness of Chance symbolizes her irrationality and unpredictability, the blindness of Justice signifies the opposite. The allusion to one blind goddess inevitably reminds us of the other and thus quietly epitomizes Jonson's earlier praise. The poem's closing emphasis on blindness nicely balances its opening emphasis on searching acuity, just as the final reference to Coke's "rise" (l. 23) recalls the opening reference to his having been "rais'd" (l. 2). In this and in every way, Jonson's epigram seems carefully conceived and thoughtfully executed.

Jonson seems careful to steer clear of any hint that he might be praising Coke as the judge who once opposed extension of the king's prerogative, and indeed the second line seems designed to remind Coke that he served at the king's sufferance. The epigram's title and its opening and closing couplets (both concerned with Coke's elevation) suggest the poem was written around the time of his actual and prospective promotions in the winter of 1613/14. As the newest privy councilor he would have been a likely recipient of one of Jonson's poems. If the poem was written to celebrate his "elevation" to the King's Bench, an "honor" he did not desire, he may even have found the terms of its praise more than a little ambiguous. Whether Jonson intended his poem as innocent praise, as a kind of consolation, as a defense of Coke's fundamental loyalty and integrity, or perhaps even as an admonition to him about how to conduct himself in his new position, it does seem clear that the epigram is not especially daring or defiant in its willingness to commend Coke publicly. Indeed, the available facts suggest that for much of Coke's tenure as chief justice it would have been perfectly safe to praise him. It was not until the spring of 1616 that he was clearly out of favor, and later that year (thanks, in part, to Bacon's further connivance) he was dismissed. Even then he was not wholly vanquished: he remained a courtier and continued to maneuver at court, because he knew as well as Jonson that the court was the center of political and social power.[19] Jonson's epigram may seem surprising when viewed by itself or in light of the scanty knowledge editorial notes can provide. When it is viewed with a fuller knowledge of the circumstances surrounding it, however, its praise of Coke becomes easier to comprehend. As in the case of the poem to Neville, we must resist the temptation to simplify the political contexts—and thus the textual intricacy—of Jonson's writing.

Bacon's triumph over Coke was hardly permanent, and in fact Coke was one of those in parliament who helped engineer Bacon's own fall from office in 1621.[20] After Bacon fell, John Williams was chosen to succeed him as lord keeper. Williams's rise had been relatively steady. He had been patronized by both Egerton and Bacon, but his most powerful backer was James. Despite some opposition from Buckingham, the royal favorite, Williams repeatedly received the king's patronage. Like both Bacon and Coke, however, he eventually suffered a dramatic reversal.[21]

19. Ibid., 370–411. White remarks that Coke's "judicial philosophy was hardly the sole cause of his political troubles"; he angered Buckingham, the new favorite, by "disposing of a lucrative clerkship without consulting him" and annoyed others by digging too deeply into Overbury's murder (Sir Edmund Coke, 7).

20. Bowen, The Lion and the Throne, 412–34. On Coke's role in the parliament of 1621, see White, Sir Edmund Coke (esp. 45).

21. On Williams's career, see John Hacket, Scrinia Reserata: A Memorial Offer'd to the Great Deservings of John Williams, D.D., 2 vols. (London: Samuel Lowndes, 1692), and B. Dew Roberts's Mitre and Musket: John Williams, Lord Keeper, Archbishop of York, 1582–1650 (London: Oxford University Press, 1938). Hacket, a basic source, was for many years Williams's protégé. For a less sympathetic and sketchier picture, see G. P. V. Akrigg, Jacobean Pageant: or The Court of King James I (Cambridge: Harvard University Press, 1962), 316–19. In Scrinia Reserata, Hacket discusses Williams's early relations with James and Buckingham (1:36–39), his links with Pembroke (Jonson's patron) and with the Earl of Southampton (1:60, 68), and his regard for John Selden (1:69) and for William Camden (2:527), Jonson's good friends.

Despite Buckingham's great power, Williams at first seems to have been wary of courting him assiduously, both because he worried that his support might prove inconstant and because he doubted that Buckingham's own status could long endure. It was James himself who finally suggested that Buckingham's friendship was worth pursuing, and Williams was not slow to act on the advice. He was instrumental in smoothing the way for Buckingham's marriage to the earl of Rutland's daughter and afterward proved a valuable adviser on parliamentary matters. But when, as lord keeper, he proved less than completely subservient, the favorite began to lose patience and by 1625 was determined to cut him down.[22] James's death early that spring had helped make Williams more vulnerable, since Charles shared Buckingham's attitude in this as in other matters. Despite Williams's initial confidence that he could survive, in the end a purely technical pretext was found, and on 25 October he suddenly lost his office.[23] An untitled poem in *Underwoods* (LXI) seems to have been prompted by this dismissal. In it Jonson addresses a man who has "seene the pride, beheld the sport, / And all the games of Fortune, plaid at Court, / View'd there the mercat, read the wretched rate / At which there are, would sell the Prince, and State" (ll. 1–4). Yet he praises the man for having "got off thence, with cleare mind, and hands / To lift to heaven" (ll. 7–8). After attacking contemporary corruption, the poem concludes that whoever is able "To teach the people, how to fast, and pray, / And doe their penance, to avert Gods rod / He is the Man, and Favorite of God" (ll. 18–20).

The skill of Jonson's poem is worth remarking. The first two couplets, for instance, cleverly balance the trivial with the deadly serious, the former both offsetting and intensifying the latter. At first glance the Court seems merely an arena where "games" are "plaid"—*for* fortune, but also *by* Fortune. Through the simple equivocation of "of," Jonson manages to suggest that the participants are at once players and played with—seekers after fortune but also her potential victims. The sense of "sport" that dominates the first couplet is radically attenuated in the second, with its imagery of bargaining that is doubly cheap but deadly treacherous. If the opening distich focuses with wry irony on the corruption of individual courtiers, the second draws out the implications of their chicanery for the state as a whole. The "rate" they accept for their perfidy is both economically and morally "wretched," while the poem's reference to "the Prince" not only exempts Charles from any responsibility for the dishonesty

---

22. Chamberlain's letters record rumors about Williams's instability years before he fell; see *Letters*, 2:426, 455, 457, 471, 532, 613. Both Hacket (*Scrinia Reserata*, 1:148, 2:5, 20) and Roger Lockyer (*Buckingham: The Life and Political Career of George Villiers, First Duke of Buckingham, 1592–1628* [London and New York: Longman, 1981], 175, 265) suggest that part of the duke's growing disdain for Williams was rooted in fear. Hacket says Williams at first tried to ignore Buckingham's coolness, lest it weaken him in others' eyes (*Scrinia Reserata*, 1:107).

23. The major modern editions of Jonson all suggest that Williams lost his office three years later, in 1628. Only Francis Cunningham (*The Works of Ben Jonson*, 3 vols. [London: Chatto and Windus, 1903]) gives the correct date of 1625. I discuss later why the poem's date is important.

surrounding him but also implies the unshakable loyalty of both the poet and the man he praises. No mention is made of Charles's role in sanctioning Williams's dismissal, which is indeed presented not as a dismissal at all. When Jonson asks "who is't not understands / Your happinesse, and doth not speake you blest, / To see you set apart, thus" (ll. 8–10), he depicts Williams's fall as election to a higher grace. His question implicitly challenges the misguided values of any reader who sees the fall in a different light, and its artless tone seems calculated to highlight Jonson's uncommon moral acuity. In adopting so sanguine an attitude, he consoles Williams the individual while bolstering the threatened reputation of Williams the public man. God becomes an alternative patron, Williams his ideal servant; the relationship between this king and this "Favorite" obliquely mirrors— but also shows up—the one between Buckingham and Charles.

Like everything else in the poem, the religious references function tactically. By implicating himself and the country at large in the general sinfulness he condemns, Jonson makes his indictment of court corruption both more effective and more defensible. The religious passion that pervades the epigram's final half gives his voice an authority it would lack if he simply spoke as the disappointed client of a fallen patron. Just as he incites Williams to pray to God, so his own poem becomes a model for that act, a heartfelt petition that seems itself to express the kind of "felt griefe" (l. 14) he hopes Williams's prayers will elicit in others. When the final lines call upon Williams to "teach the people" through his actions (l. 18), they remind us of the many senses in which Jonson himself has just been teaching through his words.

Never before had Jonson so emphatically praised a man so obviously out of favor; given the circumstances, his closing reference to Williams as God's "Favorite" seems particularly daring. But with this poem as with so many of his others, we need to know more about the facts of circulation before we can speculate intelligently about his intention. Was the poem widely published, or was it shown only to Williams and his circle, who could be relied on not to betray the poet's trust? Was Jonson's decision to leave "the Bishop" unidentified prompted by prudence or by some far simpler consideration? Did he identify himself as the work's author, or was his name also omitted? When—precisely—was the poem written? Immediately after Williams's dismissal, for instance, his "friends were confident that he would eventually rise again to some other great place. They believed, or Williams had told them, that the Duke, in bringing about his fall, had acted from fear rather than hatred."[24] If the epigram dates from this period, then its veiled allusion to the favorite (and indeed, its very existence) seems less risky, more comprehensible. "It was soon plain," however,

---

24. B. Dew Roberts, *Mitre and Musket*, 108–9. See Lockyer on Buckingham's great unpopularity at this time. Lockyer notes the duke's suspicion that Williams was plotting against him, not only in the 1625 parliament but also with such powerful courtiers as Pembroke, Jonson's old patron (*Buckingham*, 259, 265; see also 177, 276). Jonson's poem may thus have implied support of Pembroke.

that Williams was to be pursued even at [his estate] Buckden by the Duke's rancour and the King's displeasure. A commission was appointed to investigate his conduct and report whether any charge could be brought against him. That expedient failed; the commission could find nothing culpable in his past career. But he was continually watched and spied upon; it was reported that he kept a state unbecoming a 'cashiered courtier,' and that the Bishop's palace at Buckden was a rallying-place for those who bore a grudge against Buckingham.[25]

If the poem was written under the circumstances and at the time described here, then it seems far more provocative. Perhaps neither supposition is correct. Unfortunately, it is doubtful that we will ever know for sure. Yet the caution such uncertainty breeds is itself one of the best reasons for exploring more fully the political contexts of Jonson's poems. The more we know about those contexts, the less likely we are to make simplistic assumptions, either about them or about the poems they helped condition.

Loyalty to a generous benefactor, as much as daring and righteous indignation, may have prompted Jonson's poem. Williams had always been a learned man friendly to learned men, and he continued his patronage even after his fall.[26] Although disgraced, he enjoyed a hefty income and used it to entertain the nobles, gentry, and intellectuals who frequently visited his estate.[27] It is not hard to believe that Jonson was one of those who enjoyed his hospitality and munificence. His praise of the fallen bishop, then—while at first glance a purely altruistic and perhaps even defiant act on behalf of a disgraced courtier—proves more complicated on closer inspection. At the time Jonson probably wrote, Williams was still both wealthy and powerful and had not altogether given up hopes of someday reentering that "glorious miserye and splendid slaverie"[28] from which he had so recently been freed.

What the poems to Neville, Coke, and Williams all suggest is that appreciating the political contexts of Jonson's writing is crucial to appreciating the complexities both of his works and of his social position. The more we know about the political conditions that helped shape his works, the less likely we will be to judge either them or his character in any snap or facile way. The more closely we examine the issues of autonomy his works raise, the more complex both those issues and his works are likely to seem. Our views of Jonson's "freedom" need to be anchored, insofar as possible, in specific facts. In many cases these facts are lost to us, but enough survive to warn us away from any simple assertions that he

25. B. Dew Roberts, *Mitre and Musket,* 109. Williams's house became an informal academy for the sons of such men as Pembroke; see Hacket, *Scrinia Reserata,* 2:36. Although Charles never abandoned Buckingham, no one would have been surprised if this favorite had eventually fallen. Ironically, Hacket argues that shortly before Buckingham's death, the duke and Williams, secretly reconciled, were planning to promote each other's interests (*Scrinia Reserata,* 2:65, 80).

26. See Hacket, *Scrinia Reserata,* 1:29, 2:32, 34; see also B. Dew Roberts, *Mitre and Musket,* 124–25.

27. B. Dew Roberts, *Mitre and Musket,* 119.

28. Ibid., 106.

was either largely autonomous *or* completely subservient. In assessing his disdain for flattery, for instance, we need to ask how such disdain might actually have promoted his standing as a dependent; in dealing with his "satire" on superiors (such as the epigram "To My Lord Ignorant" or the attack on the "Court Pucelle"), we need to ponder its circumstances and the ways it might have served his political interests. And in reading all his works, we need to ask how they might have advanced his own and others' power. While appreciating the real limits to his authority, we need to consider how nearly all his works strive either to promote or to defend it.

Above all, we need to resist any temptation to resolve tensions or dissolve contradictions—even when his works themselves encourage us to do so. Jonson's social position simultaneously created and frustrated his desire for autonomy, and his claimed independence from social pressures only reflects his deep responsiveness to them. His pronounced self-regard paradoxically reflects his very real concern with others' opinions; his claimed independence provided a psychic cushion against the inherent instability of his worth in others' eyes. Since no patron was entirely dependable (if only because of death), an image of rigid independence paradoxically enhanced Jonson's flexibility, his capacity to adapt to new circumstances or different alliances. At the same time, assertions of autonomy ultimately signified a keen awareness of being enmeshed in the fabric of social power. His reputed independence made Jonson a more valuable client and ally, more confident in himself and thus more useful to others. For all these reasons, to posit crudely either his simple autonomy *or* his obvious subjection is to ignore the complexities both of his circumstances and of his works.

Michael C. Schoenfeldt

5. "The Mysteries of Manners, Armes, and Arts": "Inviting a Friend to Supper" and "To Penshurst"

In his provocative essay on Ben Jonson, T. S. Eliot remarks: "When we say that Jonson requires study, we do not mean study of . . . seventeenth-century manners."[1] I would argue on the contrary that we have much to learn about Jonson's poetry by situating it amid the discourse of seventeenth-century manners. For Jonson and his culture, politeness and politics are more than just etymologically related; manners afford the medium through which power is manifested and exerted. Jonson's *Epigrammes* XXXV, for example, praises King James as one "Whose manners draw, more than thy powers constraine."[2] Lacking the authority to constrain the behavior of others, Jonson exercises in "To Penshurst" and "Inviting a Friend to Supper" the capacity of manners to "draw" their compliance. By placing himself at the table of the great in "Penshurst" and feasting the "grave sir" to whom "Inviting" is addressed, Jonson establishes a place for the poet in the social structure of seventeenth-century England; at the same time, he uses the discourse of hospitality to disclose this structure's hostility to poetry.[3] In both poems, Jonson illustrates a concept crucial to his definition of himself and his vocation: the poet is the legislator, however unacknowledged, of behavior in the world. "The wisest and best learned," observes Jonson in the *Discoveries,* "have thought [poetry] the absolute Mistresse of manners" (H&S 8:636). In "Penshurst" and "Inviting," Jonson demonstrates how the service of this mistress can confer a prestige that the political hierarchy denies. He "articulates an ideal of civilized life in a well-ordered society"[4] in order to show that not only Robert Sidney, Lord Lisle, but also Ben Jonson, poet, comprehends "The mysteries of manners, armes, and arts."

1. "Ben Jonson," in *Selected Essays* (New York: Harcourt, Brace & World, 1950), 128.
2. "To King James," in *Ben Jonson,* ed. C. H. Herford and Percy and Evelyn Simpson, 11 vols. (Oxford: Clarendon Press, 1925–1952), 8:37. All citations of Jonson are to this edition, hereafter cited as H&S.
3. I have learned much about Jonson's sense of his role as a poet from William E. Cain, "The Place of the Poet in Jonson's 'To Penshurst' and 'To My Muse,'" *Criticism* 21 (1979): 34–48, and Richard Helgerson, *Self-Crowned Laureates: Spenser, Jonson, Milton and the Literary System* (Berkeley: University of California Press, 1983), 101–84.
4. Claude J. Summers and Ted-Larry Pebworth, *Ben Jonson* (Boston: Twayne, 1979), 166.

Jonson's careful attention to manners probably results at least in part from an acute sensitivity to his lack of the "arms," or status, of a gentleman. His grandfather, he claims in the *Conversations with Drummond,* was a "Gentleman" who "served King Henry 8," but "his father Losed all his estate under queen Marie, having been cast in prison and forfaitted." Jonson was "brought up poorly" by a stepfather who apprenticed him as a bricklayer, an occupation "he could not endure" (H&S, 1:139). Jonson relates a tale of gentility lost, as the family status plummets from serving kings to laying bricks. Much of the energy of Jonson's poetic career, and especially of "Inviting" and "Penshurst," is devoted to regaining this gentility, to washing the dust of manual labor from his skin. Frank Whigham has argued that the literature of courtesy, although intended to preclude the phenomenon of social mobility, unwittingly enabled the socially mobile to disguise their less than noble origins by offering them a pattern of imitable behavior.[5] A parallel process is at work in Jonson's literary performances. By making his own craft—poetry—the arbiter of proper behavior, Jonson converts the discourse intended to debar such a lowborn figure into the element through which he can achieve and exercise authority. Both "Inviting" and "Penshurst" dramatize this conversion, welcoming in order to expel, enclosing in order to liberate, building walls that summon rather than seclude.

The action common to "Inviting" and "Penshurst"—eating—has cultural as well as alimental importance. To celebrate his release from prison for an impolitic reference to King James in the play *Eastward Ho,* Jonson, remarks Drummond, "banqueted all his friends" (H&S, 1:140). Victorious, celebratory, and communal, the feast marked Jonson's liberation from bondage. "In the act of eating," asserts Mikhail Bakhtin, the body "triumphs over the world, over its enemy, celebrates its victory, grows at the world's expense . . . in the act of eating and drinking . . . [one] partakes of the world instead of being devoured by it."[6] Moreover, as it signals victory over the natural world, the feast also announces prestige in the political arena, for the ability to feed others is an index of social status. The English Renaissance placed particular value on what Lawrence Stone terms the "aristocratic virtue of generosity." The "prime test of rank," remarks Stone, "was liberality, the pagan virtue of open-handedness. It involved . . . above all maintaining a lavish table to which anyone of the right social standing was welcome."[7] In a letter to the earl of Newcastle, Jonson describes "those chargeable and magnificent honors of makeing feasts" (H&S, 1:212). By "makeing feasts," one displays one's magnificence, one's ability to make and maintain dependents. Furthermore, nourishment and authority share etymological as well as ideological kinship; as Stephen Orgel comments: "the King describes himself in *Basilicon Doron* as 'a loving nourish father' providing

---

5. *Ambition and Privilege: The Social Tropes of Elizabethan Courtesy Theory* (Berkeley: University of California Press, 1984).
6. *Rabelais and His World,* trans. Helen Iswolsky (Cambridge: MIT Press, 1968), 283–85.
7. *Crisis of the Aristocracy 1558–1641* (Oxford: Clarendon Press, 1965), 42.

the commonwealth with 'their own nourish milk.' The very etymology of the word 'authority' confirms the metaphor: *augeo,* 'increase, nourish, cause to grow.'"[8] Authority is achieved, sustained, and displayed in the act of feeding others.

As the giving of a feast is a sign of power, so the acceptance of another's fare is a mark of submission. Antony de Guevara, for example, warns in *The Diall of Princes:* "that day the Courtyer graunteth to dyne with any man, the same day hee bindeth himselfe to be beholding to him that bids him."[9] The act of sitting down to dinner with another is a "status ritual," at once an exhibition and trial of one's prestige.[10] In the *Conversations,* Drummond records that one of Jonson's favorite "Jeasts" involved a question of table manners: "A Justice of peace would have comanded a Captaine to sit first, at a table because sayes he, I ame a Justice of Peace, the other drawing his sword comanded him for sayeth he I ame a Justice of War" (H&S, 1:146). Jonson's fascination with this tale derived not only from his admiration for the soldier's rapier wit but also from the episode's exposure of the political coercion and social violence at the core of such apparently superficial matters as priority in seating. In "Inviting a Friend to Supper," Jonson reveals his profound awareness of this coercion even as he cloaks it in a veneer of attentive courtesy. The aesthetic and political achievement of the poem rests in the elegance with which it segregates the occasion from a constraining social world even as it recognizes these constraints and records their pernicious effects on poetry, the poet, and good fellowship.

By "Inviting a Friend to Supper," then, Jonson arrogates to himself a mode of behavior through which the aristocracy parades its power over others. He integrates the authority of nourishment with that inherent in writing. Yet he mitigates the oppression intrinsic to this situation by means of the reverence and self-deprecation through which the invitation is extended:

> To night, grave sir, both my poore house, and I
> Doe equally desire your companie:
> Not that we thinke us worthy such a ghest,
> But that your worth will dignifie our feast,
> With those that come; whose grace may make that seeme
> Something, which, else, could hope for no esteeme.
>
> (*Epigrammes* CI)

The terminology graciously acknowledges the social distance between guest and host that the invitation nevertheless proposes to span. Although "poore" and unworthy of this guest, both house and host request the presence of a visitor whose superior status will enhance rather than impoverish their own.

---

8. "Prospero's Wife," *Representations* 8 (1984): 9.

9. Trans. Thomas North (London, 1619), 619.

10. The term is from Erving Goffman, "The Nature of Deference and Demeanor," in *Interaction Ritual: Essays on Face-to-Face Behavior* (Garden City: Anchor, 1967), 57.

By entreating the guest to compensate for the host's lack of prestige, Jonson emphasizes the political component of the occasion even as he attempts to palliate it. The shrewd display of deference discharges the social burden that the situation imposes by redistributing the hierarchical privileges of guest and host. "Inviting a Friend to Supper," remarks Wesley Trimpi, "is actually a definition of a friend, not of a dinner."[11] But even as it attempts to define a friend, the poem interrogates the prospect of inoculating friendship against the diseases of a suspicious and oppressive social world. For by designating the subject of his invitation as "friend" while addressing him as "grave sir," Jonson calls attention to the bewildering convergence of amicable and onerous bonds inherent in seventeenth-century concepts of friendship. As Lawrence Stone reminds us, *friend* "did indeed often mean a loved one. . . . But it was also frequently used to mean not a person to whom one had some emotional attachment, but someone who could help one on in life, with whom one could safely do business, or upon whom one was in some way dependent."[12] *Friend,* then, could stipulate concurrently a relationship of affective equality and one of hierarchical dependency. In *The Truth of Our Times,* Henry Peacham laments that "The common and ordinary friendship of the world is measured by the benefit that one man reaps by another."[13] The confusion of emotional and political bonds inhering in the word betokens the difficulty of quarantining the occasion from the social contagion that circumscribes it.

An analogous conflation of deference and affection is exercised when Jonson courteously credits his guest with a creative power over the meal that is being offered to him:

> It is the faire acceptance, Sir, creates
> The entertaynment perfect: not the cates.

The quality of the repast, in other words, depends more on its reception than on its preparation. The social component of this dependence is emphasized by the reverential *sir*—repeated from the poem's opening line—that separates subject from verb. Such deference, however, also confers status on the poet/host as he demonstrates his command of the meticulous protocol through which invitations are extended and accepted. As Pierre Bourdieu argues, "practical mastery of what are called the rules of politeness, and in particular the art of adjusting each of the available formulae (e.g., at the end of a letter) to the different classes

---

11. *Ben Jonson's Poems: A Study of the Plain Style* (Stanford: Stanford University Press, 1962), 188. See also Richard Finkelstein, "Ben Jonson's Ciceronian Rhetoric of Friendship," *Journal of Medieval and Renaissance Studies* 16 (1986): 103–24.

12. *The Family, Sex and Marriage in England 1500–1800* (New York: Harper and Row, 1977), 97.

13. *The Truth of Our Times* (1638), in *"The Complete Gentleman," "The Truth of Our Times,"* and *"The Art of Living in London,"* ed. Virgil B. Heltzel (Ithaca: Cornell University Press, 1962), 204.

of possible addressees, presupposes the implicit mastery, hence the recognition, of a set of oppositions constituting the implicit axiomatics of a determinate political order."[14] By artfully deferring to it, Jonson brandishes his mastery of the political order that would assign him an inferior status. Moreover, Jonson's affable attribution of value to his guest constrains this guest's critical faculties, implying that whatever imperfections the meal contains are the product of the guest's sensibility rather than of the host's shortcomings. The guest is encouraged to view the repast favorably or be found guilty of an overscrupulous palate.

Even as he emphasizes his guest's imaginative power over the feast, Jonson adumbrates a pattern of his own imaginative power. Moreover, he underscores this pattern through a clever pun on "faire" (meaning both the courteous acceptance of the meal, and the meal itself, the fare). The creative act of offering a feast is compared to the equally creative act of acceptance. Similarly, just as the guest's worth will "*dignifie* our feast," so will the host offer "An olive, capers, or some better sallade . . . to *rectifie*" his guest's "palate." The assonance of "dignify" and "rectify," like the pun on "faire," indicates reciprocity between the actions of guest and host. As the guest will make the meal worthy, so will the meal "make right" the palate of the guest. "The real criterion and real subject at issue" in the poem, suggests Thomas Greene, "are the mutual acceptance of guest and host together."[15] Jonson's verbal ingenuity and attentive courtesy conjoin guest and host, meal and manner, transforming a politically unilateral occasion and a socially unequal relationship into a moment of convivial exchange.

Jonson thus manipulates the language of self-deprecation to attain equality with—if not superiority over—his politically superior guest. A related mode of manipulation surfaces in the curious combination of bounty and contingency with which the evening's fare is described. Jonson's promise of "a short-leg'd hen, / If we can get her, full of egs" oscillates between paucity and plenty with perplexing frequency. More playfully, the availability of larks is made to hinge on the deferment of the end of the world:

> And, though fowle, now, be scarce, yet there are clarkes,
>   The skie not falling, thinke we may have larkes.

This emphasis on the concurrent abundance and dependence of the repast culminates in Jonson's confession to exaggerating the richness of the fare in order to ensure his guest's attendance. By advertising the coercive hyperbole of his invitation, Jonson both deploys and defuses it:

> Ile tell you of more, and lye, so you will come:
>   Of partrich, pheasant, wood-cock, of which some

---

14. *Outline of a Theory of Practice,* trans. Richard Nice (Cambridge: Cambridge University Press, 1977), 218, n. 46.

15. *The Light in Troy: Imitation and Discovery in Renaissance Poetry* (New Haven: Yale University Press, 1982), 281.

> May yet be there; and godwit, if we can:
>> Knat, raile, and ruffe too.

Indeed, the items themselves highlight the socially exceptional nature of this supper; domestic and wild fowl such as Jonson proffers were reserved for the tables of nobility, and then only for particularly festive events.[16] Jonson's invitation emulates gentle menus as well as manners. "The meal proposed is sumptuous," remarks Joseph Loewenstein, "but it is a curiously soluble sumptuousness."[17] As he whets the appetite of his visitor with a list of foods he may not be able to provide, Jonson creates a tone of intimate yet deferential sincerity amid his rhetorical maneuvering. He also documents a gap between the extravagant banquet his imagination and hunger can summon and the far more modest meal his profession and status can supply.

The hints of economic constraint present in Jonson's emphasis on the feast's contingent nature reemerge in his pledge to nourish his guest's intellect as well as his belly:

> my man
> Shall reade a piece of Virgil, Tacitus,
>> Livie, or of some better booke to us,
> Of which wee'll speake our minds, amidst our meate.

Reading and eating are given equal weight. Yet even as Jonson "professe[s] no verses to repeate," he proposes a way in which his poetry may still become part of the evening's entertainment:

> To this, if ought appeare, which I know not of,
>> That will the pastrie, not my paper, show of.

As Roger Cognard argues, "Jonson is referring to the common practice of using the pages of unsold books as wrappings in bakers' shops."[18] The pastries Jonson serves, in other words, might bear the impression of Jonson's own poems—unbought by a public unable to appreciate them—thus presenting food for thought as well as flesh.[19] Just as Jonson may not be able to afford the lavish fare he promises because he has not sold enough copies of his poems to generate the necessary capital, so may he not be able to keep his pledge to isolate the occasion from his verses. The two broken vows measure, ultimately, not Jonson's lack of courtesy but the neglect with which poetry is received by the world. The ab-

---

16. In *All Manners of Food: Eating and Taste in England and France from the Middle Ages to the Present* (Oxford: Basil Blackwell, 1985), 56, Stephen Mennell observes of sixteenth-century English meals: "Capons, chickens, hens and a range of game fowl were to be bought for special occasions, but only for 'my Lord's table.'"

17. "The Jonsonian Corpulence, or The Poet as Mouthpiece," *ELH* 53 (1986): 493.

18. "Jonson's 'Inviting a Friend to Supper,'" *Explicator* 37, no. 3 (1979): 4.

19. Loewenstein, "The Jonsonian Corpulence," 496–99, examines this passage as a metaphor of Jonson's anxiety about imitation and the marketplace.

sence of poultry and the presence of poetry both result from Jonson's penury. This menu for mind and body exposes a tension between what Jonson would enjoy serving and what his subservient social status enjoins.

In his lengthy discussion of the evening's drink, Jonson amplifies the relationship between poetry and consumption implicit in the image of pastries imprinted with his poems:

> But that, which most doth take my *Muse,* and mee,
> Is a pure cup of rich *Canary*-wine,
> Which is the *Mermaids,* now, but shall be mine:
> Of which had Horace, or Anacreon tasted,
> Their lives, as doe their lines, till now had lasted.
> *Tabacco, Nectar,* or the *Thespian* spring,
> Are all but Luthers beere, to this I sing.

Significantly, the same wine that *takes* Jonson and his Muse will also be taken by Jonson, appropriated, made *mine.* The wine, like the poetry it inspires, involves both a loss and an acquisition of control. Moreover, Jonson's praise of the liquor allows him to interject the names of two of his classical models and the immortalizing capacity of poetry that they embody: "Of which had Horace or Anacreon tasted, / Their lives, as do their lines, till now had lasted." The wine, furthermore, makes not only tobacco and nectar but also the Thespian spring—located on Mount Helicon, sacred to the Muses—seem like "Luthers beere," underscoring the connection between the liquor of which Jonson sings and the poetic rapture this liquor provokes. The meal Jonson promises is finally a kind of secular literary communion, composed of bread bearing the imprint of his poems and the wine that inspires his poetry. Yet like the contingencies that couch the catalog of possible courses in this beggar's banquet, this feast of the word made bread illustrates not only Jonson's hospitality to his guest but also the animosity to the poet of the social world he inhabits.

The pressure exerted by this world on the poet and the event he sponsors can be felt most strongly in the series of negations with which the poem concludes:

> Of this we will sup free, but moderately,
> And we will have no *Pooly',* or *Parrot* by;
> Nor shall our cups make any guiltie men.

Only through exclusion can the occasion achieve freedom. Moderation, Jonson assures his guest, will prevent license from turning into licentiousness. The prospect of treachery is affirmed in order to be denied; as if their presence were the norm from which he deviates, Jonson guarantees his visitor isolation from spies and the social violence they represent. Indeed, as Mark Eccles has shown, Robert Poley was a government agent present when Christopher Marlowe was killed in a tavern brawl after supper and so represents a particular menace to a poet and dramatist such as Jonson.[20] The names of these spies—Pooly (poulet)

20. "Jonson and the Spies," *Review of English Studies* 13 (1937): 385–97.

and Parrot—not only betray the warbling banter through which they accomplish their perfidious deeds but also contrast with the variety of poultry that constitutes the evening's meat and drink (the Canary Isles were famous for their birds as well as their wine). Yet the metaphoric and assonantal connections among the fowls that are embraced as nutritious and the foul spies that are shunned as noxious demonstrate the difficulty of shielding the moment from the duplicity that surrounds it.

This difficulty gives point to Jonson's promise not to take advantage of his guest; rather, he declares, guest and host shall at the end of the evening possess the same status they enjoy at the beginning, just as the invitation concludes with the same phrase—"to night"—with which it begins:

> at our parting, we will be, as when
> We innocently met. No simple word,
>   That shall be utter'd at our mirthfull boord
> Shall make us sad next morning: or affright
>   The libertie, that wee'll enjoy to night.

Although Jonson invests much imaginative capital in describing the evening's menu, the main course, finally, is not the mutton, or the coney, or the lark, but something far more difficult to obtain: "libertie." By invoking the exigencies of the oppressive political world it purports to exclude, the poem invites one to enter a necessarily circumscribed chamber and to feast on the freedom such circumscription affords.

In "To Penshurst," Jonson also imagines a situation in which dining with another enhances rather than diminishes the authority of the guest. By an act of "faire acceptance" like that asked of the guest of "Inviting," Jonson converts the social duress of eating at the table of a superior into a politically propitious situation by praising his host for behavior that indulges his own appetite for food and power. In "Inviting," Jonson adopts a pose of authority—feeding others—in order to reveal his social vulnerability; in "Penshurst," by contrast, Jonson converts the gestures that display his dependency—being fed at the table of a superior—into the seal of his own nearly regal power.

This is no simple accomplishment. As Henry Peacham observes, when

> a great man inviteth you to dinner to his table; the sweetness of that favor and kindness is made distasteful by the awe of his greatness. . . . While you whisper in a waiter's ear for anything that you want, you must endure to be carved unto many times of the first, worst, or rawest of the meat. Sometime you have a piece preferred unto you from [the host's] own trencher, but then imagine his belly is full or he cannot for some other reason eat it himself, so that for true and free content you were better seek your dinner with some honest companion in Pie Corner. Besides, [great men] love [that] you should have a kind of dependency of them, that they might make use of you at their pleasure.[21]

21. *The Truth of Our Times*, 203.

"To Penshurst" assesses the humiliation inherent in this situation but converts it into an opportunity for the host's, and the guest's, glorification. In the *Conversations*, Jonson remembers that one day when he was "at table with my Lady Rutland," her husband "accused her that she keept table to poets" (H&S 1:142). The achievement of "Penshurst" is to transform keeping table to poets from a cause of accusation into a reason for approbation.

The poem approaches the dinner table indirectly, through extensive praise of the architectural and natural world that provides the setting and the sustenance of the meal. Yet the terms of this praise prepare for the table by emphasizing the political and edible aspects of the estate. "Penshurst" begins where "Inviting" ends, with a sequence of negations. The first five words—"Thou art not, Penshurst, built"—suggest momentarily that the manor is not the product of human art but springs organically from the countryside (*Forrest* II; H&S 8:93–96). This suggestion is enhanced in the subsequent lines: rather than "a row / Of polish'd pillars," Penshurst presents only an "ancient pile"; rather than boasting a roof of gold, a lantern, stairs, and courts, Penshurst "joy'st in better markes, of soyle, of ayre, / Of wood, of water."[22] Penshurst is "reverenc'd" rather than "grudg'd at" because its physical and social architectonics depend on the operations of nature rather than the obligations of politics.

Moreover, the flourishing natural world that surrounds the manor endows its lord with an independence that the host of "Inviting" would envy. The forest, for example, "serve[s]" Lord Lisle "season'd deere" (suggesting through a playful pun that the deer are always in season and that they are already prepared).[23] "Sydney's copp's," likewise, manages "To crowne" Lisle's "open table" with "The purpled pheasant," whose color suggests both its wound and the royalty its presence confers. Penshurst has a "Mount" where Pan and Bacchus hold their "high feasts." The land feeds the livestock that will nourish Lisle's guests. "Each banke doth yeeld thee coneyes," and the ponds "pay thee tribute fish." As Arthur Marotti observes, "The nature [Jonson] has portrayed is essentially *an edible one.*"[24] The language of obligation and ingestion, so much a part of dining with a superior, is here transferred to the nature that supplies the table this superior sets.

Conversely, the farmers from the surrounding area present to Lord Lisle both their fruits and "their ripe daughters," implying a naturalization of the social

---

22. According to the *OED*, "pile" designated both "a small castle, tower, or stronghold" and "a heap of things (of some height) laid or lying one upon another in a more or less regular manner." The word thus invokes the ancient, native art of castle-building as well as an artless, natural collocation of forms, both of which are contrasted with the exotic ostentation of contemporaneous prodigy houses.

23. Heather Dubrow notes this pun in her fine discussion of "The Country-House Poem: A Study in Generic Development," *Genre* 12 (1979): 163, and suggests: "one of the many reasons the world of Penshurst seems mythic is that, like so many mythic visions, it mediates between the raw and the cooked."

24. "All About Jonson's Poetry," *ELH* 39 (1971): 217.

hierarchy that corresponds to the politicization of the natural hierarchy in the poem's opening lines. At Penshurst, the very edifices that normally enforce social and physical barriers—walls—invite rather than exclude:

> The blushing apricot, and woolly peach
> Hang on thy walls, that every child may reach.

This accessibility is matched by the spontaneous offer of gifts from the country people surrounding the estate. While the ponds are represented as paying tribute and the pikes as acting "Officiously," the laborers respond to their superior with an instinctive, uncoerced fruitfulness:

> But all come in, the farmer, and the clowne:
> And no one empty-handed, to salute
> Thy lord, and lady, though they have no sute.

Despite the demands of decorum, the country people are accepted even if they are improperly dressed ("no sute"), just as their offer is not intended to pave the way for a favorable response to some "sute," or request, of theirs. The natural world absorbs the language of political obligation and so liberates the social world from its constraints:

> But what can this (more then expresse their love)
> Adde to thy free provisions, farre above
> The neede of such?

As Don Wayne remarks, these lines refer to "the payment of *rent in kind* by peasants on the Sidney lands; but its quality as rent and as the product of human labor is hidden, and instead the process is represented as the peasants' free bestowal of 'gifts.'"[25] Obligatory and distressing levies are translated into gestures of voluntary and lavish affection.

This vision of bounty and free giving culminates in Lisle's courtesy toward guests such as Jonson at his table. Lisle's "liberall boord," Jonson exclaims, "doth flow, / With all, that hospitalitie doth know!" Unlike the earl of Salisbury, who, according to Jonson, "never cared for any man longer nor he could make use of him" and who invited Jonson to dinner, yet put him "at ye end" of his table and gave him "none of his meate" (H&S 1:141), Lord Lisle treats his non-noble guest as an equal:

> Where comes no guest, but is allow'd to eate,
> Without his feare, and of thy lords owne meate:
> Where the same beere, and bread, and selfe-same wine,
> That is his Lordship's, shall be also mine.

25. Don E. Wayne, *Penshurst: The Semiotics of Place and the Poetics of History* (Madison: University of Wisconsin Press, 1984), 67. The classic statement of the poem's mystification of coercive social relations is Raymond Williams, *The Country and the City* (London: Oxford University Press, 1973), 28–34.

Lisle's hospitality—manifested most explicitly in his offer to his guests of the precise fare that he consumes—allows Jonson's presence at the table and in the poem to surface simultaneously. Exploiting the same *wine/mine* rhyme used in "Inviting," Jonson manifests his initial use of the first person (more than halfway into the poem) in the act of appropriation and ingestion, claiming for his own what Lisle courteously confers on him. As he distinguishes himself from those "faine to sit (as some, this day, / At great mens tables) and yet dine away," Jonson praises his host for the capacity and desire to satiate a corpulent guest's hunger.

Yet even such acts of hospitality as those for which Jonson applauds Lisle are to be received warily. Jonson, recalls Drummond, "used to say that they who delight to fill men extraordinarie full in their own houses, loved to have their meate againe" (H&S 1:146), implying that great lords feed their inferiors well only in order to fatten them for the slaughter. "I *have* discovered," remarks Jonson in the *Discoveries*, "that a fain'd familiarity in great ones, is a note of certaine usurpation on the lesse. . . . So the Fisher provides baits for the Trowte, Roch, Dace, &c. that they may be food to him" (H&S 8:597–98). Although feeding subordinates is a mark of authority, feeding on subordinates is the privilege of power. "He that doth [courtesies] meerly for his owne sake," insists Jonson, "is like one that feeds his Cattell to sell them" (H&S 8:578). Not only is the scorn and humiliation that Jonson experienced at Salisbury's table to be guarded against, so is the apparently beneficent condescension displayed by Lord Lisle.

In "Penshurst," Jonson does not deny the possibility of such social cannibalism; rather, he transposes it to an anthropomorphized and burgeoning nature which supplies society so bountifully that exploitation is rendered irrelevant. Instead of watching Lisle fatten his guests for the slaughter, we view his cattle feeding by the river to provide meat for his visitors. Instead of setting baits for guests whom he would then consume, Lisle manages an estate that yields pikes who "now weary of their owne kinde to eat, . . / Officiously, at first, themselves betray." Moreover, in a feast with intentional eucharistic overtones (perhaps punning on *host* without mentioning the word, as George Herbert does in "Love" [III]), Penshurst offers to its guest "thy lords owne meate." As in "Inviting a Friend to Supper," the generosity of the host makes possible a secular communion in the midst of a carnivorous social world. Lisle's sacramental hospitality inverts the potential political cannibalism of the occasion; here, inferiors consume, instead of being consumed by, their lord.

Finally, then, not just the natural hierarchy but also the social hierarchy is rendered edible. The Great Chain of Being is divulged as a Great Chain of Feeding. Both the bounty of Penshurst and the hospitality of Lisle are perfected in Jonson's mouth. As Jonson apprehensively glances at a waiter—one whose subordinate status approximates his own—he finds not the grudging of one who will be deprived by Jonson's voracious appetite (since waiters would get to eat only the leftovers), but one who gives freely, like the grounds of the estate he serves:

> Here no man tells my cups; nor, standing by,
>   A waiter, doth my gluttony envy:
> But gives me what I call, and lets me eate,
>   He knowes, below, he shall finde plentie of meate.

Just as Penshurst's architecture banishes envy (l. 1), so is emulation purged from the social distinctions that linger amid such magnificence. And if Jonson must still "call" for what he wants at table, in his room he does not even need to ask, as Lisle's hospitality anticipates all desires:

> Nor, when I take my lodging, need I pray
> For fire, or lights, or livorie; all is there.

Such immediate and total gratification gives Jonson a feeling of power not only over the estate—"As if thou, then, wert mine, or I raign'd here"—but also over the kingdom:

> There's nothing I can wish, for which I stay.
>   That found King James. . . .

The *that* connecting poet and monarch is intentionally ambiguous, temporarily eliding the vast differences in their power and status. Lisle's hospitality, rather than forcing Jonson to taste his bitter subjugation, allows him to feel like a king. "In 'To Penshurst,'" Jonathan Goldberg asserts, "the king and the poet present matching fantasies and desires that the poem and the place enclose. . . . In the poem the poet exercises royal powers."[26] Jonson's ingestion of the substance of his host is also an assimilation of his host's prestige. Although much closer socially to the waiter than to the king, Jonson is able, momentarily, to portray himself as sovereign rather than servant.

In its hospitality to poet and king, then, Penshurst demonstrates the great esteem in which its lord holds poetry. Significantly, the estate contains a tree dedicated to Sir Philip Sidney, the brother of Lord Lisle and a consummate poet and patron:

> That taller tree, which of a nut was set,
>   At his great birth, where all the *Muses* met.

Moreover, this tree testifies to the power of poetry to move its audience:

> There, in the writhed barke, are cut the names
>   Of many a Sylvane, taken with his flames.

---

26. *James I and the Politics of Literature: Jonson, Shakespeare, Donne, and Their Contemporaries* (Baltimore: Johns Hopkins University Press, 1983), 225. See also Cain, "The Place of the Poet," 39–40.

Burgeoning from a single seed into a spray of leaves (with a buried pun on "pages") and kindling flames of desire, the tree exemplifies the creative and coercive capacities of poetry. Like his more illustrious brother, Lisle offers a "defense of poetry"; as the estate nurtures and protects this tree, so does it nourish and shelter Ben Jonson. Noting that "Several of the poems in *The Forrest* are addressed to the Sidney family," David Norbrook comments: "By making public his many links with the Sidney dynasty, Jonson was establishing himself as an heir of the Elizabethan tradition of public poetry." The Sidney family tree integrates the activities of Philip Sidney's vocational and genealogical successors, embodying both Lord Lisle's hospitality to poetry and those literary talents that this hospitality allows Jonson to pursue.[27]

Like the tree, the manor, and the uncoerced and noncoercive tributes that the country people present to Lisle, "To Penshurst" seems to sprout effortlessly from Lisle's fructifying beneficence. Yet just as charitable condescension can disguise the exploitation of inferiors, so can the offering of praise authorize the manipulation of superiors. In the *Discoveries,* for example, Jonson recommends that one should praise one's prince as if he "were already furnished with the parts hee should have" (H&S 8:566). Jonson's exuberant panegyric of Lisle's estate thus offers a model of benevolent behavior which Jonson hopes Lisle will emulate. In this way, too, Jonson attains power over Lisle and so manages to "raign" at Penshurst. Don Wayne pointedly delineates the kinetics of this process: "Jonson makes his patrons *assume* the image which he is obliged to reflect for them."[28] By serving a banquet of language that mirrors as well as honors Lisle's feast, Jonson restores symmetry to a necessarily subordinate relationship.

Jonson's praise of Lisle's hospitality, then, carves a niche for the poet in the social order of Penshurst. As the worth of the guest in "Inviting" dignifies the feast, so Jonson's creative reception of Lord Lisle's fare dignifies the digestible hierarchy of the estate. While Jonson asserts that the Sidney children can "Reade, in their vertuous parents noble parts, / The mysteries of manners, armes, and arts," the operative verb ("Reade") and final noun ("arts") indicate activities far more appropriate to Jonson's text than to the noble parts of his hosts. Into the poem's fabric of praise, then, Jonson insinuates the possibility that Lisle needs him as much as he needs Lisle. In the *Discoveries,* Jonson explicates the dynamics of this conception of the poet's relationship with authority: "Learning needs rest: Soveraignty gives it. Soveraignty needs counsell: Learning affords it" (H&S 8:565). Jonson's "faire acceptance" of Lisle's hospitality dignifies the feast, the estate, and his noble hosts by making them, and what they stand for, legible. Although his eating of another's meat declares his subordination, his praise of his superior's beneficence grants him authority.

27. *Poetry and Politics in the English Renaissance* (London: Routledge and Kegan Paul, 1984), 184. It is significant that Robert Sidney, Lord Lisle, was also a poet. See *The Poems of Robert Sidney*, ed. P. J. Croft (London: Oxford University Press, 1984).

28. *Penshurst*, 154.

In the *Discoveries,* Jonson remarks: "*I have seene,* that *Poverty* makes men doe unfit things; but honest men should not doe them: they should gaine otherwise. Though a man bee hungry, hee should not play the Parasite. . . . But *Flattery* is a fine Pick-lock of tender eares" (H&S 8:596). In "Penshurst," Jonson attempts simultaneously to satisfy his hunger, to flatter, and yet to do no "unfit things." It is a difficult rhetorical stance to sustain, and Jonson often sounds uncomfortably like those "Flatterers for their bread, that praise all my oraculous Lord do's or sayes, be it true or false," whom he censures so severely (H&S 8:612).

But in "Penshurst" Jonson interlards his adulation with faint but distinct hints of discomfort with the political order the estate represents, so that his fulsome praise evinces not only covert counsel but also clandestine criticism. The hyperbole suffusing Jonson's descriptions of nature, for example, infiltrates the depictions of Penshurst's social harmony, implying that one is as removed from reality as the other, that lords will be this beneficent, estates this open, and peasants this grateful, when, and not before, eels choose to "leape on land, / Before the fisher, or into his hand." Moreover, "Penshurst" transposes but does not eliminate the social violence on which the estate's bounty depends. The "season'd deere," the "purpled pheasant," the "painted partrich" that "lyes" and is "willing to be kill'd," the carps that "runne into thy net," the pikes that "betray" themselves—all testify to the hypocrisy and latent brutality of the political, social, and natural order that Jonson attempts to render benign. In addition, the peasants' presentation of their fruits to Lisle via their "ripe daughters" anticipates just the kind of social cannibalism, where superiors ingest inferiors, that Jonson is at pains to purge from Penshurst.

Relatedly, the manor's welcome of gift-bearing peasants "though they have no sute" suggests not just the estate's accessibility and the tenants' generosity but also the rapacity of a social order that requires rent from those who cannot even clothe themselves properly. Furthermore, the praise that is "heap'd" (l. 83) on Lady Lisle for her "high huswifery" is uncomfortably echoed by those "proud, ambitious heaps" (l. 101) to which Penshurst is favorably contrasted. Likewise, the occasion for which Lady Lisle merits praise—"To have her linnen, plate, and all things nigh, / When shee was farre"—clashes disconcertingly with the poem's concluding panegyric of Lord Lisle: that he "dwells," that he, unlike other magnates, remains on his estate in the country. Jonson's elaborate vision of social and natural harmony contains elements, however repressed, of its own repudiation. Such elements disturb, but do not destroy, the vision of beneficent harmony that Jonson creates. Eddies in the "high-swolne *Medway*" bordering the estate (a river that may "faile" Lisle's "dish"), these elements signal the bitter social reality from which Penshurst attempts to isolate itself but that continues to trespass the estate's boundaries; they also mark Jonson's characteristic ambivalence toward even the most propitious manifestations of authority.

In one of his last surviving letters, a request for aid addressed to the earl of

Newcastle, Jonson broadcasts the trepidation about his dependence on authority that "Penshurst" and "Inviting" only whisper. Rather than the nearly regal power he claims for himself in "Penshurst" or the graceful disclaimers of self-worth that compose the opening of "Inviting," Jonson declares: "I my selfe beeing no substance, am faine to trouble you with shaddowes" (H&S, 1:213). He proceeds to relate "an Apologue, or Fable in a dreame" that is remarkable for its exposure of the bitter subjugation into which poetry had cast him. It begins where "Penshurst" reaches its climax, with a gift from a superior: "I being strucken with the Palsey in the Year 1628. had by Sir Thomas Badger some few monthes synce, a Foxe sent mee for a present; wch Creature, by handling I endeavored to make tame." As Jonson tries to domesticate this wild gift from a patron (foxes were thought to cure palsy, so the gift is not as outlandish as it might seem), one of his servants announces that the fox has learned to speak. Jonson finds the animal "cynically expressing his owne lott, to be condemn'd to the house of a Poett, where nothing was to bee seene but the bare walls." Jonson tries to comfort his talking fox with "good words, and stroak[ing]," but the fox tells Jonson that he needs not words but "meate." This angers Jonson, who calls the fox "stinking Vermine," to which the fox replies: "looke into your Cellar, . . You'le find a worse vermin there." Jonson goes to his cellar and discovers "all the floore turn'd up, as if a Colony of Moles had beene there." In order to rid himself of the vermin, Jonson sends for "the Kings most Excellent Mole-catcher." But when the mole catcher arrives, he tells Jonson, "It is not in my power to distroy this vermine; the K[ing] or some good Man of a Noble Nature must helpe you. This kind of Mole is call'd a *Want,* wch will distroy you, and your family, if you prevent not the workeing of it in tyme."

Beginning with an intractable gift from a patron that reminds Jonson of his poverty without relieving its distress, the letter foregrounds the harsh reality on which the fantasies of gratification and power depicted in "Penshurst" and "Inviting" are based. Rather than the fecund nature that officiously surrenders itself to Lisle's table, Jonson's basement teems only with moles, which are also called (in a pun Jonson wittily but bitterly exploits) "wants." These wants can be exterminated exclusively through the intervention of the king or some nobleman. Instead of the capacity to feast another graciously manifested in "Inviting," here Jonson is unable to supply a pet fox with meat. The nature animated by political duty in "Penshurst" is supplanted by a nature that is anthropomorphized only to force Jonson to recognize his social and political impotence.

An immense aesthetic and political distance separates the vision of the poet's relationship to power presented in this letter from that attained in "Inviting" and "Penshurst." Yet in the margins of "Penshurst"'s extravagant praise and under the surface of "Inviting"'s courteous veil lurk traces of the antagonistic social world haunting the letter to Newcastle. Just as "To Penshurst" mystifies the backbreaking labor and social violence by which the estate's bounty is achieved, rendering the payment of rent a token of affection and transforming slaughter into willing sacrifice, it also mystifies the sedulous labor and lamentable subjugation of the poet by cloaking them in "the mysteries of manners, armes, and arts." But mystification is not necessarily falsification. At times both "Penshurst" and "Inviting" seem to practice the "Art" that Jonson upbraids in the *Discoveries*—"to apparell a Lye well, to give it a good dressing; that though the nakedness would show deform'd and odious, the suiting of it might draw their Readers" (H&S 8:573). But in "Penshurst" and "Inviting," Jonson practices a far more difficult and profound art: he attires a stultifying social structure in garb that enhances its attractiveness while betraying its repugnant qualities. The vitality of these poems resides in their ability to articulate the anxieties of the poet even as they announce his nearly regal power.

"Inviting" and "Penshurst," furthermore, expose Jonson's deep distrust of the two audiences—the popular and the aristocratic—whose support was necessary for his survival as a writer. With no certain source of income beyond his ability to capitalize on his verbal performances, Jonson exploited the wide range of markets open to a writer in Renaissance England. As Joseph Loewenstein remarks, Jonson's

> career in the literary marketplace, his relation to the mechanisms of making the written word pay, was particularly various. He sold plays to acting companies. . . . He acted in plays. . . . He sold masques to the court. He also participated in the older, chancier literary market, circulating verse in manuscript and so making direct and indirect appeals for patronage. And, of course, he also sold verse to a publisher, a member of the Stationers' Company, for dissemination in print.[29]

The casual mention in "Inviting" of the bread bearing the imprint of his unsold poems betrays Jonson's acute anxiety about the aesthetic taste of the popular literary market. Similarly, the repressed but omnipresent violence of "Penshurst" divulges his uneasiness with the potentially ravenous system of aristocratic patronage. Although participating simultaneously in the diverse economies of capitalism—by virtue of being published in the 1616 *Workes*—and of clientage—by virtue of being addressed to superiors—both poems nervously decry the popular and aristocratic markets they nevertheless desire to enter.

"All art is transformation," contends Stephen Spender, "and the greatness or littleness of a poet in his poetry lies in the degree of his capacity to translate the harsh unpoetic material of the world into poetry."[30] "To Penshurst" and "Inviting a Friend to Supper" display Jonson's striking capacity for such translation. But even more impressively, these poems manifest Jonson's aptitude for inscribing in his translation those aspects of the world that remain harsh, unpoetic, and hostile. The tonal and generic range of Jonson's literary corpus has always presented something of an enigma, encompassing delicate lyricism and elegant panegyric as well as vitriolic mockery and bitter invective. In "Penshurst" and

---

29. "The Script in the Marketplace," *Representations* 12 (1985): 102.
30. "On Fame and the Writer," *New York Review of Books* 33, no. 20 (18 December 1986): 75.

"Inviting," however, these contrary impulses are tenuously conjoined. Concurrently masques celebrating the social hierarchy and satires decrying its abuses, "Penshurst" and "Inviting" consolidate the poet's divergent duties of praise and blame.

Jonson maintains a claim of independence in the world of patronage, proposes Stanley Fish, by "declar[ing] unreal the network of dependencies and obligations that to all appearances directs and regulates his every action."[31] Although accurately diagnosing the peculiar aggregation of autonomy and dependency in Jonson's poetry, this formulation hinges on an unwarranted sense of the contradictory rather than complementary relationship between poetry and politics. In "Inviting" and "Penshurst," at least, Jonson does not declare this network of obligations unreal; rather, he usurps its terminology in order to "create it perfect" even while exposing its ample and troubling imperfections. The narrow imbrication between flattery and satire is for Jonson the region of whatever fragile independence he can achieve.

"Any account of ideology in literature that assumes a sharp divide between ruling class and opposition, between writers who legitimate and writers who subvert," remarks Annabel Patterson, "will fail to deal with Jonson."[32] Indeed, the linguistically equivocal and socially intricate nature of Jonson's utterances to and about power defy the easy dichotomies by which we attempt to order our discourse about the relationships between poetry and politics. In "Penshurst" and "Inviting" particularly, we feel the inadequacy of these categories to convey the complex fusion of legitimation and subversion, encomium and indictment, panegyric and paranoia, that these poems produce. In them, Jonson attains a voice of potency by advertising his dependency as praise of another's charity.

In "An Epistle to Sir Edward Sacvile, now Earle of Dorset," Jonson also intends to convert his dependency into an opportunity to exercise his creative authority:

> And though my fortune humble me, to take
> The smallest courtesies with thankes, I make
> Yet choyce from whom I take them.
> (*Underwood* XIII)

The terminology of taking and making, seizing and creating, is the same used in "Inviting" and "Penshurst" to assert the persuasive and procreative power of the poet. But here, rather than rectifying himself and another through an inventive act of praise and "faire acceptance," Jonson can only "*make* choyce" on whom to depend. In "Penshurst" and "Inviting," however, Jonson transforms, if only briefly, the acceptance of another's bounty into a genuinely imaginative and

---

31. "Authors-Readers: Jonson's Community of the Same," *Representations* 7 (1984): 56.
32. "Lyric and Society in Jonson's *Under-wood*," in *Lyric Poetry: Beyond New Criticism*, ed. Chaviva Hosek and Patricia Parker (Ithaca: Cornell University Press, 1985), 158.

authoritative gesture, generating a nearly seamless vision of social harmony subservient to the poet who serves as host and guest. To turn dependence into victory, subordination into authority, praise into poetry, and poetry into power, was for Jonson the supreme accomplishment of "the mysteries of manners, armes, and arts."

6. Carew's Monarchy of Wit

Nothing seems further from reality than poetic compliments whose extravagance time has exposed as pure friendship. Beyond the poet's affability, however, some of Thomas Carew's poems to or about fellow authors disclose important aspects of his cultural perspective. Reading these poems in the context of the writings and speeches of Kings James and Charles, one has the sense of witnessing a new social phenomenon resulting from the convergence of political and cultural currents. These currents are complex, but the immediate effect of their confluence seems startlingly simple: the populace has discovered its voice and is using it as never before. Though this development sounds innocuous, neither Thomas Carew, courtier and coterie poet, nor the Stuart kings are pleased to hear the murmurings from below. To the kings and the poet, the new voice signals social upheaval: they see a conflict emerge between an authoritative voice and a dissident voice raised to usurp its hegemony.

James and Charles reacted to this phenomenon by reiterating certain principles, convictions arising from a master idea and meant to silence their people and, especially, their parliaments. In the political context, such a reaction, though repressive, is not surprising; in the literary domain, however, it is remarkable. A number of Thomas Carew's poems transfer his monarchs' principles into the world of letters, reflecting the royal attitude that the public voice threatens the usurpation of rightful authority. Consistently in these poems, Carew appropriates the language and the categories of the existing political and social orders, reorienting them to construct a monarchy of wit based on absolutist Stuart principles. Imitation is supposed to be a sincere form of flattery: Carew's appropriation of James's and Charles's rhetoric and political strategies would seem to be a valorization of their state. However, since the kings' absolutist stance depends on their claims of being unique sources of authority, imitating them produces a challenge to, rather than an affirmation of, their rank and governance. Covertly, Carew's poems subvert the state of his Stuart kings by positing an alternate order of authority governed by poet-kings.

In the realm of literature, two of the major factors that contributed to the emergence of a diverse public ready to express its views are well known: the growth of the popular theater and the increasing readiness of authors to publish their work made everyone a potential commentator. Even King James realized that the publication of *Basilikon Doron* made the royal book "subject to every mans censure, as the current of his affection leades him."[1] In the political world, also, the general public gained access to materials bound to provoke discussion. The first coranto was published in December 1620 and, though the publication of domestic news was illegal during this period, ways of leaking State information were devised. Parliamentary deliberations were supposed to be secret, but members circulated manuscripts of their own speeches. When these were pirated and offered for sale, they achieved a wider circulation, as did summaries of debates and other parliamentary business. Given such stimulation, it is hardly surprising that the "rabble," as Thomas Carew styled it, seemed to grow loquacious. In 1621, James twice issued proclamations intended to stop public discussion of state affairs, complaining, "There is at this tyme a more licentious Passage of lavish Discourse and bould Censure in matters of State than hath been heretofore or is fitt to be suffered."[2]

The freedom and limitation of speech had long concerned the English monarchy, inspiring Henry VIII in the 1530s to extend "the definition of treason to cover the spoken word."[3] Elizabeth and James expected their parliaments to speak only on subjects they specified and prohibited parliamentary discussion of foreign affairs and religion. James especially emphasized the impropriety, not to say the illegality, of discussion of his regal power: "As to dispute what God may doe is Blasphemie . . . So it is sedition in subjects to dispute what a King may do in the height of his power." At different times, he reminded his people of God's law that "Thou shalt not rayle upon the Judges, neither speak evill of the ruler of thy people" and told a parliament that "Men should bee ashamed to make shew of the quicknesse of their wits here, either in taunting, scoffing, or detracting the Prince of State in any point."[4] Charles was as attentive as his predecessors to the liberties and limits of his subjects' speech, but the three rulers faced a losing battle. In Elizabeth's day, the House of Commons "moved from a position of asking to speak their minds on issues put before them without fear of punishment, to a position of demanding the right to initiate discussion and influence policy on any issue they chose." Lawrence Stone remarks that by the 1620s the House of Commons had progressed from the desire to moot particular subjects to the basic question of freedom of speech.[5] It is no wonder that, as James and Charles heard their subjects encroaching on territory they deemed their own, they articulated a full complex of attitudes about speech in relation to authority.

1. *The Political Works of James I. Reprinted from the Edition of 1616*, intro. by Charles Howard McIlwain (Cambridge: Harvard University Press, 1918), 5. In quotations from this text, typographical conventions are modernized.
2. Perez Zagorin, *The Court and the Country: The Beginning of the English Revolution* (New York: Atheneum, 1970), 108, 106.
3. Lawrence Stone, *The Causes of the English Revolution, 1529–1642* (London: Routledge & Kegan Paul, 1972), 59.
4. *James*, 310, 60, 289.
5. *Causes of Revolution*, 93.

Regardless of the issues that elicited them, the statements of the kings from whose courts Carew wrote reveal some consistent assumptions about speech and authority. These are implicit in the ancient political metaphor of head and body, which James used in *The Trew Law of Free Monarchies:* "As the discourse and direction flowes from the head, and the execution according thereunto belongs to the rest of the members, every one according to their office: so it is betwixt a wise Prince, and his people."[6] Since only the head has a tongue, only the head is gifted with the power of genuine speech. And "direction" as well as discourse belongs to the head of the body politic, again, because the mind resides in the head. As far as James and Charles are concerned, authority in the State belongs only to the voice of the king; secondarily, authoritative speech belongs to those officials whom the king empowers with his singular authority. Occasionally, he empowers a group such as parliament to discuss certain topics; but such discussion in the absence of royal authority he regards as political insubordination. It seems as perverse to him as if talk were to issue suddenly from his leg. From this self-serving cluster of kingly ideas followed the corollaries whose aim was to silence the free and unwelcome expression of popular and parliamentary views: the denial that unauthorized voices are based on understanding or vital knowledge and the charge that they subvert a hierarchy based on the indisputable power and wisdom of the king.

Fundamental to the royal view of authoritative speech is the equation of comprehension with rank; explicitly or implicitly, the Crown maintained that understanding and, therefore, responsible discourse are related to status in the government hierarchy. King James's insistence on his subjects' inability to understand the essence of his power is well known: "If there fall out a question that concerns my Prerogative or mystery of State, deale not with it," he ordered the judges in the Star Chamber, "for they are transcendent matters." Charles's attitude echoed his father's. Responding to a parliamentary remonstrance in 1628, he claimed that the ability to understand key issues belonged to him alone: "Now I see you are fallen upon points of state which belong to me to understand better than you, and I must tell you that you do not understand so much as I thought you had done."[7] The equation of rank with understanding is given a clever twist and translated into the world of letters by Carew in "To my much honoured friend Henry Lord Cary of Lepington upon his translation of Malvezzi."

This poem elicits little attention today since neither Malvezzi's *Romulus and Tarquin* nor Henry Cary himself is of interest to literary criticism. Indeed, even in his own day the poet believed the translator could hope only for a small audience. It seems, at first, that in his poem Carew attributes the limited appeal of his friend's translation to its subject: Malvezzi had to learn "vulgar Italian,"

---

6. *James*, 65.

7. *James*, 332; Conrad Russell, *Parliaments and English Politics: 1621–1629* (Oxford: Clarendon Press, 1979), 385.

the demotic idiom, before he wrote his book. Even so, his material is "so sublime," his mode of expression "so new," that he is "by a good / Part of his Natives hardly understood." It stands to reason that an excellent translation will duplicate the sublimity and novelty that puzzled the Italian public and have the same effect on the English.

But Carew's consoling explanation to his friend is more complex, and typical of his attitude toward the public world at large:

> You must expect no happier fate, 'tis true
> He is of noble birth, of nobler you:
> So nor your thoughts nor words fit common eares,
> He writes, and you translate, both to your Peeres.
>
> (ll. 13–16)[8]

At first it seems that the poet locates the problem of the work's reception in the social class of its author and translator. With considerable cleverness, he seems to have "proved" that understanding is a function of social rank: the English lord, because he is a peer, understood the Italian marquesse while most of his compatriots did not, though he condescended to write in their ordinary speech. Similarly, Lord Cary's translation will not be generally understood; because of his social status he, like Malvezzi, speaks a language different from the language of common people. Only his peers, for whom the poet speaks, can understand him.

But the latter statement brings us up short, of course, and apprises us of the poet's covert agenda: he appropriates the terminology that defines the existing social system to posit a rival, challenging system. As one who understands Malvezzi and Henry Cary, Thomas Carew speaks for their "Peeres"; obviously, then, peerage in this system of aristocracy is not a matter of social rank. The true nobility of Malvezzi and Cary, the poet suggests, consists of the novelty, sublimity, and elegance of their thoughts and words; his own nobility consists of his understanding and appreciation. Their important titles are not *lord* or *marquesse,* but *translator* and *author*—titles that Thomas Carew, as *poet* or *author,* can match. The lower classes in the caste system the poet creates are all those, titled or untitled, who do not understand, at least, the talents or achievements of their superiors: certain "thoughts and words" are too large, literally, for ears of congenital smallness. Initially, it seems as if the poet's emphasis on nobility is a crude compliment to Henry Cary's social rank; in fact, it is a subtle compliment to his native talent and to his accomplishment as a translator.

The common public will not praise Lord Cary's work because they will not understand it, but this judicious discretion was not typical in state affairs. More often, Carew's kings stressed their subjects' ignorance as a compelling argument

---

8. All quotations of Carew's poems are from *The Poems of Thomas Carew, With His Masque Coelum Britannicum,* ed. Rhodes Dunlap (1949; rpt. London: Oxford University Press, 1970).

for their silence. James sought to control his people's discussion of political business because it was "of high Nature unfit for vulgar Discourse," "Matter above the Reach and Calling that to good and dutiful Subjects appertaineth."[9] Charles tried to stop the impeachment of Buckingham in the House of Commons by arguing his superior knowledge against the members' supposed ignorance: he "himself doth know better than any man living," he declared, the character of the Duke.[10] When dissidence persisted, the kings protested, as an offense against the reasonable established order, the lifting of unqualified voices against those invested with authority. James warned one of his parliaments that they should "not meddle with the maine points of Government; that is my craft. . . . I must not be taught my office." Charles complained in 1626 that eminent state counselors had been "censured and traduced in this house [of Commons], by men whose years and education cannot attain to that depth." Three years later, he professed astonishment that "young lawyers" in the House "take upon them to decry the opinions of the Judges."[11] This kind of hierarchical transgression, a topsy-turvy state of affairs wherein ignorance questions or contradicts wisdom, figures significantly in Carew's poems to Ben Jonson and to William Davenant.

Carew's poem to Jonson, "Upon Occasion of his Ode of defiance annext to his Play of the new Inne," opens with an image of authority and points to its attempted usurpation:

> Tis true (deare *Ben:*) thy just chastizing hand
> Hath fixt upon the sotted Age a brand
> To their swolne pride, and empty scribbling due,
> It can nor judge, nor write.

By virtue of his "just chastizing hand," Jonson is a judge who has fairly deliberated and meted out punishment. His decision to mark the offenders by branding discloses their status, since that form of punishment was reserved for criminals of the lowest class. The crimes that revealed their true nature (despite the status they might claim in society) and merited the humiliating chastisement are obvious: they attempted the usurpation of functions properly undertaken by their superiors. Empty scribblers have presumed to write, and "sotted" heads, minds "foolish, doltish, and stupid" (*OED*), have presumed to judge. If Charles was shocked that young lawyers offered their opinions against experienced judges, we can only imagine his consternation if convicted malefactors had spoken out to judge their judges. Such an instance of insubordination Carew perceives in Jonson's situation. The entire age has meddled in matter above its reach and calling. The populace has tried to usurp the authority belonging only to those who can judge and write.

9. Zagorin, *Court and Country*, 107.

10. Samuel Rawson Gardiner, ed., *The Constitutional Documents of the Puritan Revolution, 1625–1660*, 3d ed. (Oxford: Clarendon Press, 1906), 4.

11. *James*, 315; *Constitutional Documents*, 5, 93.

Carew's contempt for the public voice is evident in the way he hides his agreement with its appraisal of *The New Inn.* The age cannot judge or write,

> and yet 'tis true
> Thy commique Muse from the exalted line
> Toucht by thy *Alchymist,* doth since decline
> From that her Zenith, and fortells a red
> And blushing evening, when she goes to bed.
>
> (ll. 4–8)

As far as the poet is concerned, the benighted public has no right to express its views even if, as it happens, they coincide with his own and are, therefore, correct. Carew cleverly manages not to identify his evaluation with that of the incompetent public: by not commenting at all on *The New Inn,* he avoids echoing the voice he has discredited. In spite of this maneuver, however, his criticism of Jonson's entire dramatic work aims at its present nadir, his reference to a "blushing evening" clearly indicating the shame of a humiliating failure, despite the compliments that follow.

Carew's magisterial remarks on the "sotted Age," his confident overview of Jonson's work, and the reasonable distinctions he perceives among his friend's plays all declare an authority equal to the "just chastizing hand" of Jonson. But when he suggests that he is a better judge than the emotionally involved father of the works under discussion, his claim to power is complete. He urges Jonson to accept from his superior a version of what he would not accept (quite properly) from his inferiors: that his plays, "though one brain strike / Soules into all . . . are not all alike." Having asserted his authority, Carew proceeds to judgment:

> Why should the follies then of this dull age
> Draw from thy Pen such an immodest rage
> As seemes to blast thy (else-immortall) Bayes,
> When thine owne tongue proclaimes thy ytch of praise?
> Such thirst will argue drouth. No, let be hurld
> Upon thy workes, by the detracting world
> What malice can suggest.
>
> (ll. 23–29)

If the thickheaded public tried to usurp the judicial office, Jonson's fault was to acknowledge the decision handed down from a kangaroo court. Worse, his "ytch of praise" ceded to the "dull age" the power to grant or withhold something he prized. In effect, and for all his "defiance," Jonson submitted to a body whose judicial capacity he and the poet deny.

Carew goes on to demonstrate that Jonson can never hope to be justly valued by the pugnacious crowd: while the mob scorns the playwright as a plagiarizer, the poet honors him as a conqueror of foreign powers bringing home "rich spoyles" (ll. 33–42). Carew's language, making Jonson a king winning trophies, demonstrates that in thought, language, and discrimination, a major chasm separates the general public and true poets. Since the chasm exists, Carew advises Jonson to look to the future. "Let others glut on the extorted praise / Of vulgar breath, trust thou to after days":

> Thou art not of their ranke, the quarrell lyes
> Within thine owne Virge, then let this suffice,
> The wiser world doth greater Thee confesse
> Then all men else, then Thy selfe onely lesse.
>
> (ll. 47-50)

He enjoins Jonson to acknowledge the distinctions separating him from vulgar writers, and "the wiser world" from vulgar audiences. A surfeit of praise is available to scribblers of the hastily written trash enjoyed by the ignorant public. But the hunger for commendation that Jonson revealed in his "Ode" should be satisfied by the esteem of the "wiser world." How the elder poet must have hated Carew's imitation of his own manner: the seamless combination of criticism, praise, and advice is delivered in accents as measured, deliberate, and conclusive as any of Jonson's.

In Carew's view, there can be no such thing as universal acclaim: the gap between the vulgar and the wiser worlds is so wide that they cannot approve or applaud the same things. He concedes that the louder voice belongs to the witless rout. But ultimately, he asserts, the truly powerful voice belongs to Jonson's (and his own) small class, whose authority will be upheld by "after dayes," long after the applause of the mob has been forgotten. The poet stresses the ignorance of the public and its incapacity to judge, not to suggest that Jonson is above appraisal, but to assert his own claim to deliver the authoritative verdict. Displacing the public voice that would usurp the privilege of making literary judgments, he claims a unique authority for those who can judge and write, for true poets.

When Charles ordered the House of Commons to stop prying into Buckingham's affairs, he suggested that in a well-ordered state, people who do not understand should acknowledge their limitation and allow themselves to be guided; therefore, he told the Commons to "cease [its] unparliamentary inquisition" and to "commit unto his Majesty's care, and wisdom, and justice" any necessary reformations.[12] In "To my worthy Friend, M. D'Avenant, Upon his Excellent Play, *The Just Italian,*" Carew exalts as desirable a similar popular docility in literary affairs and appropriates his monarch's all-knowing and angry paternalism. He dispatches quickly with the great merit of Davenant's play to concentrate on his real subject, the public who disliked it. The age, Carew believes,

> Requires a Satyre. What starre guides the soule
> Of these our froward times, that dare controule,

---

12. *Constitutional Documents,* 5.

Yet dare not learne to judge? When didst thou flie
From hence, cleare, candid Ingenuitie?
I have beheld, when pearch'd on the smooth brow
Of a faire modest troope, thou didst allow
Applause to slighter workes; but then the weake
Spectator, gave the knowing leave to speake.
Now noyse prevailes, and he is tax'd for drowth
Of wit, that with the crie, spends not his mouth.

(ll. 4–14)

From the beginning, the poem's diction suggests political confrontation: though "Garlands" "crowne" Davenant's "triumphant worke" (ll. 2–4), the times "dare" to criticize it. The age's preference for satire is only one indication of its contentious nature. Calling the times "froward," Carew accuses his obtuse contemporaries of being refractory or ungovernable, a trait whose relevance to theatergoing is not immediately clear. The people challenge and criticize freely, without any knowledge of standards for judgment, as a consequence merely of their malevolent disposition to belittle and censure. This verbal aggressiveness Carew describes as a new attitude, contrasting the present public with a past audience characterized by "Ingenuitie." The word means "straightforwardness" and "sincerity," but in the seventeenth century, its primary sense was related to social class. The first definition the *OED* cites is "the condition of being freeborn; of honourable extraction or station." As he did in the poem to Jonson, Carew implies that the public behaves like the social dregs. The vanished audience he misses was "a faire modest troope," its gentility and modesty evident in the applause it gave to plays "slighter" than Davenant's. But primarily the audience was genteel and modest, as far as Carew is concerned, because it knew and kept its humble place; the "weake Spectator," acknowledging his limitations, deferred to the opinion of the "knowing." Meekly accepting the judgment of his betters, he kept his lowly mouth shut.

But now the public forgets its well-deserved modesty, pretends to have wit, and produces "noyse"—an annoying and meaningless eruption of sound. Carew expatiates on the public ignorance and tastelessness with a zest exceeding the "scorne, and Pity" he declares it merits (ll. 15–32). In the final consolation he offers Davenant, he explains his vehemence:

Repine not Thou then, since this churlish fate
Rules not the stage alone; perhaps the State
Hath felt this rancour, where men great and good,
Have by the Rabble beene misunderstood.
So was thy Play; whoose cleere, yet loftie straine,
Wisemen, that governe Fate, shall entertaine.

Obviously, Carew wishes he could organize his world according to the ideal scheme also favored by his monarchs: a public accepting the guidance of a few "understanders," trusting the judgment of that overclass entirely. It is against this ideal hierarchy that the "froward" audience of Davenant's play rebelled. Perhaps the unspecificity of Carew's remarks about the "great and good" statesmen reflects a necessary discretion; certainly, it facilitates his equation of literary and governmental affairs. The criticism of Davenant's play as an "impious reach" or conception (l. 23) is the equivalent of the criticism of blameless state officials when their "reach" or "policy" *(OED)* has been misunderstood. As the weak spectator tries to usurp the critical function of the knowing in the theater, the rabble tries to usurp the evaluative capacity of men able in governmental matters. Carew makes the acts of rebellion seem equal. But, as if the elevation of literary affairs to the level of government were not subversive enough, he suggests that the authorities facing the insurrections are not equal. "Men great and good" may be on a par with "Wisemen"; but the first rule only the State while the second "governe Fate." The stage, a relatively small and insignificant sphere, is left to the churls. In this poem, Carew almost admits that the theater is part of the only state whose power concerns him; he almost declares the supremacy of the literary domain governed by wise men like himself.

James objected to his subjects' unrestricted speech as a direct challenge to his authority, as a "breach of prerogative royal," and Charles was equally alert to the threat: "under the pretense of privilege and freedom of speech . . . [the Commons] take liberty to declare against all authority of Council and Courts at their pleasure."[13] But ultimately, as dissidents insisted on their ability to understand and their right to speak, Charles could respond only with renewed and more specific restrictions. When the parliament of 1628–1629 persisted in discussing the Church's Articles, he had them printed with a declaration stating his intention to silence "any unnecessary disputations, altercations, or questions . . . which may nourish faction both in the Church and Commonwealth." To avoid the peril of faction, the king restricted all deliberation on the Articles to authorized Convocation. His aim, he explained later, was to "tie and restrain all opinions to the sense of those Articles, that nothing might be left for private fancies and innovations."[14] Like his monarchs, Carew saw danger in the expression of "private fancies." Imitating the autocratic urge to control unauthorized interpretation, in "To the Reader of Master William Davenant's Play," he reveals a desire to impose his judgment that parallels his monarchs' desire to rule absolutely.

Addressing the member of the public, the poet takes the talkative bull by the horns to instruct him on how to read Davenant's *The Witts* :

> It hath been said of old, that Playes are Feasts,
> Poets the Cookes, and the Spectators Guests,
> The Actors Waitors: From this Simile
> Some have deriv'd an unsafe libertie

13. Russell, *Parliaments and Politics,* 135; *Constitutional Documents,* 94.
14. *Constitutional Documents,* 75, 89.

To use their Judgements as their tastes, which chuse
Without controule, this Dish, and that refuse:
But Wit allowes not this large Priviledge,
Either you must confesse, or feele it's edge.

Carew substitutes, for an image of unrestricted sociability, an image of political power. The trouble with Ben Jonson's simile, according to him, is that it inspired some people to confuse taste with judgment; it caused them to confuse a social situation in which compulsion is irrelevant with an intellectual situation in which certain strictures must apply. This misunderstanding has resulted in "an unsafe libertie." Carew's use of "unsafe," surely a word too strong in this context, may hint at a concern with a situation far more important than current approaches to the stage; it suggests that he sees liberty "without controule" in any sphere as a threat to desirable order. Against the potential anarchy of individual freedom, he introduces the powerful figure of a monarch. Wit is personified as a stern king who does not grant individuals the right to deny his power. He demands that it be acknowledged, if not appreciated. The phrase "feele it's edge" suggests that too much liberty is "unsafe" because this king has a sharp punishment for rebels who resist his control.

It is the poet, of course, who tries to curb the excessive freedom assumed by incompetent readers who think they can judge literary work as they judge sausage. As the dictator of rules for aesthetic judgment, Carew insists that everything is not open to individual interpretation but has a character or quality that is indisputable, given perceptive powers acute enough: "Things are distinct, and must the same appeare / To every piercing Eye, or well-tun'd Eare" (ll. 11–12). He will permit individual taste and personal preference only so long as "the Good / And Bad, be by your Judgement understood" (ll. 19–20). Finally, after devoting twenty lines to these stern, restrictive cautions to the reader, Carew turns to the play that occasioned the poem:

But if, as in this Play, where with delight
I feast my Epicurean appetite
With rellishes so curious, as dispence
The utmost pleasure to the ravisht sense,
You should professe that you can nothing meet
That hits your taste, either with sharpe or sweet,
But cry out, 'tis insipid; your bold Tongue
May doe it's Master, not the Author wrong;
For Men of better Pallat will by it
Take the just elevation of your Wit.

(ll. 21–30)

Claiming superior powers of discrimination, Carew assures the reader that even if he exercises only his taste, he will find something in Davenant's play to his liking. The reader need not concern himself with evaluation; the poet gives him the authorized judgment. In spite of the dicta of Wit, the reader may still think he has the freedom to judge the merit of this work published to the world at large. But Carew "allowes not this large Priviledge" and threatens accordingly. The reader is free only to agree with him, the monarch whose authority in the domain of wit is unquestionable. The bold tongue that dares to disagree can hurt only its own master by revealing his dim-witted inferiority. Using his "edge" to threaten readers with their exposure as tasteless and indiscriminate, Carew devises a way to "controule" public liberty.

The writings of James and Charles suggest that, in spite of how often they were challenged, they assumed a society divided into two classes: the small elite they headed, whose power and authority derived from the royal rank, knowledge, and wisdom; and a huge underclass, whose submissiveness should logically follow from their station and their presumed ignorance. Such a perspective came naturally to men who believed they ruled by divine right. When dissident voices angered the Stuarts, subjecting them to criticism, hampering their freedom to act, or trying to define and therefore circumscribe their power, the kings tried to suppress them as threats to their authority. The poems I have discussed suggest that Thomas Carew also assumed a two-class division: the small elite of fine authors that he headed (in his own estimation), king-authors endowed with knowledge, wisdom, and taste; and the rest of the populace, good subjects when they permitted themselves to be guided, bad when they expressed their own unfounded opinions.

Assuming that authority should be the natural right of a talented and intellectual elite, Carew responded to, or even anticipated, the popular voice raised in criticism against his friends. Jealously protecting the hegemony in literary affairs that he believed should belong to himself and his artistic peers, he wrote poems that are political statements as much as they are consolations or compliments. These reveal a strong contempt for a socially heterogeneous public expressing its views despite its supposed ignorance; simultaneously, they disclose a covert hostility toward the Stuart sociopolitical system. Two opposed groups confront each other in Carew's poems: the commons and the peers; those who cannot judge or write and the wiser world; the weak and the knowing spectators; the rabble and the wisemen; the indiscriminate and the men of better palate. The poet points to the attempted overturning of the hierarchical distinctions implied by *inferior* and *superior, ignorant* and *wise, the rabble* and *the great* with images of social insubordination that are themselves gestures of rebellion: low-class offenders censure their judge, the mob criticizes men "great and good," and libertines defy a king. But for Carew, the rout and the rabble who rebel against their betters are the ignorant and indiscriminate in every social echelon. Their superiors are the talented authors.

The complex reasons why Carew would wish to undermine, in however abstract a fashion, the social structure on which he depended cannot be determined fully. But we know that he was dismissed in 1616 by Sir Dudley Carleton, his patron, for having "foolishly put to paper certain aspersions" on the character of Carleton and his wife. At least once, in other words, Carew had responded with a form of verbal aggression to a situation in which he felt at a disadvantage. He was certainly at a social disadvantage as a courtier. He "came of good family," but the recent knighthoods of his father and his elder brother would have been unimpressive at the Stuart court. The poems discussed above suggest that he was very conscious of the difference between the superiority he assumed for himself as a poet and the inferiority others assumed for him in the social hierarchy. The poems also demonstrate that, between the time Carleton dismissed him and the time he wrote these poems, Carew improved his "talent for adroitly managing his own repressed competitiveness, for making gestures that covertly challenge the powerful, even while they gratify them."[15] It must have delighted Carew to flout the intellectual and æsthetic inferiority of people who assumed social superiority to himself, and to get away with it.

Speaking for his author-peers, the wiser world, and the discriminating, Carew claimed absolute authority in the world of letters. In this regard, he was bound to be more successful than his rulers. Carew appropriated the absolutist rhetoric of his kings to create a monarchy whose power surpasses theirs. As James's and Charles's repeated complaints and warnings show, a king cannot always control his subjects. But a poet, it seemed to Carew, can control his subjects absolutely: against the rebellious outbursts directed at his friends, he triumphed. He managed in his poems to discredit his subjects' dissenting voices and to supplant their unauthorized views with his own. Against their usurping clamor, he managed to have the last word. It is appropriate that Carew reserved his highest praise for John Donne. As Carew described Donne's kingdom, the poet-king did as he liked and not a peep was heard from the passive subjects upon whose wills he "Committed holy Rapes." Whatever the reality, in the elegy Carew made Donne's dominion total: only after his death do libertines dare to rebel against his "strict lawes," using stories that Donne had "silenc'd" absolutely. Carew appreciated that kind of power, especially because he could create and wield it himself. Manners and good sense forced him to suggest that his author-friends share his status, but one feels that theirs are courtesy-titles. Carew's poems exalt and preserve his taste, his judgment, his word, his authority. His compliments notwithstanding, Thomas Carew is the king, the sole and absolute ruler of the monarchy of wit that he created.

---

15. Rhodes Dunlap, "Introduction," in *The Poems of Thomas Carew*, xxi, xiii. The remark about "repressed competitiveness" I appropriate from Katharine Eisaman Maus's discussion of Ben Jonson, Mosca, and Jeremy in *Ben Jonson and the Roman Frame of Mind* (Princeton: Princeton University Press, 1984), 9.

Michael P. Parker

7. Satire in Sextodecimo: Davenant, the Dwarf, and the Politics of "Jeffereidos"

On 5 April 1630 Giovanni Soranzo, the Venetian ambassador to the court of Charles I, dispatched the following news to the doge and senate:

> Some two months ago there went to France Mons. Garnier, husband of the nurse of the queen here, in order to fetch a midwife for the coming confinement. With him went a dwarf of the queen, a marvellous sight and the most perfect imperfection of nature that ever was born, and therefore much beloved by his mistress. On their return a week ago they fell in with some Dunkirkers and were taken prisoners. The news moved the queen to tears, and it was necessary to send a courier to Brussels for their release, and the Spanish ambassador was asked to write letters in their favour. But scarcely had the booty reached Dunkirk than the Infanta gave orders for its release and all have arrived safely, except the baggage, which might amount to 20,000 ducats, for presents which the dwarf had received in France, an advantage for which he went there, and for other things which their Majesties here had sent for their service. But the other English who were in the same boat were held and ransomed. Although this accident seems of slight importance, yet as it touched the Court so nearly, it made the hurt more sensible, owing to the shame of being misused every day. It caused so much disturbance that one of the lords here, laughing at their weakness, remarked to me that they were more upset at Court than if they had lost a fleet.[1]

The dwarf in question was Jeffery Hudson; before a month had elapsed the young playwright and poet William Davenant had composed the mock epic "Jeffereidos, Or the Captivitie of Jeffery" to commemorate his seaborne misadventures. The poem achieved immediate popularity. On 24 April 1630 Joseph Mead wrote to his friend Sir Martin Stuteville, "There is a poem which I cannot yet get, called 'Geffreidos,' describing a combat between Geoffrey, the queen's dwarf, and a turkey-cock at Dunkirk."[2] For the remainder of the century "Jeffereidos" ranked among the most mentioned and quoted of all Davenant's works.

To modern eyes the popularity of "Jeffereidos" is as puzzling as the seventeenth-century fascination with dwarfs. The poem is unfinished; its humor

---

1. *Calendar of State Papers, Venetian (CSPV), 1629–32,* 315–16.
2. Thomas Birch, *The Court and Times of Charles I,* 2 vols. (London: Henry Colburn, 1848), 2:77.

seems both crude and cruel; there appears to be no point to its rambling narrative. A less cursory reading of the poem, however, combined with an examination of the social and political context in which it was written, suggests why the court took the loss of Hudson so much to heart and why Mead was so eager to obtain a copy of Davenant's work. Simply stated, "Jeffereidos" is a critique of Caroline foreign policy in early 1630, and Hudson himself is a satiric surrogate for his royal master. Davenant's mock-epic treatment of the dwarf's captivity burlesques what many contemporaries saw as the king's truckling to Spain. By seeking to undermine Charles's peace negotiations with Philip IV and advocating the alliance with France urged by Henrietta Maria, "Jeffereidos" constituted a significant step in the formation of a party to publicize and further the queen's political aims. Davenant's use of Jeffery Hudson as the vehicle for political satire attests to the significance court dwarfs held for their contemporaries. The dwarf appears to have been a species of fool, with the distinction that he was not so much a maker of jests as the object of them. The closeness of the dwarf to the monarch, moreover, gave a point to these jests: there were few ways in which one could "touch the Court so nearly."

Caroline writers were quick to make use of the opportunities that Jeffery and the other court dwarfs offered. Much matter in these dwarfs—they were seen as texts to be interpreted and glossed. Robert Heath composed an epigram on Jeffery Hudson; Edmund Waller wrote a wistful poem on the marriage of the dwarfs Richard Gibson and Anne Shepheard in 1640 that can be read as a lament for the passing of the royalist Arcadia. More substantial is *The New-Yeeres Gift*, a 115-page duodecimo volume written by the pseudonymous Microphilus, perhaps Thomas Heyward, and published by N. and I. Okes in 1636. A mock encomium "where-in is proved Little Things are better then great," the work is addressed to "Little Jefferie," whose portrait adorns the frontispiece. *The New-Yeeres Gift* achieved enough popularity to be reissued in a second edition in 1638.

The literary interest in the dwarfs is primarily a phenomenon of the seventeenth century, but the practice of keeping dwarfs at the English court dates back at least to the reign of Mary Tudor, who appointed the forty-two-inch-tall John Jervis a page of honor.[3] No English monarch, however, indulged in the collecting mania that prevailed at some Continental courts. Charles IX of France counted nine dwarfs among his attendants; Marie de Medici possessed three couples; in 1566 Cardinal Vitelli is reported to have hosted a banquet in Rome at which the guests were served by thirty-four dwarfs.[4] The interest of Charles and Henrietta Maria in dwarfs was perhaps spurred by the troupe of *enanos* assembled by Philip IV of Spain, which Charles viewed during his visit

3. C. J. S. Thompson, *The Mystery and Lore of Monsters, with accounts of some Giants, Dwarfs and Prodigies* (London: Williams and Norgate, 1930), 191.

4. Ibid., 188–89.

to Madrid in 1623. Jeffery, the most famous dwarf at the English court, joined the queen's retinue about 1628.

Many of the events in the life of Jeffery Hudson have an apocryphal ring, and a number of details seem to have been borrowed from the histories of Tom Thumb that were popular in the early seventeenth century.[5] According to the earliest and most reliable accounts, those of Thomas Fuller and James Wright,[6] Jeffery was born in 1619 in Okeham, Rutlandshire; as Fuller delights in pointing out, he was "the *least* man of the *least* County in England."[7] Hudson's father was a butcher who kept and baited bulls for George Villiers, the duke of Buckingham; both his parents were of normal stature. According to one account, his mother, "when pregnant with him . . . was not cumbersome, nor concern'd herself about a Midwife; for truly my little Gentleman was beforehand with them, and flew into the World like a Cork out of a Bottle."[8] When Hudson was nine years old his parents presented him to the Duchess of Buckingham at Burley-on-the-Hill. Not long afterward the duchess served up Hudson "in a cold baked Pye to King Charles and Queen Mary at an entertainment." The queen immediately took Hudson into her service, in which he remained for over twenty years. At this point in his life Hudson reportedly stood eighteen inches tall; he was, in modern parlance, a midget, "without any deformity, wholly proportionable."[9]

The roles played by the dwarfs at court were as multiple as the motives that impelled Charles and Henrietta Maria to install them among their attendants. Dwarfs were, first and foremost, figures of fun. The various exploits of Tom Thumb published in the 1620s and 1630s are, in essence, jestbooks; *The New-Yeeres Gift* derives much of its humor from the italicization of every use of words such as *low, little,* and *short,* and the biographers of Hudson and other dwarfs indulge in the same hoary jests. But the keeping of dwarfs possessed broader cultural implications as well. The European fascination with dwarfs, as Leslie Fiedler notes, is largely a late Renaissance phenomenon, and one might discern in the fashion an unconscious response to the political, military, and religious turmoil of the early seventeenth century.[10] The cultivation of the miniature appears to stem from a nostalgia for the seeming order of childhood, from a

5. The earliest printed version of the Tom Thumb story to survive dates from 1621.

6. Fuller, *The History of the Worthies of England Endeavoured by Thomas Fuller, D.D. First Printed in 1662. A New Edition, with a few Explanatory Notes,* ed. John Nichols, 2 vols. (London: F. C. and J. Rivington, 1811); and Wright, *The History and Antiquities of the County of Rutland: Collected from Records, Ancient Manuscripts, Monuments on the Place, and other Authorities* (London: Bennet Griffin, 1684). The two accounts agree on most details; Wright, however, claims to have known Hudson personally and to have heard from his own mouth the story of his later adventures.

7. Fuller, *History of the Worthies,* 2:244.

8. "The History of Jeffery the famous Dwarf in K. Charles I's Time," *Gentleman's Magazine* 2 (December 1732): 1120.

9. Fuller, *History of the Worthies,* 2:244.

10. *Freaks: Myths and Images of the Secret Self* (New York: Simon and Schuster, 1978), 48–49.

desire for mastery in a world no longer readily mastered.[11] It is likely no coincidence that Charles and Henrietta Maria's dwarf-collecting was concurrent with England's withdrawal from Continental politics. The miniature, unlike European statecraft, lent itself to easy comprehension and control. Such a predilection, however, carries a price. Soranzo's comment that the court was more upset by Jeffery's capture than by the loss of a fleet attests to a warping of perspective, a diminished ability to distinguish between the trappings of royal power and that power itself.

The imperfection of dwarfs also held a moral lesson for those who could decipher it. As Microphilus argues, "in the *Greater world,* which is the Creators Library, (the severall creatures being as so many Bookes in it) have wee not rarer Documents from the little *decimo-sexto's,* the Ant and the Dove, then from the *Great Folio's,* the Elephant and the Whale?" (pp. 5–6). Applying the same trope of nature as an open book specifically to dwarfs, Robert Heath assures Jeffery,

> in your lesse self I see
> Exprest the lesser worlds Epitomie.
> You may write man, ith' *abstract* so you are,
> Though printed in a smaller Character.
> The pocket volume hath as much within't
> As the broad Folio in a larger print,
> And is more useful too."[12]

Microphilus carries this process of textualization to an extreme in a lengthy passage in which he considers the reasons for maintaining dwarfs in courts. Asserting that "Your *little low person . . .* is *natures humble pulpit,* out of which shee reads graces diviner lectures to *High-aspiring* Mortals," he claims that dwarfs are kept in courts for "use" and "service" as well as for "wonder and merriment":

> So (at all times) the residence of *dwarfes* in Courts hath a two-fold Representment, *Theologicall,* and *Politicall,* the first to the *Soveraigne,* the second to the Subiect: For the first, as *Philip* King of Macedon betimes every morning had a *little boy* came unto him, and cryed, *Philippe, memento te esse mortalem, O Philip, remember how thou art mortall:* So *little dwarfes* (boyes in proportion, though perchance men in discretion) being about a Monarch, though silent, yet their very persons (being with Princes of the same naturall extraction) are as a voice crying *Rex, memento te esse minimum: O King remember how thou art little,* borne like others *little,* to teach thee to Heaven, humility, to Earth, humanity: For the second, the civill regard in relation to the subiect: the residence of *dwarfes* about Monarchs hath beene by those who are grounded Politicians accounted *emblematically* necessary, to denote those who desire to approach neere Princes ought not to be ambitious of any *Greatnesse* in themselves, but to acknowledge all their Court-lustre is but a beame of the Royall

11. See Susan Stewart, *On Longing: Narratives of the Miniature, the Gigantic, the Souvenir, the Collection* (Baltimore: Johns Hopkins University Press, 1984), 65–69.

12. *"To Jeffry the Kings dwarfe,"* ll. 1–7, in the Epigrams section of *Clarastella; together with Poems occasional, Elegies, Epigrams, Satyrs* (London: Humphrey Moseley, 1650), 16.

Sunne their Master, which when, and to whom, he please hee can send forth or withdraw. (pp. 99–100; 102–6)

The facetious touches notwithstanding, Microphilus approaches very near to seriousness here: the swipe at court favorites and the nod to Stuart theories of kingship come across as utterly straightforward and devoid of ironic intent. The dwarf is, in effect, a tangible emblem of the doctrine of the king's two bodies: he *is* the body natural, and his physique serves as a daily reminder of all the ills to which the flesh is heir. This alienation of the body natural from the person of the monarch provides the dwarf with a function complementary to that of the licensed fool. He is a licensed jestingstock, a royal surrogate who can be baffled and abused with impunity. But the advantages were not all on one side. The relationship that Microphilus describes is what E. Tietze-Conrat terms the "motif of interchangeability": from Egyptian times dwarfs and fools at courts have frequently been treated as doubles of the monarch and accorded every royal honor.[13] Although deformed and different, the butt of every callous courtier, the dwarf is nonetheless invested with the arcana of majesty.

Jeffery Hudson's relationship with the royal family appears to have been compounded of such a mixture of intimacy and insult. Hudson—almost always referred to as "Little Jeffery"—was thrust into the role of surrogate child to the queen. He was presented to Henrietta Maria about the time of her miscarriage in May 1629; he was sent to fetch the queen her French midwife; he was bound up in all the intimate dealings of procreation and birth at court.[14] The queen, moreover, apparently played with Jeffery as she was unable to play with her children, who were bound by the strict routines of the royal nursery. In Sir Anthony van Dyck's portrait of Henrietta Maria and Jeffery, now in the National Gallery in Washington, the only clue that the dwarf is other than a normal child is the monkey he holds on a leash, but that one detail carries a weight of significance. Jeffery is not an immature adult, but the middle term between man and beast; the analogy between Jeffery and his monkey and between the queen and her dwarf requires no further gloss.

Hudson's relationship with the young Prince of Wales, born 29 May 1630, is even more unusual. The two seem paired in a symbiotic nexus like the babe and changeling of English faery lore. While the infant Charles II displayed Herculean precocity—"he is so fat and so tall, that he is taken for a year old, and he is only four months," his mother wrote to Madame de St. Georges in September 1630—Jeffery remained the perpetual child.[15] In July 1634 the Dutch ambas-

---

13. *Dwarfs and Jesters in Art*, trans. Elizabeth Osborn (London: Phaidon, 1957), 8–13. Tietze-Conrat notes that as a mark of this relationship court dwarfs were frequently granted titles—and not always in jest—such as *king, count,* or *marchese*.

14. Jeffery played a part in royal marriage ceremonies as well. At the bedding of Princess Mary and the Prince of Orange after their marriage in 1641, Jeffery produced a pair of shears to cut the princess's chemise and allow the ritual of consummation to proceed. See Quentin Bone, *Henrietta Maria, Queen of the Cavaliers* (Urbana: University of Illinois Press, 1972), 126.

15. Ibid., 77.

Sir Anthony van Dyck, *Queen Henrietta with Her Dwarf,* National Gallery of Art, Washington, D.C., Samuel H. Kress Collection.

sador Albert Joachimi "made an amusing mistake when he took leave of the queen, as he paid his respects to her little dwarf, who happened to be there under the impression that he was the young prince."[16] Charles II was four at the time; Jeffery was fifteen. Paintings of the pair underline the similarities and the differences. Both the prince and the dwarf are frequently portrayed with dogs, but whereas Charles displays the stuff he is made on by subduing a huge mastiff with a gesture of the hand, Jeffery is dragged across the canvas by a leash of the king's terriers.[17]

These three seventeenth-century ways of looking at the court dwarfs—as a source of amusement, as extensions of the king, and as emblems of some larger truth—come together in Davenant's "Jeffereidos." The poem consists of two cantos, each a little over a hundred lines long, chronicling the events of the dwarf's captivity. Davenant promises a third canto describing Jeffery's "delivery" at the close of part 2, but this conclusion was never written.[18] It has long been thought that Davenant's health prevented him from completing his mock epic, but I think that the real reasons the work was left unfinished were political rather than medical.

The capture of Jeffery and of the queen's midwife could not have come at a worse time in Anglo-Spanish relations. During the ascendancy of the Duke of Buckingham, Britain had waged an aggressive, ultra-Protestant foreign policy on the Continent. By 1627 the nation was at war not only with Spain but also with Spain's traditional enemy, France, in a vain attempt to succor the Huguenot rebels of La Rochelle. Buckingham's assassination and the fall of La Rochelle to Richelieu's forces in 1628 effectively sapped English desire to prosecute the war with France; thanks in part to the mediation of Henrietta Maria with her brother, Louis XIII, Charles brought the conflict to an end with the Treaty of Susa, signed 14 April 1629. The war with Spain was more difficult to resolve because of Charles's insistence on the return of the Spanish-held fortresses in the Palatinate to his brother-in-law, the Elector Frederick. The Spanish dispatched the painter Peter Paul Rubens to London in June 1629 to negotiate a truce that would lay the groundwork for a permanent treaty between the two nations.

Rubens's mission was complicated by the arrival in London of the French ambassador, the Marquis de Chateauneuf, who urged the king to join France in an alliance against Spain and promised the return of the Palatinate by arms. The appeal of the French offer was vitiated by the king's distrust of Richelieu and the

16. *CSPV, 1632–36, 251;* letter of 28 July 1634 from Francesco Zonca to the doge and senate.
17. In Van Dyck's *The Five Children of Charles I* and Mytens's *Charles I and Henrietta Maria Departing for the Hunt,* respectively.
18. Wright refers to "Jeffereidos" as "a very pleasant Poem consisting of three Canto's" (*History and Antiquities,* 105). Nothing in his account, however, suggests he has actually seen the third canto, and I think his description is based on Davenant's promise of a conclusion at the end of canto 2.

recognition that another military campaign on the Continent would require calling a new parliament to levy funds. For nine months the rival ambassadors schemed and lobbied members of the government and the court. Rubens drew on his artistic talents to inure Charles to the idea of a truce with Spain, presenting the connoisseur king with a number of compositions from his own hand. The French faction coalesced around Henrietta Maria: as Rubens advised the Spanish prime minister Olivares in a letter of 22 July 1629, "It is to be noted that the King of England is extremely devoted to the Queen his wife, and that she has great influence over His Majesty and is strongly opposed to Spain."[19] The "Puritan" party at court supported Henrietta Maria in her advocacy of a French alliance, in part from an idealistic desire to bolster the cause of militant Protestantism on the Continent, in part from the pragmatic belief that only arms could recover the Palatinate for the king's sister.[20]

Despite the opposition of the queen, Rubens eventually succeeded in negotiating a limited truce and the exchange of ambassadors with full powers to draw up a peace treaty. Knighted by Charles for his services, Rubens left London on 3 March 1630. Two weeks later, on 18 March, Jeffery was captured by the Dunkirkers. Although acknowledging the sovereignty of the Spanish crown, the Dunkirk pirates were accustomed to acting on their own; England and Spain were still legally at war, and the booty on the ship was considerable. Aware that the incident could undermine the treaty negotiations between the two nations, the Archduchess Isabella, governor of the Spanish Netherlands, quickly secured the release of Jeffery and the midwives, but the damage had already been done. The Venetian ambassador's comments on the court's sense of "shame" at "being misused every day" suggest how deeply the incident was resented in London as an insult to the king and nation.

"Jeffereidos" exploits this frustration and outrage to rally the French party gathered about the queen. The first canto of the poem describes the taking of the English ship by the Dunkirkers, the seizure of Jeffery from his hiding place under a pewter candlestick, and his interrogation by his captors. Although the Dunkirk privateers were Flemish in race and language, Davenant refers to their captain as "a crafty Diego"; the appellation is calculated to stir up latent hispanophobia among English readers. The Diego, however, is not as crafty as he looks. Certain that Jeffery is an important and powerful captive, he resolves to take appropriate measures:

> Victors, and Vanquished! I bid
> You all give eare, to wisdome of Madrid!

19. *The Letters of Peter Paul Rubens,* trans. and ed. Ruth Saunders Magurn (Cambridge: Harvard University Press, 1955), 316.

20. R. M. Smuts, "The Puritan followers of Henrietta Maria in the 1630s," *English Historical Review* 93 (1978):28–34. For a brief discussion of the literary activities of the queen's coterie, see Martin Butler, *Theatre and Crisis, 1632–1642* (Cambridge: Cambridge University Press, 1984), 25–30.

> This, that appeares to you a walking Thumbe,
> May prove the gen'rall Spie of Christendome:
> Then calls for Chaines, but such as fitting seeme
> For Elephants, when manag'd in a Teeme.
> While puissant *Jeff'ry* 'gins to wish (in vaine)
> He had long since contriv'd a truce with Spaine.
> His Sinewes faile him now; nor doth hee yeeld
> Much trust unto his Buckler, or his Shield;
> Yet threatens like a second Tamberlaine,
> To bring them 'fore the Queenes Lord-Chamberlaine;
> Because without the leave of him, or her,
> They keepe her Houshold-Servant prisoner.
>
> (1.33–46)[21]

The humor is at the expense of both Diego and Jeffery. The Spaniard lacks the sense to size up his captive; Jeffery, on the other hand, proves a coward. He talks big but fails to take up arms: he is, quite literally, *vox et praeterea nihil,* a voice and nothing else. The allusion to the Spanish truce (which had, in fact, been agreed on by this date) reinforces the suggestion that fear alone would force an Englishman to seek terms from Diego.

Convening a makeshift court on their arrival in Dunkirk, Diego next presses Jeffery to reveal

> Some secrets that concerne the English State.
> But O! true, loyall Heart! he'ld not one word
> Reveale, that he had heard at Councell-bord.
>
> (1.72–74)

He similarly refuses to explain the reason for his visit to France, though the poet comments in an aside that

> divers think, when there,
> The Cardinall did whisper in his eare
> The Scheame of all his plots, and sought to gaine
> His company along with him to Spaine;
> For thither he'll march, if he can by th'way
> Sweep a few durty Nations into th'Sea.
>
> (1.83–88)

To Davenant's audience, which knew the true reasons behind Jeffery's mission to the French court, such speculations were ludicrous. The treatment of Richelieu is more subtle. While portraying him as a villainous schemer—a characterization, incidentally, in which Henrietta Maria would have concurred—Davenant does suggest that the cardinal is a man of action who will overrun

---

21. The text is taken from A. M. Gibbs, ed., *Sir William Davenant: The Shorter Poems, and Songs from the Plays and Masques* (Oxford: Clarendon Press, 1972).

Spain when he is ready. The contrast with Jeffery is profound. The canto ends with the invocation of the other great bugaboo of seventeenth-century England, the Roman Catholic Church. Jeffery is interrogated by a Spanish monk, who declares, "That shrivled face hath Schysme in it!" and seeks to arraign the dwarf on charges of heresy. When Jeffery again refuses to talk, the pirates grow impatient and dispatch him to Brussels mounted on a lapdog.

Jeffery's misadventures in canto 1 draw on all the commonplaces of dwarf humor, a fact Davenant acknowledges in his oblique allusion to Tom Thumb, but they also touch on graver issues. Jeffery represents England and its king trapped in the toils of European diplomacy. Although he rages like Tamerlaine, Jeffery is unwilling to resort to arms; although he inspires a certain fear and respect among his captives, he is in the end merely a dwarf. Caught between the blandishments of the supersubtle Richelieu and the threats of Spain, Jeffery hardly knows where to turn. In casting the dwarf as the emblem of the nation, Davenant captures the sense of frustration and impotence that poisoned English public opinion at the end of the 1620s. The failure of Buckingham's Protestant foreign policy and the inability of the king's government to take new initiatives led to the feeling noted by Soranzo of "being misused every day." England, for Davenant, was no more than a Jeffery on the European stage: a shrunken, dwarfish, poppet of a nation.

This interpretation of "Jeffereidos" breaks from traditional readings of the poem and of the poet. Davenant is usually regarded as an apologist for the Caroline regime, not as its critic, and "Jeffereidos" has been described as devoid of "sharp social and personal criticism."[22] But in 1630 the court itself was divided as to the course of foreign policy and, in light of his later association with the queen's household, it is not surprising to find Davenant supporting the position that Henrietta Maria herself advocated. In his ode "To the King on New-yeares day 1630," Davenant wishes Charles "Long proffer'd Peace, and that not compass'd by / Expensive Treaties but a Victorie."[23] These lines undoubtedly allude to the furious diplomatic activity conducted by Rubens and later by the regular Spanish ambassador, Don Carlos de Coloma, at the close of 1629 and the beginning of 1630. The ode concludes, moreover, with the hope that in the coming year the fame of Gustavus Adolphus, the champion of European Protestantism, will be "No more our envy, nor our shame" (l. 28). Davenant appears to advocate a renewed military effort to secure peace and the Palatinate; at the very least, this poem must be read as a call for a more active and aggressive policy on the Continent. In this aim the ode seems very much of a piece with the first part of "Jeffereidos." It is in canto 2, however, that the poet suggests the course that England should follow.

The opening of the second canto of "Jeffereidos" elaborates on the indignities

22. By Gibbs in ibid., xlvii.
23. Ibid., 31; ll. 9–10.

the dwarf suffers in his captivity. Jeffery's canine mount trips over a hair, stumbles, and falls to his death. As the dwarf sprawls on the ground, the Spaniards taunt him with his misfortunes:

> And *Diego* too, whose grave and solemne Brow
> Was ever knit, grew loud and wanton now:
> O for a Guard (quoth he) of *Switzers* here,
> To heave that Giant up! but come not neere,
> For, now enrag'd, he may perchance so tosse us
> As you would thinke you touch'd a live Colossus!
> This *Jeff'ry* heard, and it did stir his gall
> More than his Coursers death, or his owne fall.
>
> (2.29–36)

While Jeffery laments his fate, the most dangerous foe yet closes upon him:

> A Foule of spatious wing, bloody, and bold
> In his aspect; haughty in gate, and stiffe on
> His large spread Clawes he stood, as any Griffon,
> Though by kinde a Turkey.
>
> (2.50–53)

In its initial terms the description recalls the dragons that rampage through the pages of *The Faerie Queene,* but the final anticlimactic clause, "Though by kinde a Turkey," firmly reminds the audience that this is the world of mock epic, not romance. The account of the combat, indeed, derives from a number of classical and popular sources: Homer's *Batrachomyomachia* (first translated into English by Chapman less than ten years previously), the battle between the pygmies and the cranes, and the struggles of Tom Thumb with various cows, crows, and sausages. Davenant's narrative, however, employs details that develop the political message of canto 1. The Turkey pecks at the dwarf, and he is forced to draw. Battle is joined when "*Jeff'ry* the Bold,"

>   his Arme uprear'd,
> Then cryes St. *George* for England! and with that word
> He mischief'd (what I pray?) nought but his sword,
> Though some report he noch'd the Foes left wing;
> And Poets too, who faithfully did sing
> This Battaile in Low-Dutch, tell of a few
> Small Feathers there, which at the first charge flew
> About the field; but doe not strictly know
> That they were shed by fury of that blow.
>
> (2.68–76)

On an initial reading the fray seems merely bathetic, but the dwarf's cry of "St. *George* for England" translates the episode to a more serious plane. Jeffery's charge and the piddling damage he inflicts upon his enemy allude to England's abortive military forays onto the Continent during the five preceding years:

despite the martial posturing and the loud threats, Buckingham and Charles had accomplished little more in their campaigns than to notch the Spanish wing and scatter a few feathers at Cadiz.

The allusion is, however, even more pointed. From the very beginning of his reign Charles I had evinced an interest in the Order of the Garter and its patron, St. George: he redesigned the decoration, reformulated the rules for its display, and commissioned new plate for the order's official ceremonies.[24] During his nine-month stay in England, moreover, Rubens designed his well-known *Landscape with St. George*. The canvas casts the armored Charles I as the saint and depicts him rescuing "a plumped-up . . . Henrietta Maria" of a princess;[25] the expiring dragon lies trodden underfoot. The preliminary sketch attracted a great deal of attention, and the finished painting was eventually purchased for the royal collection. In the spring of 1630, it would have been impossible not to read Davenant's allusion to St. George as a comment on the king's appropriation of the myth. Rubens presents St. George—and the king—at the moment of triumph: the dragon slain, all that remains is to enjoy the spoils of victory. In assenting to a peace with Spain, the painter asserts, Charles vanquishes war itself and emerges a hero. Davenant's "Jeffery as St. George," on the other hand, is a burlesque of the same scene. Victory is only an illusion; the enemy, angered and more dangerous than ever, waits to return the blow. And that enemy, should the reader forget, is *Diego*—Spain.

While Jeffery gloats on his seeming victory, the Turkey strikes back:

> *Jeff'ry* strait was throwne; whilst faint and weake,
> The cruell Foe assaults him with his Beake.
> A Lady-Midwife now, he there by chance
> Espy'd, that came along with him from France.
> A heart nours'd up in War, that ne're before
> This time (quoth he) could bow, now doth implore:
> Thou that deliver'd hast so many, be
> So kinde of nature to deliver me!
>
> (2.91–98)

Only the French alliance tendered by Chateauneuf, Davenant suggests, can "deliver" England from the sort of harm and insult that Spain offers to Jeffery. This is the position, of course, that the queen and the Ultra-Protestant party, for very different reasons, espoused during the spring of 1630.

Davenant, however, declines to sketch out the results of such an alliance, at least at this time. Although the real Jeffery Hudson and the queen's midwives had been released and sent on their way to London by the date "Jeffereidos" appeared, Davenant leaves the poetic outcome in suspense:

24. Roy Strong, *Van Dyck: Charles I on Horseback* (New York: Viking, 1972), 60–61.
25. Sir Oliver Millar, *The Age of Charles I: Painting in England, 1620–1649* (London: Tate Gallery, 1972), 57.

> But stay: for though the learn'd Chronologer
> Of Dunkerk doth confesse him freed by her,
> The subt'ler Poets yet, whom wee translate
> In all this Epick Ode, doe not relate
> The manner how; and wee are loth at all
> To vary from the Dutch Originall.
> Deeds they report of greater height than these;
> Wonders, and truth; which, if the Court-wits please,
> A little helpe from Nature, lesse from Art,
> May happily produce in a Third part.
>
> (2.99–108)

Davenant apparently never composed the promised conclusion to "Jeffereidos"; A. M. Gibbs speculates that the poet's notorious bout with syphilis, which cost him his nose and nearly his life, struck him down at this time and prevented him from producing the third and final canto.[26] But Davenant's failure to produce a conclusion, I think, was primarily political. At the time cantos 1 and 2 were composed, England had not yet agreed to the Spanish treaty; the diplomatic imbroglio over the taking of Jeffery and the midwives raised expectations that the English government might scuttle the negotiations altogether. Davenant prophesies such a development in Jeffery's French "delivery"—the hoped-for alliance with France—but since "the subt'ler Poets yet . . . doe not relate the manner how," the details of the happy ending must wait. The final lines of the poem tease the reader with intimations of more momentous matters that the author has been forced to hold back: these "subt'ler Poets"—diplomats? courtiers in the queen's party?—report deeds "of greater height than these; / Wonders, and truth."[27] If "Nature" cooperates—if the French alliance comes to pass—Davenant will release the happy story of Jeffery's, and England's, delivery.

Nature did not, in fact, cooperate. In the end, Rubens's canvases and counsel carried more weight than Davenant's polemic. After a summer of negotiation, the English agreed to a peace with Spain; the Treaty of Madrid was signed on 5 November 1630. At the banquet given by Don Carlos de Coloma to celebrate the signing of the treaty, Henrietta Maria appeared dressed in her most somber

---

26. *The Shorter Poems*, xxiii-xiv.

27. Davenant's insistence that "Jeffereidos" is merely translated from the "Low-Dutch" works on several levels. On one hand, the poet's assertion is of a piece with the mock-epic character of the poem. As Marvell's "Character of Holland" attests, the seventeenth-century Englishman regarded the Dutch as mercenary, greedy, boorish, and dull—in sum, the antithesis of heroic. On another level, the reference to the "Dutch Originall" that Davenant translates in "Jeffereidos" may point very specifically to one of the instigators of the poem. Albert Joachimi, the ambassador of the United Provinces in London, worked ceaselessly to undermine the Spanish treaty negotiations since one of the conditions of the agreement would be the cessation of English military and financial aid to the Netherlands (Rubens, *Letters*, 287). Joachimi, moreover, would have been in an excellent position to relay information to the queen's circle about the treatment of Jeffery and the midwives in Brussels. Such an allusion might serve to legitimize the political position Davenant stakes out in the poem by attributing it to one of the most knowledgeable and influential diplomats at court.

attire to indicate her displeasure. Although her first major attempt to influence foreign policy had failed, the coterie that the queen gathered about her continued to grow in power and influence throughout the first half of the 1630s. This coterie, moreover, would continue to make use of poetry and dramatic performances to set forth its political program; styling himself "her Majesties Servant," Davenant would eventually emerge as its preeminent literary spokesman. After the mysterious eighteen-month hiatus following the composition of "Jeffereidos," Davenant resumed his career in 1632. By the middle of the decade he had become the preferred writer of masques for both king and queen, unabashedly promoting the cult of heroism that provided the language for political discourse at the late Caroline court. But Davenant retained his skeptical bent in poems like "The Souldier going to the Field" and in the main antimasque of *Britannia Triumphans:* in that "Mock-romanza," a knight, a damsel, a giant, and a dwarf—this last very probably played by Jeffery—give chivalry such a going-over that the main masque never quite regains its seriousness.

And Jeffery? In the end, he literally outgrew the role he had played so long at court. Davenant's characterization in "Jeffereidos" notwithstanding, Hudson proved himself no puling pip-squeak in the tumults of the succeeding decades. After serving as a "Captain of Horse" in the king's army during the Civil War, he accompanied Henrietta Maria into exile in France. In Paris he was insulted by a brother of Lord Crofts, whom he challenged to a duel. Crofts arrived on the field armed only with a squirt; Hudson met him "with Powder and Ball, and shot him dead on the Spot."[28] He was, as Fuller remarks, "though a *Dwarf,* no *Dastard.*"[29] Expelled from the court for his part in this incident, Hudson had the misfortune to be captured yet a second time by pirates, on this occasion by the Turks. According to Wright, this "was a much more fatal Captivity than the first" since due to the "hardship, much labour, and beating" he endured while a slave on the Barbary coast, "he shot up in a little time to that highth of stature which he remain'd in his old age, *viz.* about three foot and nine Inches." The modern reader might join Wright in contemplating this "Paradox, how that which hath been observed to stop the growth of other persons, should be the Cause of his";[30] it is psychologically significant, perhaps, that Jeffery was able to grow only after he left the court that had relegated him to the role of eternal child. Eventually redeemed, Hudson made his way back to England, where he retired to Rutlandshire and lived on a pension allowed him by the second duke of Buckingham. A Roman Catholic, he was arrested in 1679 for complicity in the Popish Plot. After a brief confinement in the Gatehouse at Westminster, Hudson was released and died in 1682.[31]

28. "The History of Jeffery," 1120; see also Fuller, *History of the Worthies,* 2:244, and Horace Walpole, *Anecdotes of Painting in England* (London: Alexander Murray, 1871), 115.

29. Fuller, *History of the Worthies,* 2:244.

30. Wright, *History and Antiquities,* 105.

31. *Dictionary of National Biography,* s.v. Jeffery Hudson.

In a song in Ben Jonson's *Volpone,* Nano the dwarf explains why he should claim precedence over his master's other entertainers, the hermaphrodite and the eunuch:

> First, for your dwarfe, hee's little, and wittie,
> And every thing, as it is little, is prittie;
> Else, why doe men say to a creature of my shape,
> So soone as they see him, it's a pritty little ape?
> And, why a pritty ape? but for pleasing imitation
> Of greater mens action, in a ridiculous fashion.
>
> (3.3.9–14)[32]

In "Jeffereidos" Davenant provides such a "pleasing imitation . . . in a ridiculous fashion" of the various poses struck by the king and his government in their desperate attempt to extricate England from the Spanish war. But Davenant has a serious aim as well. He uses the dwarf not merely to parody contemporary politics but also to direct them; he manipulates the facts of Jeffery's captivity to shadow forth a way to "deliver" the nation from the frustration and shame of its inglorious sloth. Davenant here treads on perilous ground: at moments one is unsure whether the dwarf imitates Charles, or Charles the dwarf. In this very boldness, however, "Jeffereidos" suggests that the scope allowed to dissident voices at court was not always so narrow as we sometimes believe. A consensus of shared values, in fact, perhaps encouraged a measure of dissent over policy and its implementation. Jeffery Hudson's position as a standing gloss on the actions of his prince made him a choice vehicle for expressing such disagreement. As Microphilus notes, we find the most rare and meaningful documents in the little decimo-sextos. It needs only a subtle poet, such as Sir William Davenant, to interpret them aright.

---

32. The text is that of C. H. Herford and Percy and Evelyn Simpson, eds., *Ben Jonson,* 11 vols. (Oxford: Clarendon Press, 1925–1952), 5:70.

Sidney Gottlieb

8. The Social and Political Backgrounds
of George Herbert's Poetry

In the preface to the first edition of *The Temple*, Nicholas Ferrar is curiously defensive as he introduces Herbert's volume to its readers: "The world therefore shall receive it in that naked simplicitie, with which he left it, without any addition either of support or ornament. . . . We leave it free and unforestalled to every mans judgement."[1] Ferrar's defensiveness derives at least in part from his awareness that the "naked simplicitie" of *The Temple* might seem anomalous to readers accustomed to books set in a network of social relations by often elaborate prefatory materials, dedications, and commendatory poems. The absence of such indicators of patrons, friends, and intended readers supports Ferrar's construction of Herbert's "independencie upon all others" (p. 4): presumably Herbert's absolute dependence on God precludes any other dependency. Ferrar goes on to mention Herbert's noble birth, prestigious Cambridge oratorship, and connections at court only to dismiss them as inconsequential to his choice of life and to his poetry. The poems in *The Temple*, he suggests, describe "those inward enforcements" to a holy life and holy verse, "for outward there was none" (p. 3).

I take the "naked simplicitie" of *The Temple* and Ferrar's comments as contributing causes but more as emblems of a persistent attempt, stretching from Ferrar and Izaak Walton through the modern revival of interest in Herbert by typological and "New" critics, to "de-contextualize" Herbert. Recently, however, the prominence of new historical approaches to seventeenth-century authors in general and a number of fine exploratory studies of Herbert in particular have demonstrated the pressing need for and great value of "re-contextualizing" Herbert, interpreting his poetry with a fuller awareness of its originating

1. *The Works of George Herbert*, ed. F. E. Hutchinson (1941; corr. rpt. Oxford: Clarendon Press, 1945), 3. All quotations from Herbert are from this edition and will be indicated by line or page number in the text.

I am grateful to Joseph Summers and Louis Martz for their generous help and useful criticism as I continue to work on the broad subject indicated by my title here. In addition, Richard Helgerson, Jonathan Post, Stanley Stewart, and George Walton Williams read earlier versions of my essay and offered encouragement as well as advice. The research and writing of this essay have been supported by an NEH Summer Stipend, an ACLS Travel Grant, and a Huntington Library Short-Term Fellowship.

circumstances.[2] Stephen Greenblatt's observation about Wyatt—"that there is no privileged sphere of individuality" in his works "set off from linguistic convention, from social pressure, from the shaping force of religious and political power"[3]—is, it seems to me, directly applicable to Herbert, and a great amount of available material supports, even demands, a revised understanding of Herbert's deep personal and poetic involvement with public issues and worldly affairs.

In what follows, I will focus only on a few themes and poems. But my interpretations and emphasis are generated by three basic premises that should be at least briefly sketched out, especially because each to an extent challenges premises often implicit in conventional approaches to Herbert.

First, a full examination of Herbert's life, aided greatly by Amy M. Charles's meticulous biography, nevertheless undermines her assumption that Herbert had only a "secondhand knowledge of the world of affairs." The Herbert family was for generations accustomed to a life of political service and reward, and George's ties with his brothers Edward and Henry, his cousins William and Philip, earls of Pembroke, and John Danvers, his stepfather (later one of the regicides and even at this time a crafty and controversial man on the move), as well as his personal friendships with such men as Bishop John Williams and Francis Bacon, gave him a close view of a world where neither naiveté nor unqualified retreat was advisable or possible. We should in no way think of Herbert as a recluse, uninterested in day-to-day worldly affairs—even at Bemerton, which as Charles wisely remarks is not "in any sense a retreat from the problems of the world."[4]

Second, despite the attempts of some historians to picture the early seventeenth century as a calm before the storm of the Civil War, we should acknowl-

2. Studies that focus on social and political dimensions of Herbert include: Diana Benet, "Herbert's Experience of Politics and Patronage in 1624," *George Herbert Journal* 10, nos. 1 & 2 (1986/1987): 33–45; Jonathan Goldberg, "Herbert's 'Decay' and the Articulation of History," *Southern Review* (Australia) 18 (1985): 3–21; Sidney Gottlieb, "Herbert's Case of 'Conscience': Public or Private Poem?," *Studies in English Literature* 25 (1985): 109–26; Kenneth Alan Hovey, "Church History in 'The Church,'" *George Herbert Journal* 6 (1982): 1–14, and "Holy War and Civil Peace: George Herbert's Jacobean Politics," *Explorations in Renaissance Culture* 11 (1985): 112–19; Cristina Malcolmson, "George Herbert's *Country Parson* and the Character of Social Identity," forthcoming in *Studies in Philology;* Leah Sinanoglou Marcus, "George Herbert and the Anglican Plain Style," in *"Too Rich to Clothe the Sunne": Essays on George Herbert*, ed. Claude J. Summers and Ted-Larry Pebworth (Pittsburgh: University of Pittsburgh Press, 1980), 179–93; Michael C. Schoenfeldt, "'Subject to Ev'ry Mounters Bended Knee': Herbert and Authority," in *The Historical Renaissance: New Essays on Tudor and Stuart Literature and Culture*, ed. Heather Dubrow and Richard Strier (Chicago: University of Chicago Press, 1988); Stanley Stewart, "Herbert and the 'Harmonies' of Little Gidding," *Cithara* 24 (1984): 3–26; Claude J. Summers and Ted-Larry Pebworth, "Herbert, Vaughan, and Public Concerns in Private Modes," *George Herbert Journal* 3 (1979/1980): 1–21, and "The Politics of *The Temple:* 'The British Church' and 'The Familie,'" *George Herbert Journal* 8, no. 1 (1984): 1–15.

3. *Renaissance Self-Fashioning: From More to Shakespeare* (Chicago: University of Chicago Press, 1980), 120.

4. *A Life of George Herbert* (Ithaca: Cornell University Press, 1977), 107, 157.

edge that Herbert lived during extremely troubled times. For example, not enough has been made of Herbert's attendance at the tumultuous 1624 session of parliament, the experience of which no doubt lies behind his haunting line in *The Country Parson* that there is "no School to a Parliament" (p. 277). Nicholas Tyacke and David Norbrook show convincingly that the 1620s and 1630s were marked by increasing political and ecclesiastical pressure.[5] Herbert's poems bear signs of not only the controversies of these times but also the various directives to stifle controversies. In addition, Herbert could hardly have been unaware of the major economic and social problems of the early seventeenth century: devastating economic depression especially in the cloth industry; continuing distress and unrest caused by enclosure, disafforestation, and monopolies; and outbreaks of plague, compounded by years of bad harvests. These dismal facts of life are concretely registered in some of Herbert's poems that are often thought of as personal, abstract, or liturgical.[6]

My third premise is that a considerable amount of Herbert's work confirms that his characteristic literary gesture was neither submissive retreat nor inaction. His letters and orations show how knowledgeable he was about numerous public issues (such as the project for draining the fens around Cambridge) and how boldly he confronted even extremely sensitive questions: the oration welcoming back Charles from Spain is a fine example of Herbert's courage and honesty, as he praises peace to a man clearly bent on war (pp. 444–55). The witty boldness and public concerns of this oration, and of the *Musae Responsoriae,* "Inventa Bellica," and the poems to the Queen of Bohemia, become transformed but by no means disappear in *The Temple,* and these neglected works need to be assimilated into rather than bracketed apart from our study of the better-known lyrics.

With these premises in mind, we might be more inclined to broaden the meaning of some of the allegorical poems in *The Temple.* Allegory is of course frequently a genre of political displacement. That this is true for Herbert as well as, say, Sidney, Spenser, and Jonson is not always acknowledged. For instance, Rosemond Tuve says of Herbert's poem "Peace" that it "travels no unfrequented by-ways of the fancy, rather the broad high-road of accepted Christian symbolism." Read typologically, the poem is, in Tuve's words, "a Holy Communion poem" about the "apostles' mission" and the "'mystical Body' of Christ."[7]

But a typological approach gives no help with interpreting the opening sections in which the poet casts his eye on the real world around him. Herbert's

5. Tyacke, "Puritanism, Arminianism and Counter-Revolution," in *The Origins of the Civil War,* ed. Conrad Russell (New York: Harper and Row, 1973), 119–43; Norbrook, *Poetry and Politics in the English Renaissance* (Boston: Routledge and Kegan Paul, 1984). Tyacke elaborates on his ideas in *Anti-Calvinists: The Rise of English Arminianism, c. 1590–1640* (Oxford: Clarendon Press, 1987).

6. See the references in my "Herbert's Case of 'Conscience.'"

7. *A Reading of George Herbert* (Chicago: University of Chicago Press, 1952), 164, 162.

well-known love of peace, both political and religious, and the experience of greeting an embarrassed and angry Prince Charles, just returned from Spain, by praising his peacefulness—a gesture that some critics feel cost Herbert any chance for advancement—provide a vital background to a poem that flees from the world of power only after anatomizing it. Helen Vendler suggests that in "Peace" "Herbert's allegory is tranquil,"[8] but that is not true of the first three stanzas. The "clouds" that "break and scatter" the rainbow of peace in stanza 2 evoke disturbing historical conditions, and the third stanza, suggesting there is something rotten at court, is even more audacious than Herbert's oration to Charles:

> Then went I to a garden, and did spy
> A gallant flower,
> The Crown Imperiall: Sure, said I,
> Peace at the root must dwell.
> But when I digg'd, I saw a Worm devoure
> What show'd so well.
> (ll. 13–18)

The stunning irony and critical force of Herbert's use of the "Crown Imperiall" to suggest that the royal powers in England were not capable of bringing the country to true peace become more apparent when we place this poem alongside contemporary works that use the identical image to construct emblems of "Caroline optimism."[9] In James Shirley's masque *The Triumph of Peace* (1634), for example, Astrea enters with "a crown imperial in her hand"; and in the conclusion of Ben Jonson's masque *Love's Triumph Through Callipolis* (1631), a "Crown Imperiall" joins with a palm tree, roses, and lilies to create a peaceful "shade" that will be "propitious" to the kingdom.[10] Thus, at approximately the same time Caroline poets and artists were creating the fiction of peaceful "halcyon days,"[11] Herbert seems to have written "Peace" as a sobering, allegorical but demystifying anti-masque.

The range of allegorical references also needs to be expanded for such a poem as "Humilitie." It seems much less like the heavy-handed "schematic and algebraic" story Vendler discovers[12] if we read it not as a medieval, simply moralistic beast fable but as at least in part a deeply satiric picture of credibly ludicrous

8. *The Poetry of George Herbert* (Cambridge: Harvard University Press, 1975), p. 97.

9. Graham Parry, *The Golden Age Restor'd: The Culture of the Stuart Court, 1603–42* (Manchester: Manchester University Press, 1981), 167.

10. Shirley, *The Triumph of Peace*, in *The Dramatic Works and Poems of James Shirley*, ed. William Gifford (London: John Murray, 1833), 6:276; Ben Jonson, *Love's Triumph Through Callipolis* in *Ben Jonson*, ed. C. H. Herford and Percy and Evelyn Simpson (Oxford: Clarendon Press, 1941), 7:742.

11. For the carefully crafted myth of "halcyon days," see C. V. Wedgwood, *Poetry and Politics under the Stuarts* (Ann Arbor: University of Michigan Press, 1964).

12. *Poetry of George Herbert*, pp. 65, 67.

courtiers offering bribes before a real, royal "azure throne" (l. 2), endangering a precarious balance of power. "Humilitie" is also part of a well-developed sequence—including "Content," "The Quidditie," "Frailtie," and "Constancie"—that is highly critical of life at court. Reading Herbert's allegories requires that we learn his figurative language, and the above examples suggest that that language has secular as well as spiritual or typological referents.

References to the contemporary world in *The Temple* are by no means always filtered by allegory. Herbert's poems are characterized by an "informed topicality," to borrow a useful term from Claude Summers.[13] Almost from the beginning, critics of the metaphysical poets have examined their voracious borrowings from many fields of recondite knowledge, but, ironically, not much attention has been paid to how these poets also ransacked the world of everyday public experience. Many critics and readers of Herbert seem content with the notion that public poems such as "The British Church" and "Church-rents and schismes" are rare in *The Temple*. On the contrary, in one way or another a substantial number of Herbert's poems reflect on a wide range of controversial issues and topical affairs: the use of intercessors in religion ("To all Angels and Saints," a strategically evasive poem, as Stanley Stewart points out);[14] tithes, increasingly a disputed subject because they were used not only for charity but also to support the conservative church establishment (ll. 385–86 of "The Church-porch," "Charms and Knots"); church order and discipline ("The Familie," "Church-rents and schismes"); holy communion ("The H. Communion"); priestly vestments and conduct ("Aaron," "The Priesthood"); preaching vs. praying ("The Windows," "Conscience," "Prayer" [I] and [II]); the dangers of both Roman Catholicism and Puritanism ("The British Church," "Sion," "Divinitie," "The Church Militant"); and the proper relationship between Church and State ("Lent," the opening of "The Church Militant"). This background of controversy may also be the right context to use in trying to account for the blend of millenarianism and nostalgia that surfaces in such poems as "Whitsunday," "The World," "Decay," "The Jews," "Home," and "The Church Militant"—a blend that of course characterizes the poems of Henry Vaughan, written later during even more troubled times. Herbert's poems, in short, repeatedly confirm Christopher Hill's observation that, like the great tragedians of the time, "the metaphysical poets . . . are not dealing with 'the human condition,' with 'man,' but with specific problems which confronted rulers and their subjects in a specific historical situation."[15] There is not enough space here to discuss at length Herbert's many topical references, both general and specific, to places, events, and controversies. A few examples will have to suffice.

Despite the important work by such critics as Raymond Williams and James

13. "Herrick's Political Counterplots," *Studies in English Literature* 25 (1985): 167.
14. "Herbert and the 'Harmonies' of Little Gidding."
15. "The Pre-Revolutionary Decades," in *The Collected Essays of Christopher Hill, Volume I* (Amherst: University of Massachusetts Press, 1985), 24.

Turner on the literary consequences of the enclosure movement, modern readers still need to be reminded that the tremendous disturbances brought about by a shift in the traditional patterns of land use penetrate even lyric and devotional poetry.[16] Some of Herbert's references to land enclosures are worrisome, as in "The Invitation," where destruction is threatened when one breaks through boundaries (ll. 19–21), or in the following stanza of "The Church-porch," ostensibly but not exclusively about marriage:

> If God had laid all common, certainly
> Man would have been th' incloser: but since now
> God hath impal'd us, on the contrarie
> Man breaks the fence, and every ground will plough.
> O what were man, might he himself misplace!
> Sure to be crosse he would shift feet and face.
>
> (ll. 19–24)

Herbert often uses highly charged political language even when he is analyzing or expressing deeply felt personal themes, and the figures here evoke not so much personal as social disturbances. The images of man impaled within enclosures and then turning to fence-breaking and lawless disruption of property, plowing "every ground," provide a dramatic view not only of a man turned upside down but also of a world turned upside down. To say the least, this political background of enclosure adds a new dimension to the work of such critics as Robert Higbie and Frank Huntley, who have already pointed out how recurrent in Herbert's poems are images of enclosure and "violent containment."[17]

An awareness of Herbert's "informed topicality" reinforces our understanding of how carefully he sets many of his poems in a concrete social landscape that allows him to reflect and to reflect on both spiritual and physical or economic distress. Arnold Stein has noted about Herbert, "Social ills . . . do not move him to distinguished expression. He is a passionate observer chiefly of those recesses of the mind and heart from which his own decisive actions emerge."[18] But this unnecessarily separates the inner and outer worlds and underestimates how much of a lyric's power comes from the convergence of these worlds. "Home," for example, demonstrates such a powerful convergence. Vendler gives parts of "Home" her highest praise, suggesting that the "cries" seem "written by exhausted bones and joints."[19] Hutchinson usefully grounds

16. Williams, *The Country and the City* (New York: Oxford University Press, 1973); Turner, *The Politics of Landscape: Rural Scenery and Society in English Poetry, 1630–1660* (Cambridge: Harvard University Press, 1979).

17. Higbie, "Images of Enclosure in George Herbert's *The Temple*," *Texas Studies in Literature and Language* 15 (1974), 627–38; Frank L. Huntley, "George Herbert and the Image of Violent Containment," *George Herbert Journal* 8, no. 1 (1984): 17–27.

18. *George Herbert's Lyrics* (Baltimore: Johns Hopkins University Press, 1969), 85.

19. *Poetry of George Herbert,* 265.

the personal lament in the liturgy, in this case from Advent services (p. 515). But I suggest that "Home" is moving because it synthesizes personal, liturgical, and historical details. The description of "this weary world" is poignant because it is more than the vision of a feverish spirit or a formulaic liturgical complaint. The wasteland pictured in "Home" would have been all too familiar to the men and women of Herbert's parish during this period of bad harvests:

> Nothing but drought and dearth, but bush and brake,
>   Which way so-e're I look, I see.   .
> . . . .
> We talk of harvests; there are no such things,
>   But when we leave our corn and hay:
> There is no fruitfull yeare, but that which brings
>   The last and lov'd, though dreadfull day.
>   (ll. 49–50, 55–58)

Perhaps social ills *alone* did not move Herbert to his finest expression—he did not, after all, write poems like Milton's "On the late Massacre in Piemont" or Blake's "London"—but his work is nevertheless characterized by what L. C. Knights calls his "acceptance of 'life at hand,'"[20] demonstrated by his frequent integrations of communal, public experience into his poems. Even such a poem as "Lent," which at first glance seems deeply personal, is set in an important public controversy and not only tries to work out an individual's connection to a church ritual but also examines the social context of the ritual and the social consequences of the individual's actions.

Despite the disarming opening of the poem, as if there could be nothing more natural than announcing "Welcome deare feast of Lent," Herbert quickly jumps into a public debate. Lent and the practice of fasting raised many problems in early seventeenth-century England: some felt that both were popish innovations to be abandoned, and even those who wanted to retain them disagreed on the extent to which Lent should be observed, the uses to which fasting should be put, and the particular "Authoritie" (a word used twice in Herbert's poem) responsible for ordering and enforcing various fast days. Far from being what Vendler describes as one of Herbert's "more unsuccessful attempts at individuating the liturgy,"[21] "Lent" is, at least through its first five stanzas, a bold piece of public argumentation. Herbert links personal "Temperance" with obedience to social "Authoritie" (l. 2) and defends conformers to the generally accepted traditions from the disruptive criticisms of noisy nonconformers.

What is particularly interesting, though, is the way Herbert develops the theme of Lenten fasting from a matter of individual to a matter of social concern. Vendler suggests that the concluding lines are masterful because "a poem,

---

20. "George Herbert," in *Explorations* (New York: New York University Press, 1964), 145.
21. *Poetry of George Herbert*, 150.

for [Herbert], is only 'helped to wings' when it is entirely personal (even if the personal is couched rhetorically in the abstract or the plural."[22] Here is the last stanza:

> Yet Lord instruct us to improve our fast
> By starving sinne and taking such repast
>   As may our faults controll:
> That ev'ry man may revell at his doore,
> Not in his parlour; banquetting the poore,
>   And among those his soul.
>   (ll. 43–48)

I find these lines successful for exactly the opposite reason than the one Vendler gives. The speaker incorporates others into the poem, not as part of a rhetorical or abstract figure but through a gracious act of charity: fasts at this time were used not only to help develop self-control but also to help conserve food supplies and thus provide for the hungry poor. It should seem perfectly characteristic of Herbert to end a poem with a vision of shared delight, of "banquetting the poore, / And among those his soul." Wit and compassion reinforce one another: in a telling bit of wordplay not fully activated until these final lines, we see that only social charity, the movement from one's "parlour" to one's "doore," turns a "fast" into a "feast." The beauty and touching sentiment of "Lent" are thus fully apparent only when we read the poem as something more than a private meditation.

   This concern for charity and the rites and habits of the community comprises an often overlooked "festive" dimension of *The Temple* (marked in "Lent" by the use of the term "revell" [l. 46] and by the concluding vision of a joyous social banquet). Despite what may have been his natural austerity and detachment, Herbert had many qualities of what Patrick Collinson calls the "sub-professional" cleric, who typically "identified with the community of which he was a part" and shared its round of work and leisure.[23] Herbert notes, for example, that "The Country Parson is a Lover of old Customes, if they be good, and harmlesse" (p. 283), and he evidently had no qualms about "beating the bounds" of the parish during Rogation time, a ceremony frowned on by contemporary Puritans, but one that had, in Collinson's words, "a truly Durkheimian significance as a symbolic affirmation of the community of the parish."[24]

   We find such "symbolic affirmations" throughout *The Temple.* Discussion of "Whitsunday," for example, is often directed, if not preempted, by Tuve's masterful analysis of the iconographic contexts of the otherwise mysterious "pipes of gold," and so on.[25] Yet the poem is also grounded in the experience of Whit-

22. Ibid., 151.
23. *The Religion of Protestants: The Church in English Society 1559–1625* (Oxford: Clarendon Press, 1982), 104.
24. Ibid., 109.
25. *Reading of George Herbert,* 169–75.

suntide celebrations, marked in many rural locations by church ales, dancing, and, to borrow Herbert's words, "Feasting all comers" (l. 8) and "good joy" (l. 22). The nostalgic tone of the poem helps set it specifically in a period when traditional holidays were threatened. There are, to be sure, apocalyptic moments scattered throughout, but the concluding plea—"Restore this day, for thy great name, / Unto his ancient and miraculous right" (ll. 27–28)—can be answered in time as well as in eternity, and Herbert, as much as he is calling for heavenly "fire," may be reflecting on the social and political pressure toward maintaining traditional holidays that culminated in Charles's reissuing of *The Book of Sports*. In many ways strikingly similar to "Whitsunday," "Sunday" is also, as Leah Marcus points out,[26] one of Herbert's most festive poems, and it is only against the background of the heated debate over holidays and the proper uses of the sabbath that we can appreciate the boldness of Herbert's affirmation that "Thou art a day of mirth" (l. 57).[27] Both "Whitsunday" and "Sunday" confirm Herbert's immersion in, not his insulation from or attempt to flee, history. Holidays and Sundays, well observed, support the life of the community and the visible church: they are "The fruit of this" world as well as "the next worlds bud" (l. 2).

Until now I have emphasized the *representation* of social and political details in Herbert's poems, and indeed much analysis remains to be done on the concrete historical circumstances that are more than occasionally the setting and subject of *The Temple*. The importance of this approach—as "old-historical" as it may seem—is acknowledged even by Fredric Jameson, who defends what are often referred to as the "cobwebs of topical allusion" and then shifts metaphors to suggest that "if the modern reader is bored or scandalized by the roots such texts send down into the contingent circumstances of their own historical time, this is surely testimony as to his resistance to his own political unconscious."[28] Yet as Jameson and other modern historical critics go on to insist, social and political forces influence poets in extremely complicated ways, and we need to study not only textualized "facts" in poems and in history but also elisions, absences, and formal and thematic displacements. I would like to conclude by briefly suggesting some of the ways in which these approaches can be applied to Herbert.

The revisions in Herbert's poems, for example, provide a useful perspective on how he responded to various social and political pressures. Some revised

26. *Childhood and Cultural Despair: A Theme and Variations in Seventeenth-Century Literature* (Pittsburgh: University of Pittsburgh Press, 1978), 110–11.

27. I am grateful to Richard Strier for his reminder that "mirth" was by no means the sole property of the Laudians and that certain types of individual and communal joy were important to Protestants who are often mistakenly thought of only as the dour enemies of the traditional pastimes. I do not mean to suggest that Herbert's statement that Sunday is "a day of mirth" identifies him as a consistent Arminian, Laudian, or proponent of the *Book of Sports*.

28. *The Political Unconscious: Narrative as a Socially Symbolic Act* (Ithaca: Cornell University Press, 1981), 34.

lines perhaps show Herbert pulling back from topics grown uncomfortably controversial, and if he was revising his poems for publication he might well have been cautious: for example, the reference to "ffrench sluttery wch so currant goes" (l. 368) in the Williams manuscript version of "The Church-porch" would certainly have been imprudent, as Hutchinson notes, "after Charles I's marriage to Henrietta Maria in June 1625" (p. 482), and it was duly canceled. Other places in "The Church Militant" were conspicuously toned down via revision; though the final version of the poem is often wickedly satiric, it is generally more cautiously argued than the Williams manuscript version. For example, in the later version Rome is contrasted with Greece and Egypt, which give way to "Mahometan stupidities" (l. 153), an insatiable attraction to "carnall joy" (l. 149). Rome avoids "this contagious infidelitie" (l. 158), although we soon find out that it falls to other assaults by sin. In the Williams manuscript, though, Herbert's criticism of Rome is more ironic and far-reaching. Rome rests on a "Rock" (l. 159) of "Traditions" that have no legitimate sanction or authority. Herbert's figure is particularly interesting:

> Traditions are accounts wthout our host.
> They who rely on them must reckon twice
> When written Truths shall censure mans devise.

In commonplace Protestant fashion Herbert attacks Catholic traditions as costly innovations, unauthorized by Scripture. These lines, which refer directly (as Herbert notes a few lines later) to specific "controversies sprung of late" (l. 166), were eliminated, blunting the satire.

Similarly, not long after this section in the Williams manuscript Herbert sketches in impressive detail the figure of Sin gaining popularity and power, "carr[ying] all mens eyes" (l. 189). Most ominously, rulers are swayed, not by force but by guile, which

> did bewitch both kings & many a nation
> Into a voluntarie transmigration.
> All poste to Rome. . . .
>
> (ll. 193–95)

Herbert revised these very pointed lines, and although he retained his sharp and unflattering picture of subservience in high places—"Princes submit their necks / Either t' his publick foot or private tricks" (ll. 195–96)—he may have thought better of referring directly to a king bewitched by Catholicism, a claim many were coming to make about Charles, and paying the price for such insinuations or criticisms. In the revised lines, Rome is able to "bewitch and finely work each nation" (l. 193), but there is no longer specific mention of a king.

Some of the more significant revisions can also be related to social and political conditions. Elsewhere I have argued that the poems at the end of "The Church" in the Williams manuscript and those in the same place in the Bodleian manuscript establish two dramatically different conclusions.[29] The earlier conclusion is hesitant, broken up by worries about human unworthiness, the inefficacy of the will, predestination, and perseverance. The revised conclusion eliminates these concerns, replacing them with an emphasis on the powers of the human will and the joy of a sacramental relationship with God.

This development, though, is not strictly a private, personal matter and in fact seems closely coordinated to broader movements of the 1620s. Tyacke argues persuasively that the Protestant consensus, based on a common "Calvinist heritage," began to break up just before the mid-1620s, largely because of the growing prominence of Arminianism, whose proponents contested and then virtually banned predestinarian teaching in favor of an emphasis on free will and efficacious church ceremonies.[30] Though they do not of course simply reflect these historical circumstances, Herbert's revisions at the end of "The Church" often conspicuously parallel them and must be studied with them in mind.

I am not trying to undermine Herbert's independence completely, but it is worth examining how his choices are, to use the modern terms, overdetermined and bounded. Even his decision to write devotional poetry, announced in the early sonnets canonized by Walton, took place during a time when, as Arthur Marotti points out, religious verse was, because of the interests of the new king, replacing love poetry "as a major literary means of expressing social, economic, and political ambition."[31] Social and political conditions in the very least have an "agenda setting" function, as Christopher Hill and Annabel Patterson have recently demonstrated: outside forces may not always determine what we think, but more often than we would like to admit they influence what we think about—and what we do not think or write about.[32] Some of what is often described as Herbert's lack of contentiousness, for example, may well be less a matter of temperament than of circumstances, and various poetic decisions may have been at least in part swayed by political or ecclesiastical pressures. "Perseverance," for instance, a very moving, troubled poem about the controversial topic of whether or not one could fall from grace, may have been dropped from *The Temple* at a point when it was no longer of personal concern to Herbert. But it is surely relevant to note that especially in the late 1620s there were public directives to avoid all potentially inflammatory topics of debate, including matters of theological disagreement such as predestination, church ceremonies, and

29. See my "The Two Endings of George Herbert's 'The Church,'" in a festschrift for Joseph Summers, ed. Mary Maleski (Binghamton: Medieval & Renaissance Texts and Studies, forthcoming).

30. "Puritanism, Arminianism, and Counter-Revolution," 129.

31. "'Love is not love': Elizabethan Sonnet Sequences and the Social Order," *ELH* 49 (1982): 420.

32. Hill, "Censorship and English Literature," in *Collected Essays, Volume I*, 32–71; Patterson, *Censorship and Interpretation: The Conditions of Writing and Reading in Early Modern England* (Madison: University of Wisconsin Press, 1984).

communion. In late 1628 King Charles reissued the 39 Articles with a prefatory declaration ordering that "all further curious search be laid aside."[33] Laud ordered the suppression of a work on perseverance by the Bishop of Down in 1631, and also in 1631 Bishop Davenant of Salisbury apparently got into trouble, according to Thomas Fuller, "just for mentioning the word election in a sermon at court."[34] Such pressure may have encouraged Herbert to drop from his volume not only "Perseverance" but also such potentially controversial poems as "Trinity Sunday" and "The H. Communion."

Herbert did not habitually flee from controversy, but he was deeply aware of external events and pressures and was often cautious, with good reason, in his responses, as we see memorably expressed in "The Priesthood." The persona's hesitancy about his ability to serve God is explained to a certain extent by the dangerous times within which the poem is set:

> Wherefore I dare not, I, put forth my hand
> To hold the Ark, although it seems to shake
> Through th' old sinnes and new doctrines of our land.
>
> (ll. 31–33)

The biblical allusion to 2 Samuel 6:6, noted by Hutchinson (p. 534), safely displaces but also powerfully concentrates attention on Herbert's contemporary predicament. In Samuel, Uzzah tries to steady the ark as it is carried by oxen, but he is instantly killed by an angry God (6:7). This spectacular warning did not paralyze Herbert: it did not keep him from becoming a priest or, for that matter, a poet. But his deep awareness that he lived and wrote in troubled times—that the ark was shaking and that any attempt to steady it was problematic, if not dangerous—is registered throughout *The Temple* in a variety of complicated and interesting ways.

The poems of *The Temple* are, to use an unfortunate but perhaps necessarily shocking term proposed by Daniel Javitch, "impure": "entangled in the world of strife," implicated in the world of getting and spending, moving and shaking, rising and falling under the eyes of the king and his functionaries as well as of God and his.[35] But if *The Temple* is "impure poetry," it is also poetry with a much more impressive breadth and lively relevance than we usually grant to Herbert as a devotional lyricist writing only about the "spiritual Conflicts" between himself and his God.

33. *The Constitutional Documents of the Puritan Revolution 1625–1660*, ed. Samuel Rawson Gardiner, 3d ed. rev. (Oxford: Clarendon Press, 1906), 76.

34. Hugh Trevor-Roper, *Archbishop Laud: 1573–1645* (1940; rpt. London: Macmillan, 1963), 238; Thomas Fuller, *The Church History of Britain*, 6 vols. (Oxford, 1845), 6:75, quoted in Peter White, "The Rise of Arminianism Reconsidered," *Past and Present*, no. 101 (November 1983): 53.

35. "The Impure Motives of Elizabethan Poetry," in *The Power of Forms in the English Renaissance*, ed. Stephen Greenblatt (Norman: Pilgrim Books, 1982), 225–38.

Donald M. Friedman

9. *Comus* and the Truth of the Ear

A perusal of the footnotes to John Carey's edition of *Comus*[1] reveals an extraordinary number of appearances of the phrases *first recorded use of the word* and *first recorded use of the word in this sense*. In general Milton is not known for a penchant for neologism, although Bishop Burnet disapproved of his making many "new and rough words" and Dryden noted that "unnecessary coinage . . . runs into affectation."[2] Later criticism has objected, rather, to excessive Latinism, to a high level of abstraction, to the marmoreal quality of Milton's poetic style, to its unwieldiness in registering complex and varying currents of feeling and sensation, or to its monumental subservience to dead ideas. He has been accused of writing in a language other than English rather than of adding wantonly to the word-hoard of native English.

Nevertheless, the percentage of neologisms in *Comus* is the highest in any of Milton's poems of whatever genre, length, or period.[3] Even allowing for inevitable error in the *OED*'s recording of first appearances, the incidence of newly created words and manipulations of established words is high enough to seem noteworthy and to raise questions about Milton's purposes and the role of such words in the design of *Comus*. It may be, for example, that what have been

1. John Carey and Alastair Fowler, eds., *The Poems of John Milton* (London: Longmans, Green, 1968). The text of *Comus* is on pp. 168–229. All citations to Milton's poetry are to this edition.

2. Burnet, *History of His Own Time* (Dublin, 1742), 1:93; Dryden, *A Discourse Concerning the Original and Progress of Satire,* in *Of Dramatic Poesy and Other Critical Essays,* ed. George Watson, 2 vols. (London: J. M. Dent, 1962), 2:84.

3. *Neologism* should be understood to encompass everything from pure coinages to transfers from one part of speech to another, to transferred senses, to participial inventions. According to Carey's and Fowler's notes, the incidence of new words and new usages in Milton's major poems is usually below 1 percent; it rises in *Lycidas* to 1 percent and in *Comus* to 3 percent, or ten times higher than in *Paradise Regained* and six times higher than in *Paradise Lost.* Carey records seven neologisms in the brief epic's 2,070 lines; Fowler notes only two dozen "first occurrences" in the more than 10,000 lines of *Paradise Lost.* Fowler is less interested, or less assiduous, than Carey in pursuing this aspect of Milton's diction in his editing of *Paradise Lost;* with the aid of William B. Hunter's "New Words in Milton's English Poems," *Essays in Honor of Walter Clyde Curry* (Nashville: Vanderbilt University Press, 1954), 241–59, one can find many more than are noted, but not so many as to affect the point materially. *Comus* has little more than 1,000 lines but records nearly thirty "first uses." Hunter lists more words as new but includes trivial changes, like the addition of an adverbial *y.* In any case, Carey and Fowler's edition makes it clear that in writing *Comus* Milton went conspicuously beyond his usual practice in coining and altering words.

accepted as the "Shakespearean" qualities of the verse of *Comus* are in part an unusually free and imaginative handling of vocabulary, a kind of diffused homage to Shakespeare's flair for illuminating latent meanings by dislodging words from familiar syntactical contexts and even from strict grammatical place. Critical tradition, most recently in John Guillory's *Poetic Authority*,[4] has long identified this filiation with the masque's consideration of fancy and particularly with the rhetoric of the tempter Comus himself. But the occurrence of neologisms is fairly widespread in the text. In fact, the Elder Brother and the Attendant Spirit are responsible for the largest number of them, including the invention of the words *embodies* and *imbrutes,* which Angus Fletcher thinks are crucial to the masque's inwardness and therefore to its metaphoric structure.[5] In short, the echoing ghost of Shakespeare does not appear to have direct bearing on Milton's own minting and transforming of words. In any event, the occurrence of neologisms is not notable in those passages in which the so-called Shakespearean traits are most apparent, as for instance in Comus's speech on nature's "full and unwithdrawing hand" (ll. 705 ff.) or the Lady's entering lines (ll. 169 ff.) with their echoes of *The Tempest*.

It is plausible that Milton shared Jonson's conviction of the supreme importance of the masque text over the "shows, mighty shows" the earlier poet inveighs against in his expostulation with Inigo Jones. But even granting the primacy of poetic language for Milton, in this uncharacteristic genre as elsewhere, such a position does not require anything like the egregiousness of neologism that we find in the masque. It is true that coining new words and using familiar words in unfamiliar senses have at least one effect that is consonant with a preoccupation with poetic diction on the part of a young, ambitious, and philosophically intent writer: they call attention to his language. But unlike multicolored rhetorical passages or learned allusions, they do so in a way that may not be flattering to the audience and that may cause some unease, as well as fostering a sense of discovery or satisfaction at difficulty overcome. It is at best a risky business, especially since unsettling an audience is a different matter from surprising a reader with a word hitherto unencountered. Spoken neologisms are something of a test, with all that implies for creating anxieties and at the same time devising a way to sort out the attentive and quick-minded from the slow and conventional. In the terms announced by the Attendant Spirit as he opens the masque with some reluctance, new words are one means of distinguishing between those who "with low-thoughted care" are "confined . . . in this pinfold here" and those few others who "aspire" (ll. 6–12) to lay their hands on the key of eternity. The Spirit may promise later in the masque that Heaven will stoop to virtue should it prove feeble; but these opening lines have the true early Miltonic

4. (New York: Columbia University Press, 1983), 68–93. See also Paul Stevens, "Magic Structures: Comus and the Illusions of Fancy," *Milton Quarterly* 17 (1983): 84–89.

5. *The Transcendental Masque: An Essay on Milton's Comus* (Ithaca: Cornell University Press, 1971), 247.

ring, with their approving glance at aspiration and their seconding of the virtuous violence that will seize the way to immortality. The "just hands" of *Comus*
are first cousins to the "forc'd fingers rude" of *Lycidas* three years later. Insofar
as the introduction of new and unusual words into a text commissioned for a
ceremonial and celebratory occasion can be seen as deliberately invasive, threatening to upset comfortable conventions of what is heard and what is understood, Milton's use of neologisms in *Comus* may be connected with his desire to
challenge his audience to listen to his masque attentively and correctly, and thus
to hear it aright. Characteristically, his didactic intent takes the form of a trial of
interpretation, a test of the ability to distinguish between sound and sense.

Milton has long been a focus of the study of relations between the author and
the social and political circumstances of the society in which he wrote. But
Comus has lain apart from this current of scholarship; the debate over its meaning has circled around such questions as the source of its neoplatonism or the
ethical structure of its value system. Recently, however, the work that once was
cast as *The Transcendental Masque* was retitled *The Puritan Masque;*[6] in several
surveys of the literature of the late English Renaissance that attempt to uncover
its Reformation roots,[7] *Comus* is now being seen as in part a reaction not only to
aristocratic privilege and the verbal and fiscal excesses of Charles's court but
also quite specifically to the controversy of the 1630s over the publication of the
Book of Sports.[8] In a similar but more domestic vein, *Comus* has been set back
into the context of the contemporary history of the Egertons and of the possible
facts of its actual performance.[9] What began as the rediscovery of a great sexual
scandal has developed into a view of the masque from a number of perspectives,
all of which consider it as a product of a particular time and place.[10]

One of the less obvious ways in which this kind of analysis fits with the literary interpretation of the masque is the history of the text. The differences
among the texts of *Comus* raise questions about the nature and rapidity of

6. The references are to Fletcher, *Transcendental Masque*, and to Mary Ann McGuire, *Milton's Puritan Masque* (Athens: University of Georgia Press, 1984).

7. See Richard Strier, *Love Known* (Chicago: University of Chicago Press, 1983); Barbara Lewalski, *Protestant Poetics and the Seventeenth-Century Religious Lyric* (Princeton: Princeton University Press, 1979); and Alan Sinfield, *Literature in Protestant England* (London: Croom Helm, 1983).

8. McGuire, *Milton's Puritan Masque,* 9–59; Leah S. Marcus has treated the controversy in *The Politics of Mirth: Jonson, Herrick, Milton, Marvell, and the Defense of Old Holiday Pastimes* (Chicago: University of Chicago Press, 1986).

9. See William B. Hunter, Jr., *Milton's Comus: Family Piece* (Troy, N.Y.: Whitston, 1983); Cedric Brown, *John Milton's Aristocratic Entertainments* (Cambridge: Cambridge University Press, 1985); David Norbrook, *Poetry and Politics in the English Renaissance* (London: Routledge and Kegan Paul, 1984), chap. 10; and essays by Norbrook, Jennifer Chibnall, and John Creaser in *The Court Masque,* ed. David Lindley (Manchester: Manchester University Press, 1984).

10. See Barbara Breasted, "*Comus* and the Castlehaven Scandal," *Milton Studies* 3 (Pittsburgh: University of Pittsburgh Press, 1971), 201–24. John Creaser has argued in "Milton's *Comus:* The Irrelevance of the Castlehaven Scandal," *Notes and Queries,* n.s. 31 (1984): 307–17, that the sensa-
tional case described by Breasted was not as influential for the masque as she suggested.

Milton's development between 1634 and 1637, when the first published text appeared, in addition to questions about decorum, performance exigencies, and even the changing political and personal climate, all of which may have played a part in creating the variant texts. Recently Cedric Brown proposed that the additions to the Lady's second speech and to the Spirit's epilogue in 1637 reflect Milton's increasingly energetic and unrestrained will to attack the monarchical and Laudian establishment.[11] Later and less conjectural evidence of this is the criticism of the clergy in *Lycidas,* a criticism that Milton raised to the level of prophecy in the headnote to the poem in the 1645 edition, where he claims he had foretold their ruin eight years earlier.

Such studies have been guided by Christopher Hill's detailed alignment of Milton's political thinking with the body of dissenting opinion whose most radical lineaments became sharply visible in the expansive atmosphere of the 1640s.[12] A number of studies have found reason even in Milton's relatively early work to discuss an underlying and developing republicanism and thus to sharpen our sense of his opposition to the monarchy and the court, a strain of feeling that parallels his putative views on ecclesiastical organization and policies.

Some commentators more fully committed to the political analysis of literary works emphasize that Milton tended to become more conservative in his views of government as the hopes of the Civil War period evanesced into the interregnum and were transformed ultimately into the Protectorates and the Restoration. By "conservative" I believe is meant the movement in the late pamphlets and the later poems toward a faith—strong in its disillusion—in the inner integrity of a few just men, as a political analogue to the inward paradise that must replace the remembered and yearned-for Eden. The argument of these critics and political theorists is that whatever aspect of Milton's thought can be considered revolutionary in one of that word's ordinary senses was always primarily millennial.[13] For them, Milton's hopes and specific designs for political reform were driven by the great engine of reformation rather than by any general analysis of economic structures and dispositions of political power. David Aers and Gunther Kress, for example, argue that the millennial note struck in *Areopagitica,* in its vision of the new nation shaking its eagle-locks in impatience to complete the work of the Reformation, is strikingly and centrally different from the manifestos and proposals of the Diggers and the Levellers, in which biblical prophecies were connected to social and economic measures that would establish Christ's kingdom on earth by redistributing the rich man's wealth to the

11. *Milton's Aristocratic Entertainments,* 132–52.

12. This has been a theme of much of Hill's lifework. The central text for our purposes is *Milton and the English Revolution* (London, 1977).

13. See Mary Ann Radzinowicz, "The Politics of *Paradise Lost,*" in *Politics of Discourse: The Literature and History of Seventeenth-Century England,* ed. Kevin Sharpe and Steven Zwicker (Berkeley: University of California Press, 1987), 204–29; and Fredric Jameson, "Religion and Ideology," in *1642: Literature and Power in the Seventeenth Century,* ed. Francis Barker et al. (Essex: University of Essex, 1981), 315–36.

poor and restoring the Adamic—even prelapsarian—vice-regency of man by giving all a share of the divine creation.[14]

I would like to offer support for this line of commentary, although for reasons rather different from the ones adduced. It seems fairly clear that in 1634 Milton was still enchanted by the possibilities of moral and spiritual conversion, in the nation and in the individual, if England could be taught how to fulfill its destined reformative task. This is not to say that this latent power of conversion was not understood to have implications for purely social and political reform. It would be difficult to believe that Milton, especially by the time he composed *Arcades, Comus,* and *Lycidas,* was not alert to the accelerating currents of Caroline politics and Laudian ecclesiastical moves. But the question is one of intellectual and emotional balance; and Milton was at this point still imagining his fictions through a perspective that might be called neoplatonic, by which I mean a noticeable separation between his ideas of what is right in nature and what is true in supernature. This is one reason that the Lady's speeches in *Comus* about just distribution of the earth's bounty are, however impassioned, also platitudinous. To be sure, her arguments rest on long and familiar traditions, Stoic among others. One may also grant that not only their argumentative content is important but also the reappearance of such arguments in the local context of the debate with the enchanter and in the larger context of the seventeenth-century revival of stoic ethics and metaphysics.

But the point is that the Lady's speeches are fairly reliable indices of the weight given in Milton's thinking to visions of the inherent decency and decorum of nature and of the sublime form of virtue. The masque is filled with images of natural beauty, order, and excess; we and the Lady are also allowed to see embodiments of numinous reality. But the varying displays of imagery, if not balanced or in tension with one another, are not integrated either, as they will tend to be in the later poems, particularly the epics. What will emerge as Milton's mortalism—that is, his revision of traditional Creation doctrine so that God is seen to create the universe out of his own substance—is still in *Comus* in the process of formation. Nevertheless, the process had already begun by the time Milton composed his masque. I take this to be part of the reason that he assigns to the Elder Brother the confident assertion that evil must inevitably recoil against itself, mixing no more with goodness and consuming itself with "eternal restless change." If this is not true, he says, then "the pillared firmament is rottenness" (ll. 595–98). Further on in his career Milton was less categorical about the disjunction between good and evil, between change and stasis, between earth and heaven. But even here his youthful enthusiasm for visible virtues and the power of stasis and order to resist the temptations of sensuous mutability is projected as one agent in a dialectic. There is evidence that he is

14. "Historical Process, Individual and Communities in Milton's Early Prose," in *1642,* 283–300.

aware of the necessity of trial for such beliefs, just as there is evidence that he is aware of the political and social resonances not only of this masque itself and its chosen subjects but also of the setting, the occasion, the personage honored, and the relations of all three to the state of the nation in 1634.

It is a commonplace that Milton's works, most familiarly the longer, later ones, are built on grand polarities. But we are less comfortable describing how these polarized values and ideas operate in particular poems. Many have felt and reported on "tensions" in the poems between pagan and Christian values, classical and romantic epic conventions, or any of the myriad counterpoised concepts in which the canon is so rich. Perhaps it would be fairer to say that there is genuine oscillation from one set of values or point of view to another, oscillations over long periods of time, within whole works, and sometimes within particular speeches or delimited discursive passages. The familiar Miltonic devices of mirroring and imitation, as in the throne scenes of books 2 and 3 of *Paradise Lost,* or the successive appearances of disguised shepherds in the opening scenes of *Comus,* can be regarded as a structural analogy of this intrinsic dialecticism. *Paradise Regained,* from this viewpoint, tries to empty out the polarity by seeking, through negation and silence, the new form of heroism promised in *Paradise Lost,* to replace aggressive achievement by detachment and renunciation. Again characteristically, Milton imagines this process in the form of a sharpened and narrowly defined confrontation between two grand antagonists. Some of the late prose works show that, under the pressure of events both external and internal, the resolution of the problem of representing a universal dialectic in a strictly defined form continued to escape Milton; politics tended to come adrift from the religious values that had earlier either underpinned his ideas or even dominated them, as in the early pamphlets.

It is possible to organize our rough descriptions of many of Milton's major works along lines that parallel or duplicate the relationships between recurrent themes in those works. In some sonnets, for example, we see the working out, in terms of Milton's own struggle to reconcile poetic ambition with patience and attendance on the divine will, of the incommensurabilities of divine foreknowledge and the freedom of the human will. Similarly, the jostling between the moral imperatives of rational choice and the intuitive foundations of true knowledge goes on from poem to poem, pamphlet to treatise, throughout Milton's mature career. His poetic record is one of living daily with these struggles of thought and belief, fashioning his work out of the fierce contentions and irreconcilable impulses that he could not escape.

In *Comus,* nevertheless, and possibly because of both its occasion and its genre, he was able to avoid driving directly into the impasses that the epics had to have the courage to deal with. The Lady, for instance, can refuse to confront Circe's son with the "flame of sacred vehemence" in her exposition of the doctrine of virginity because he has "nor ear, nor soul to apprehend / The sublime notion" (ll. 794, 782–783). The failures of both the Attendant Spirit and the brothers can be redeemed by a local tutelary deity and their triumph celebrated, although the tempter, like the Blatant Beast, is still abroad. But even though the masque's ability to reap some rewards it has not in fact earned might be linked with its neoplatonic inclination to leave a gap between dogma and praxis, between belief and experience, Milton also uses the masque as an agent of instruction, as an instrument of change, education, testing, conversion. In this respect he is engaging his habitual will to harness incommensurables by nurturing within the preeminent form of courtly compliment a clearly didactic criticism of the masque genre itself, of the occasion, and of the personage honored.

To this extent the recent politicizing critics of *Comus* are correct in arguing that a fundamental attack on ostentation and worldly arrogance marks the differences between Milton's masque and its Jonsonian models. Victory in *Comus* is achieved by stooping heaven *and* feeble virtue, not by powers of education and conversion inherent in the figure of power to whom the masque is presented. The Earl of Bridgewater may be agent and representative of the monarch and his power; but his children's victory over "sensual folly and intemperance" (l. 974) is won only in his presence, not by his virtue. This is no mirror of magistracy that instructs by presenting images of the ideal to those who should embody it in their exercise of authority. It is, rather, a universal mirror of the journey-and-trial by which Milton figured life on earth as a shadow of its providential design in heaven. Insofar as this is so, the manipulations of language in the masque, especially as they challenge the audience to coordinate what they hear, what they see, and what they know, are vital to the educative task Milton has chosen to undertake.

There has always been ambivalence in the notion of Milton, the revolutionary rhetor and eventual regicide, composing as a major work of his early maturity a masque for one of the king's deputies and his aristocratic family. This ambivalence is revealed as suggestively in the forms its didacticism takes as it is in the Lady's appeal to a rational naturalism (she has recently been described as a republican) and in the Spirit's initial neoplatonic disdain for "this dim spot," which slips quickly, with only a brief, grudging, "But to my task," into patriotic praise of this "greatest" isle, "the best of all the main" (ll. 5–28). Stanley Fish would have it that these signs of ambivalence are part of a larger design—trying to get us to get things straight—and are commensurate with other noted puzzles and problems in the masque's structure and apparent meaning.[15]

Fish is right, I believe, in asserting that in *Comus* Milton is asking us to do something difficult; but that task is related in more substantial ways to currents of literary and intellectual history than his general formula allows. As we have seen, Milton shared with Jonson the belief that the masque text is its soul, the designs and dances its visible body. These traditional technical terms bespeak

---

15. Stanley Fish, "Problem Solving in *Comus,*" in *Illustrious Evidence,* ed. Earl Miner (Berkeley: University of California Press, 1975), 115–31.

the hierarchy of creative power and virtue both poets subscribed to. In Milton's case we must expand the category of poetic text to include music and the words of songs, not only because of the central participation of Lawes in the design of the masque but primarily because of the poet's early and lifelong devotion to the "Sphere-borne harmonious sisters, Voice and Verse,"[16] a devotion signaled in *Comus* by the crucial placement of its songs and by the structural interplay between the Lady's song to Echo and the Spirit's invocation of Sabrina. The former departs from the convention of such songs as we can observe it in, for example, *Cynthia's Revels,* where the voice of echo tags the last words of the singer's line; nothing answers the Lady—except, that is, the risen Sabrina, who comes at the Spirit's musical call, "Listen and save" (1. 888). This salutary nymph, third and last of the group of maidens first abandoned then translated to a higher sphere, announces simply "I am here," and proceeds to the action for which she has been summoned, thus suiting her deed to the spoken word that she has heard.

Milton's unmistakable concern with the discourse of poetry in *Comus* is connected at several moments not only to his self-conscious alignment with the Jonsonian doctrine of the soul and the body of the masque but also with his understanding of the many ways in which radical Protestant doctrines of the saving power of the word might be applied to the secular offices and works of the poet. Just a few years later Milton made a resounding manifesto out of this idea, in the opening paragraphs of book 2 of *The Reason of Church Government;* but it may be useful to remember that as well as asserting that the ability to compose poems is a gift of God "of power beside the office of a pulpit" to teach and to celebrate, Milton also suggests that the "call of wisdom and virtue" may be "not only in Pulpits" but in "Theaters," "or what other place, or way may win most upon the people to receive at once both recreation and instruction."[17]

I am not suggesting a simple, direct identification of the masque and the Puritan sermon, although some years ago William Haller did not shrink from urging such a comparison. He said of the Puritan preachers, who during the years when *Comus* was written and subsequently revised for publication were moving into ever more vigorous controversy with Laud's ceremonial impositions, that "they too cast the lessons of their inner experiences into the image of the pilgrim, seemingly lost, but not abandoned by God, encountering temptation and danger but journeying steadfastly toward heaven, led by a light within. [Milton] could no more have escaped hearing a great many sermons in which spiritual wayfaring was depicted than he could have escaped reading the Bible itself."[18] One of Haller's examples, in a different context, is the Elizabethan divine Edward Topsell, who spoke of preachers as "the stars that give light in the

---

16. "At a Solemn Music," l. 2, in *Poems,* 161–65.

17. *Complete Prose Works of John Milton,* ed. Douglas Bush et al. (New Haven: Yale University Press, 1953–1982), 1:816, 820.

18. *The Rise of Puritanism* (New York: Columbia University Press, 1938), 318.

night, the captains that are foremost in service, the soules that shield others from danger. Now if there be no stars, and no captains, and no shields, how shall we walk in the night of this world, or fight the battle of Christ, or be saved from the fiery darts of satan?"[19] *Comus* tells us that some forms of virtue give off their "own radiant light"; if it should prove too weak, a "bright aërial spirit" clad in "pure ambrosial weeds" will be sent to guide and illumine it further. And there is always Sabrina.

We know from the passage in *The Reason of Church Government* and from other explicit and implicit evidence that Milton regarded both the inspiration and the responsibilities of the preacher and the poet as interfused; the transference of power from one role to the other drew energy from his sense of being "church-outed" during the period of *Comus* by the new ascendancy of the bishops. It may be useful, then, to think of the poetic design of *Comus* as drawing specifically on the imperatives that governed the art of preaching as Milton understood it.

It is easier to distinguish among individual preachers than it is to sustain a distinction between Anglican and Puritan styles of preaching, but by and large there is an explicit disagreement about the preacher's freedom to interpret a biblical text. The Anglican argues that while Scripture is generally perspicuous the inspired preacher can open a text by imaginative comparisons and examples and by rhetorical skill so that the hearts of his congregants will be moved. The prototypical Puritan insists rather on the primacy of the literal sense of Scripture and, while not scorning the power of rhetoric to move the passions, will argue that the application of the text is perceived only because of the power of God's word to speak through the preacher, as it speaks through the Bible and preeminently through the incarnation of Christ, who is to the Father as the spoken or written word is to the unknowable word of God. Thus Luther called Christ as Word *sermo* rather than *logos*, insisting that the spirit is heard within the spoken word, the process of speech; Calvin followed him in this emphasis on the power of the spoken word to reach the heart through grace; and Reformation Protestantism developed these positions, particularly in the Netherlands and in England, into a fiery campaign for the freedom of pulpit preaching and the foundation of faith on the direct apprehension of the word, supported by the confirming power of reason.

Milton's implication in this complex of thought is marked at every stage of his poetic career, from the earliest scholastic exercises to *Samson Agonistes;* he must have been tempted to regard his own life as an allegorical commentary on the theme, as he tried to find inner vision inspired by the muse to replace his eyes' lost sight. But nowhere is the question of the relation between seeing and hearing posed so clearly and concisely as in the opening of book 12 of *Paradise Lost*, when Michael, noticing that Adam's "mortal sight" is failing, says that he will

19. Quoted in ibid., 143.

henceforth relate the providential history he has been sent to tell, rather than passing it before Adam's eyes as a series of visions. The critical consensus is that the transition marks the change from a survey of the instances of sin and destruction that will flow from the original disobedience of Adam and Eve, to the history of God's redemptive plan for humankind, as seen in the history of the world that succeeds Noah's flood and reaches its typological fulfillment in the incarnation of Christ.[20] These are matters of faith for Adam, and so they must be conveyed to his understanding by the medium of the word. Insofar as they are matters of faith for Milton's audience as well, as Joseph Summers pointed out long ago, the shift to narration places us and Adam in comparable positions as we are given the opportunity to learn the saving knowledge God has sent through the angelic voice.

Such arguments are based traditionally on a number of scriptural texts, the most prominent being Romans 10:17: "So, then faith cometh by hearing, and hearing by the word of God." It was quoted repeatedly, along with others from Revelation, from many prophetic books of the Old Testament, and from the Psalmist's verses that warned those that have ears and hear not of the dangers they faced in closing the channels of grace. To the scriptural sanction was added, in Protestant sermon theory, a moral epistemology that distinguished between kinds of knowledge on the basis of the modes of perception that apprehended them. The eye transmits images and thus presents to the mind static representations of a reality whose meaning must yet be determined. The ear records the word directly; insofar as the word is an image of thought, it comes before the sight-symbol in the order of intelligibility.

The Protestant impulse toward iconoclasm, then, took some of its impetus from its theory of preaching; and that theory ran contrary to traditional psychology and its hierarchical arrangement of the senses. Vision was distrusted because of its links to the imagination and hence its vulnerability to the deceptions of fancy and deliberate guile. Reason was accessible to the divine word when it was spoken in unmediated form, and was also then guarded against the uncertainty and unpredictability of the fancy.

Some of these strictures are reflected in Michael's shift from vision to narrative; if human history is presented to Adam—even to his vision as clarified by the three medicinal drops from the well of life—as a sequence of tableaux, he can comprehend its meaning only as compared to what he already knows, and by virtue of his inherent ability to reason. Of course, he makes mistakes; but to conduct the process of education is not Milton's only point. In the strict sense,

20. See Joseph Summers, *The Muse's Method: An Introduction to Paradise Lost* (Cambridge: Harvard University Press, 1962), 186–224; Barbara Lewalski, "Structure and the Symbolism of Vision in Michael's Prophecy, *Paradise Lost,* Books XI-XII," *Philological Quarterly* 42 (1963): 25–35; Mary Ann Radzinowicz, "Man as a Probationer of Immortality," in *Approaches to Paradise Lost,* ed. C. A. Patrides (London, 1968), 31–51; Raymond Waddington, "The Death of Adam," *Modern Philology* 70 (1972): 9–21, which includes useful bibliographical notes.

what is being revealed to Adam is the evidence of things seen; the evidence of things not seen, the sum and substance of faith, can be presented to his rational soul only by the word, and that is conveyed in narrative and spoken by a living voice. The words that it utters, and the concepts that those words symbolize, transcend both the stasis of images and the illusory sequence of history; they occur in time but speak of meanings that transcend individual events. Michael's narrative thus establishes different relationships between sense and the object of sense, just as its typological structure establishes new bonds between an event and its true meaning.

In those crucial few lines in book 12, then, Milton places his poem firmly within a complex of doctrinal and psychological tendencies that urge the primacy of the spoken word in communicating saving truth. Michael's choice of narration is in some measure a response to, and an acknowledgment of, the questions Milton has raised throughout the epic about the powers of rhetoric, the danger of the word when it is spoken without divine sanction or purpose. In *Comus* the question lies close to the heart of the masque, for it is the focus of the debate that is at the center of the drama of imprisonment and enfranchisement.

Nothing is more congenial to Milton than to find a way of adapting or recasting a literary convention so that it remains itself while changing noticeably to serve his purpose. We have seen that the fable of *Comus* has affinities with the emblematic figure of the endangered spiritual pilgrim of the sermons; we may also note that a scene of darkness and confusion is often to be found at the beginning of court masques, for similar reasons of allegory and because it allows for dazzling and didactic transformations to splendid, illuminated palaces where the king can be shown as the conqueror of darkness. It is characteristic of Milton to imitate that trope and turn it upside down at the same time by taking us from the drear wood to Comus's palace—at first. Milton develops the meaning of initial darkness, familiar from Dante's wood and Plato's cave, by emphasizing the importance of hearing correctly when the shapes of things can no longer be seen. The first imperative the Attendant Spirit utters is "Listen,"[21] as he explains the origin of his mission in the genealogy of Comus, telling us of the art of Circe and the threat to the human countenance that hides in "the thick shelter of black shades embowered." As if to make the realities of this darkness visible, the Spirit, when he puts off his "sky-robes" a few lines later to put on the habit of Thyrsis, submits his powers to the conditions of the pinfold and, as he "hears" the tread of "hateful steps" as Comus approaches, becomes "viewless," neither seeing nor seen.

This event is repeated as a variation a few lines later when Comus himself senses the approach of the Lady; as he beats time for the antimasque of bestial

21. *Listen* occurs only five times in Milton's poetic corpus—once when Raphael warns Adam *not* to listen to Satan. The other occurrences are all in *Comus,* as are all of Milton's uses of *list* as an imperative. Some years ago Angus Fletcher called *Comus* "a study in listening" (*The Transcendental Masque,* 166).

dancers he says that he *feels* "the different pace of some chaste footing" (ll. 145–46). The Trinity manuscript shows that Milton first wrote "hear," which suggests that he had already realized that Comus's ability to hear correctly would have an essential bearing on the Lady's later speech (added in revision) in defense of the "sun-clad power of chastity" and the "sage and serious doctrine of virginity."[22] There Comus is repulsed by being told that he has not "ear, nor soul to apprehend the sublime notion" (ll. 781–786).

Comus knows that his "charms," as he calls them, work best when they are used to "cheat the eye with blear illusion, / And give it false presentments" (ll. 155–56), especially when such illusions are bolstered by the deceptive use of "well-placed words" "baited with reasons not unplausible" (l. 162). Milton is not merely demonstrating the superiority of ear over eye in the perception of truth, but showing us the vulnerabilities of each and guiding his audience toward the right employment of reason in recognizing the truth that comes from faith in the virtue of virtue. The Lady enters almost immediately, searching for the source of the noise of Comus's rout, relying on the truth of her ear, as she puts it, but recognizing fully that the sound was of "riot and ill-managed merriment"; this of course is the sound that Comus has heard as a "light, fantastic round" and compared to the music of the spheres.

Milton then uses music again as a mirror that both images and distorts. The Lady, having imagined and then seen the forms of her guardian virtues, in this "single darkness" where nothing physical can be seen distinctly, decides to make such "noise" as she can. What follows is her song to Echo, which transcends the Ovidian myth by translating the nymph into a grace note to "all heaven's harmonies." In this instance, like Satan when he is struck "stupidly good" by the sight of Eve's beauty, Comus's ear also proves true momentarily; he is struck by a "home-felt delight" because of the beauty of the Lady's song and is mistaken only in believing that "such divine enchanting ravishment" cannot be the utterance of "any mortal mixture of earth's mould" (ll. 243–44). In short, unlike the Lady, he is incapable of grasping the meaning of the sounds that have enraptured him; his ear is true in a limited sense, but not in the way that is vital in the masque, the way that unites perception and reason so that the true ear matches the truth of the word it hears.

The point is made most clearly, and succinctly, by the speed with which the Lady falls victim to Comus's deceptions as he plays the false shepherd, an image that will be corrected for us in the next scene when the Spirit enacts the true shepherd as he guides the lost brothers to their sister. That correction of our understanding, it should be noted, includes our recognition that the Spirit is also disguised and merely pretends to be a shepherd, so far as we can see. What he

22. See S. E. Sprott, ed., *John Milton, A Maske: The Earlier Versions* (Toronto: University of Toronto Press, 1973), 66.

does and what he says, of course, are quite different in intent and in moral valence: and that is the point.

That it is the point is made clear when next we see the Lady. Two things have changed: she is now immobilized in an enchanted chair; and she is totally undeceived about the nature of Comus. The result is another image of ambivalence. She has fallen victim to his expert imitation of a good shepherd; but his actions have contradicted his rhetoric and proved it false. Thus, when offered the "cordial julep" to refresh her "mortal frailty," she rejects it because of the truth her faith has garnered from experience: "none / But such as are good men can give good things" (ll. 701–2). This perception, or rather this knowledge that has replaced opinion, both permits and urges her to respond to Comus's naturalist argument in favor of indulgence and the enjoyment of the world's bounties. Her counterargument, based on Augustinian principles of the use of nature, illuminates the false logic of Comus's position; but she launches it not merely to defeat him but also because, as she says, she hates "when vice can bolt her arguments, / And virtue has no tongue to check her pride" (ll. 759–60). She must speak out against the corruption of words and their rational form; and she does so despite the awkward fact that she is still imprisoned in body by the sorcerer.

As if to demonstrate beyond doubt the freedom of her mind, though her "corporal rind" remains "immanacled," Milton has her defend the power of chastity but makes a great point of finding Comus incapable even of listening to the exposition of such a doctrine. As the Lady says, he has "nor ear, nor soul to apprehend" such speech. Her utmost condemnation is to tell Comus that his wit and rhetorical skills have so tainted his soul by undermining his reason that he is not "fit to hear" himself "convinced." In other words, only good men can hear good things and know why they are good. Milton's insistence on this doctrine helps to explain why, after much revision of the Spirit's epilogue, and just before the penultimate lines on Cupid and Psyche transcending Venus and Adonis in the vision of the "happy climes" from which he is descended and to which the audience is invited to aspire—why at precisely that juncture Milton inserted the parenthetical line, "List mortals if your ears be true" (l. 996). Here again the syntactic ambiguity is to the point: "Listen carefully, for if you understand this you are one of those who can hear truly" and "Listen carefully, those of you who have true ears and are therefore those to whom I have been sent." In either case, what acts as a teaching serves also as a test, as a sorting device, and as an exhortation to "Love Virtue," who alone is free, as the members of the audience presumably would like to be and indeed probably think themselves. The sign of grace, and perhaps of election, is the ability to make sense of what is spoken, to listen to the word truly.

I would like to return, finally, to where we began, to the coinages and transfers of meaning and parts of speech that were lumped together as neologisms, and to remark on their groupings, the ways they are placed in the masque's discourse, and on their contributions to Milton's dramatization of the doctrine of the truth of the ear. In *Comus* Milton actually invents only a few new words: several new verbs, such as *immanacle, shroud, embodies;* a new noun, *cateress;* and a larger number of new adjectives. There is a large group of gerunds, and in this respect Milton conforms to the general pattern of word formation during his lifetime. In the two hundred years prior to 1700 most new words entered English by adding a suffix; but in the half-century before the Restoration the highest percentage of new words were formed by adding a prefix, and that is what we find often in *Comus*, a new word made by adding "un" or "in." Milton also creates compounds, particularly adjectival ones; but the largest group of neologisms in the masque is made up of words that change their sense or meaning rather than their form, as when the Elder Brother pictures Wisdom as she "plumes" (l. 377) her feathers, or the Lady compares Comus's rhetoric to an art of "dazzling fence" (l. 790). These words, which both are and are not what they seem, are spoken, almost all of them, by Comus, the Lady, or the Elder Brother; they cluster mainly about the debate at the center of the masque.

Nor is this device restricted to words that change their meaning slightly. Stanley Fish noted that in reading *Comus* we are "learning to perceive essential differences in the context of surface similarities,"[23] and the surface of *Comus* is dotted with similarities: disguised shepherds, endangered virgins, starry quires and their depraved imitators, glozing courtesy that is mistaken for "honest-offered" courtesy, even smoke that can be the sign either of true courtesy found in "lowly sheds" or of a "frail and feverish being" lived out in earth's sinful "pinfold."[24] Perception is figured in the masque as a distorting mirror, one that challenges the enlightened reason to find the truth in the image, when the image itself is deceptive. We know that the shepherd who is Comus in disguise is evil because of what he does; and we have the advantage over the Lady in recognizing the deceptiveness of his speech only because we have heard his confessional opening speech. Otherwise we might be no more proof against his false rhetoric than she is. However, from the point that she, too, is given evidence of his true motives, she makes no mistake in distinguishing between "dear wit, and gay rhetoric" (l. 789) and true utterance; she also remains silent for the rest of the masque, as the invocation and response of Sabrina do the work of restoring her to her natural state and the source of her virtue.

What this suggests is that in a poem about the crucial importance of identifying the truth, and about the obstacles placed in the way of that task, Milton has woven at least part of his fabric with ideas about the spoken word, as it resonates to theological doctrines with which he was familiar and as it holds within it the

23. Fish, "Problem Solving in *Comus,*" 121.
24. See Stephen Kogan, *The Hieroglyphic King: Wisdom and Idolatry in the Seventeenth-Century Masque* (Madison, N.J.: Fairleigh Dickinson University Press, 1986), 240 ff.; see also James A. Clark, "Milton naturans, Milton naturatus: the debate over nature in *A Mask presented at Ludlow,*" *Milton Studies* 20 (Pittsburgh: University of Pittsburgh Press, 1984), 3–27.

means of edification common to poets and pastors. The poem calls constantly on its auditors to listen and to hear truthfully. At the center of its fable is a test of the ability of the focal character to tell true argument from false; and it is filled with similar, epicentric testings and with calls and challenges to attention. As a kind of harmonic counterpoint to his design of crisis and accurate listening, Milton has included an extraordinary number of words meant to fall slightly aslant on the ear, words that must be construed without adequate guidance, and words that inhabit familiar shapes and sounds yet turn out to mean in a slightly different way from the expected. To understand them the hearer has to make his way forward, relying to some extent on what is already known, but trusting his guide to lead him securely to the new meaning. He must, therefore, act with faith, but also with a reasonable respect for what he knows to be true. He must risk, and make choices, and decide where meaning lies. To make sense of Milton's neologisms he must make sense of what the masque presents. In this the reader, the hearer, the community of listeners, like the characters of the masque itself, must train the ear to be true, while at the same time responding to the word that has been created.

Comus is constructed concentrically, the entries, trials, and releases of its participants circling around the debate in the wood. Similarly, its conceptual and political implications move outward from that central scene in ever-widening circles of significance. In much recent writing on the masque that significance has been connected to specific events and persons in the increasingly strained relations between Charles and his subjects[25] and between Archbishop Laud and the sectarians, as well as to a general characterization of Milton's developing thought on questions of civil and religious liberty.

We have seen that *Comus* is unlike most other examples of its genre not only in ways that were determined by the occasion but also because of Milton's perspectives on both the subject and the literary form of the masque. Sometimes the effects of these differences are difficult to distinguish; *Comus* lacks many of the trappings of the typical court masque in part because it was performed in a setting where those trappings were presumably hard to come by, but in part because its honored figure is not the king, but his representative. It is more important, however, that Milton shapes the masque's fable, as we have seen, so that its "triumph . . . O'er sensual folly, and intemperance," the fulfillment of its educative myth, is accomplished by those under trial with the aid of tutelary figures from within the fable, not by projected images of the authority before whom they perform.

This shift in the center of the masque's power and in its representation of that power is consonant with its emphasis on the vital importance for both characters and audience to make sense of the sounds and appearances of the masque.

---

25. Marcus argues that Milton was urging Bridgewater to continue to act on what she believes was the earl's "unwillingness to work with Laud" (*Politics of Mirth,* 176).

To judge solely by appearances—either visual or rhetorical—is to accept an image for the reality beneath or behind it. To rest in the image is to imagine history as arrested and thus to allow hierarchy to stand for the ordering of meaning and value. To hear or to see accurately is to be able to set experience beside knowledge, to submit to the processes of time and the speaking of its meaning through the flux of history, to open the self to the divine word by surrendering the mediations of "premeditated" structures of all kinds, from liturgies to legislatures to bishoprics to literary genres.

The decentering of the monarch in *Comus* is clear in both material and figurative senses; the dislodging of established modes of worship and belief is less apparent but no less implicit in what I have described as Milton's use of neologisms to test those whose "ears be true," those who can find the direct way to listen to the word and are less vulnerable to, and thus less dependent on, the utterances of represented authority. Radical Protestant reliance on Scripture always contained a latent challenge to hierarchical, hieratic structures; at a time when political issues were growing more nearly inextricable from religious matters, such reliance carried with it a strong anti-monarchical impulse. Milton had not left the established Church when he wrote *Comus,* and it would take some years, the Italian journey, and the outbreak of the Civil War before his vision of a reformed religion would reach maturity. But the emergent shape of that vision can be seen in the masque; when Milton addresses himself to the importance of accurate perception he is setting himself apart from those who seek "the dark, the bushie, the tangled forrest," those who "would imbosk,"[26] and urging both spectators and readers to look for truth, to listen for its unmistakable voice.

26. *The Reason of Church Government,* in *The Complete Prose Works of John Milton,* 1:569.

Achsah Guibbory

10. The Temple of *Hesperides* and Anglican-Puritan Controversy

Herrick's modern readers have often harbored suspicions that he was not a deeply religious man, even though he was an Anglican priest.[1] Certainly some of his playfully erotic poetry and his carpe diem poems seem to encourage these suspicions. As if to dispel them, Herrick appended to *Hesperides* an epigram echoing Martial and suggesting that the licentiousness of his poetry contrasted with the propriety of his life: "To his Book's end this last line he'd have plac't, / *Jocond his Muse was; but his Life was chast.*"[2] Though this epitaph suggests a sharp division between Herrick's poetry and his life, between imagination and actual experience, there was a close relationship between his poetry and his life as an Anglican priest. I want here to continue the work that has been done to historicize Herrick's poetry, to re-embed it in the sociopolitical context in which it was written and published, by showing how *Hesperides* is deeply concerned with issues that were the subject of intense Anglican/Puritan religious controversy. Not all the poems of *Hesperides* are involved with these controversies; but a surprisingly large number are, and they respond to them with varying degrees of explicitness, intensity, and indirection.

Herrick is, of course, a poet not a propagandist, but his artistic imagination was deeply stirred by contemporary controversy and conflict. For all the poems expressing a preference for the world of art, imagination, and fantasy (for example, "*Art above Nature, to* Julia," "*The Lilly in a Christal*"), there is in *Hesperides* a surprisingly persistent concern with the "real" world of experience and discord. (One could even say that his preference for the world of imagination depends on the insistent presence of that "real" historical world that Herrick typically sees as threatening, ugly, and disappointing.) Herrick's poetry often becomes entangled in the realm of political and religious conflict. Beneath the

---

1. Roger Rollin, for example, comments, "There is no way of knowing" if "Herrick *was* a 'religious man'. . . . Economic rather than deep-seated conviction may have motivated Herrick to take holy orders" (*Robert Herrick* [New York: Twayne, 1966], 125).

2. J. Max Patrick, ed., *The Complete Poetry of Robert Herrick* (New York: Norton, 1968), *Hesperides* 1130 (cf. Martial's "Lasciva est nobis pagina: vita proba est," 1.5.8). All references to Herrick's poetry are to this edition. Hereafter, references to *Hesperides* are cited as H and poem number, with references to *Noble Numbers* cited as N and poem number.

playful festivity of his poems, their delight in fantasy, and their detailed re-creations of ancient rites and customs lurks a concern with issues that were at the time highly controversial and that Herrick invokes through words that had become heavily charged with polemical meaning. Read in the context of controversy over the nature of religious worship and the church, much of the poetry of *Hesperides* takes on polemical significance.

The general anti-Puritan import of Herrick's poetry, or of specific poems, has not gone unnoticed,[3] but there is as yet no full study of the specific and complex anti-Puritan thrust of his poetry. Written for the most part from the 1620s through the 1640s, the period that witnessed the intense Puritan/Anglican controversies that culminated in the Civil War, and published in 1648, the year after Herrick, like many other Anglican priests, was ejected from his parish by the Puritans, *Hesperides* reveals a strongly anti-Puritan stance. It contains political poems praising Charles I and supporting Royalist positions, as well as satirical epigrams like *"Upon Zelot"* mocking the supposed "purity" of these "Precisians" (H 666). But Herrick opposes "Puritan" or "Precisian" sensibilities in a variety of less obvious ways—in his eroticism and his libertine poems; in his frequently blatant "paganism"; in his recurrent concern with various "mixtures" and "minglings," which contrasts sharply with the Puritan insistence on purity and separation between carnal and spiritual, holy and profane. These are all important aspects of Herrick's "anti-Puritanism" that need further attention, but I will focus here on the fascinating connections between *Hesperides* and practices in the Anglican Church as it had developed under the leadership of William Laud, Archbishop of Canterbury. Sometimes explicitly, more often covertly, Herrick's poetry accommodates, indeed supports, the Laudian positions that the Puritans vehemently criticized.

Although we usually think of Herrick as primarily a secular poet, he repeatedly draws analogies between poetry and religion, calling his book of poems a *"Sacred Grove"* (H 265). But *Hesperides* is not only a garden. It is also, significantly, a *"Temple"* (H 496, 445) in which Herrick is enacting a "Poetick Liturgie" (H 510), performing numerous "ceremonies" and "rites" and urging others to perform them. In styling himself a "priest" of poetry, Herrick is following Ben

---

3. On Herrick's anti-Puritan political poetry, see Claude J. Summers, "Herrick's Political Poetry: The Strategies of His Art," in *"Trust to Good Verses": Herrick Tercentenary Essays,* ed. Roger B. Rollin and J. Max Patrick (Pittsburgh: University of Pittsburgh Press, 1978), 171–83, and "Herrick's Political Counterplots," *Studies in English Literature* 25 (1985): 165–82. Leah S. Marcus, *Childhood and Cultural Despair* (Pittsburgh: University of Pittsburgh Press, 1978), 120–39, also discusses the political implications of Herrick's anti-Puritanism. Rollin has argued that *"The Christian Militant"* is a "veiled satirical portrait of the arch-Puritan" (*Robert Herrick,* 128). Robert H. Deming (*Ceremony and Art: Robert Herrick's Poetry* [The Hague: Mouton, 1974]) discusses the anti-Puritanism of Herrick's ceremonies (pp. 141–57) but does not examine contemporary Anglican-Puritan controversies that are crucial to understanding the anti-Puritan elements of Herrick's poetry.

Jonson, who similarly proclaimed himself "priest" of "the *Muses.*"⁴ But Herrick's actual position as an ordained Anglican priest gives the title added resonance. Moreover, Herrick goes much further than Jonson in developing this analogy between poetry and religion, making it central to his volume of poetry. It is no coincidence that the terms Herrick appropriates to his poetry *(ceremonies, rites, liturgy)* are exactly the words that figured so prominently in Laudian controversy.

As readers have long noticed, the "religion" of *Hesperides* is hardly "pure" but rather curiously mixed. Herrick incorporates elements from folk superstition, paganism, Roman Catholicism, even Old Testament Judaism. Classical, pagan customs especially permeate *Hesperides.* The volume itself, with its classical name and its frontispiece depicting the hill of Parnassus, the spring of Helicon, Pegasus, and the poet about to be crowned with wreaths, flaunts its classical, "pagan" appearance. It includes numerous poems, many of them prayers, addressed to the gods and goddesses of classical mythology—Jove, Juno, Apollo, Minerva, Vulcan, Bacchus—asking them for various kinds of aid and protection.

> Mighty *Neptune,* may it please
> Thee, the *Rector* of the Seas,
> That my Barque may safely runne
> Through thy watrie-region;
> And a *Tunnie-fish* shall be
> Offer'd up, with thanks to thee.
>   ("*Another* [short Hymne] *to* Neptune," H 325)

Rather than keeping the ancient past and its classical gods in their distant place, Herrick insists on their immediate connections with the present, as, for example, when he asks Aesculapius to come and help Pru Baldwin recover from her sickness (H 303). Declaring "I am a free-born *Roman*" in his poem on "*His returne to London*" (H 713), Herrick announces the "pagan" character of his poetry, its intimacy with the ancient pagan world at a time when Puritans were vehemently attacking all things that, to them, smacked of paganism.

The Puritan hostility to the pagan runs through earlier writers like the influential William Perkins, but it is particularly vivid and extreme in Herrick's contemporary William Prynne, who aroused the anger of Laud and of many of the king's supporters. Underlying Prynne's lengthy attack in *Histriomastix* (1633) on stage plays, court entertainments, and other "lewd" or "prophane" recreations or practices is his violent dislike of all "pagan" customs. Herrick's "classi-

---

4. See "Epistle to Katherine, Lady Aubigny" (*Forest* XII), "To the Immortall Memorie . . . of . . . Sir Lucius Cary, and Sir H. Morison" (*Under-wood* 72), and "An Ode to James Earle of Desmond . . ." (*Under-wood* 27) (in *The Complete Poetry of Ben Jonson*, ed. William B. Hunter, Jr. [New York: Norton, 1963]).

cism," his sense of continuity with literary and cultural traditions, sharply opposes the assumption of Puritans like Prynne that we must make and keep absolute separations between the Christian and the pagan, the sacred and the secular. Prynne quotes liberally from 2 Corinthians 6:14–16 to support his "separatist" position: "*what fellowship hath Righteousnesse, with Vnrighteousnesse? What communion hath Light with Darknesse? What concord hath Christ with Belial? what part hath hee that Beleeveth with an Infidell? or what agreement hath the Temple of God with Idoles?*"[5] In Prynne's own writings as well as in the biblical passages he favors, there is a rhetoric of division and opposition, an insistence on purity.

How far this is from Herrick, with his preoccupation with minglings, his eclecticism, his emphasis on the harmony among customs from various religions that all acknowledge divine control over the universe—all qualities evident in "Corinna's *going a Maying*" (H 178). Whereas Puritans rejected May Day rites as pagan and therefore profane, in Herrick's poem the celebration of May becomes a sacred act of "Devotion." Corinna is invited to participate in a May ritual that embraces all of nature, and nature is seen as instinctively alive with devotional impulses: "Each Flower has wept, and bow'd toward the East," "all the Birds have Mattens seyd, / And sung their thankfull Hymnes." The customary divisions between man and nature, between secular and sacred are blurred as Corinna is invited to "put on [her] Foliage" and join these acts of ceremonial devotion. The poem itself enacts an intermingling, as it assimilates the rituals and language of folk and pagan traditions, classical mythology, the Old Testament and Christianity. In the world of "Corinna's *going a Maying*," matins, beads, and Christian priests keep company with Titan and Aurora. The point of "Corinna's *going a Maying*," and of *Hesperides* more generally, is that we cannot neatly divide the pagan and the Christian, the secular and the sacred.

If Herrick can be accused of importing "heathenism" into the temple of *Hesperides* where he presides as priest, that is precisely what the Puritans charged the Laudian prelates with doing to the English Church and its liturgy. The Puritans, critical of Laud and the other high church Anglicans who became so powerful in Charles I's reign, felt that the English Church had become contaminated with "popish" practices of the Church of Rome, which Puritans saw as the present-day incarnation of ancient pagan idolatry. Insisting on an absolute separation between the Christian church and all forms of "heathenism," these Puritans wanted to purify what they saw as a mixed, and therefore contaminated, church. Henry Burton, for example, declared in his *Replie* to Laud that Christians must "utterly renounce all *communion*" and "*separate* themselves" from all Roman Catholic "*Heathenisme*," even if that meant separating from the Church of England, which had become polluted with "Roman" ceremonies and

---

5. *Histriomastix* (London, 1633), 33. See also William Perkins, *Workes* (London, 1612), esp. *A Warning Against the Idolatry of the Last Times*.

practices.[6] Sharing this fear that the prelates were bringing the English Church back to Rome, Prynne similarly insisted, "God, and the Devil, Christ, and Belial, are contrary, are inconsistent: therefore the service, and ceremonies of the one, are altogether incompatible with the other."[7]

It is precisely such attitudes that Herrick rejects in his complex interminglings of Christian and classical, his incorporation of "pagan" rites into the temple and liturgy of *Hesperides*. Perhaps some might say that Herrick simply exemplifies the mentality Prynne and Burton were attacking, but *Hesperides* provides striking evidence of Herrick's having a consciously anti-Puritan stance that verges on the polemical. *Hesperides,* with its "mixed" religion, is in a sense a poetic counterpart of the Laudian Church of England.[8]

There are many fascinating parallels between *Hesperides* and the popish, heathen "innovations" with which Laud was charged in his trial—too many parallels to be merely coincidental. Prynne, in his account of Laud's trial in which he himself took part, described in detail all of Laud's supposed "endeavours to set up and introduce all kinds of Popish Superstitious Idolatrous ornaments, furniture, ceremonies in our church, formerly cast out of it upon the reformation." In cathedrals, universities, parishes, and private chapels, Laud brought in the "superstitious *Rites* and *Ceremonies*" of Rome.[9] Is not this what Herrick is doing in *Hesperides,* importing the practices of both pagan and ecclesiastical Rome into a volume of poetry that is, he insists, both a *"Temple"* and a "Liturgie" (H 496, 510)? That Herrick is drawing attention to these controversial matters is evident not only in the particularity with which many poems describe the classical rituals but also in the curious fact that the polemically charged words *rites* and *ceremonies* appear even in the titles of poems that do not actually include liturgical rites, such as *"The Funerall Rites of the Rose," "Ceremonies for Candlemasse Eve," "The Ceremonies for Candlemasse day,"* and "Ceremonies for Christmasse."

Puritans insisted that Christ "in his *death* destroyed *All Ceremonies* in Religion,"[10] and they criticized the Laudian bishops for their "curious formality

6. Henry Burton, *A Replie to a Relation of the Conference Between William Laude and Mr. Fisher the Jesuite* (n.p., 1640), 36–37.

7. Prynne, *Histriomastix*, 33.

8. Leah Marcus has suggested, quite rightly, that *"The Fairie Temple; Or, Oberon's Chappell"* is "a defense of the high church position" ("Herrick's *Hesperides* and the 'Proclamation made for May,'" *Studies in Philology* 76 [1979]: 64). Marcus, in this article and in *The Politics of Mirth: Jonson, Herrick, Milton, Marvell and the Defense of Old Holiday Pastimes* (Chicago: University of Chicago Press, 1986), has shown how Herrick's poems of country festivity support Laudian policy. But whereas her emphasis is on the connections between Herrick's poetry and Laud's political policy, mine is on the connections with Laudian religious attitudes and practices, which were, of course, intimately involved with politics.

9. William Prynne, *Canterburies Doome* (London, 1646), 58, 70.

10. Burton, *Replie*, sig. C1v. Cf. Milton's anti-prelatical tracts, e.g., *Of Reformation* (London, 1641), which condemns "senceless *Ceremonies*" and "outward rites" (*John Milton: Selected Prose*, ed. C. A. Patrides, new rev. ed. [Columbia: University of Missouri Press, 1985], 81).

and punctuall observance of their holy rites"[11]—a charge that Herrick lays himself open to when, for example, he instructs Julia in the order of the church "Rites" for purification after childbirth:

> Put on thy *Holy Fillitings*, and so
> To th'Temple with the sober *Midwife* go.
> Attended thus (in a most solemn wise)
> By those who serve the Child-bed misteries.
> Burn first thine incense; next, when as thou see'st
> The candid Stole thrown ore the *Pious Priest;*
> With reverend Curtsies come, and to him bring
> Thy free (and not decurted) offering.
> All Rites well ended, with faire Auspice come
> (As to the breaking of a Bride-Cake) home:
> Where ceremonious *Hymen* shall for thee
> Provide a second *Epithalamie.*
>
> ("Julia's *Churching, or Purification,"* H 898)

Herrick's insistence in this poem and in many others (H 957, 627, 870) that the rites be properly and fully performed is a poetic validation of the Laudian position on religious worship.

Herrick was, of course, aware that performance of ceremonies and rites could degenerate into a superficial observance of externals. And so in *"To keep a true Lent"* (N 228), he asks his reader:

> 3 Is it to fast an houre,
> Or rag'd to go,
> Or show
> A down-cast look, and sowre?
> 4 No; 'tis a Fast, to dole
> Thy sheaf of wheat,
> And meat,
> Unto the hungry Soule.
> 5 It is to fast from strife,
> From old debate,
> And hate;
> To circumcise thy life.

Herrick is not actually rejecting the observance of this fast—indeed an earlier poem in *Noble Numbers* clearly sanctions the keeping of Lent by naming Noah as "the first" to "ordaine the Fast of forty Dayes" (*"The Fast, or Lent,"* N 195), implying that the tradition is worthy of being continued. Rather the point of the questions in *"To keep a true Lent"* is that ritual practices are valuable only where the spirit gives life to the literal observance. Herrick shares the seeming inconsistency of other Anglicans who, seeing in ceremony the potential for linking the

---

11. Henry Burton, *For God and King* (London, 1636), 98.

physical with the spiritual, recognized that ceremonies were "indifferent" for salvation, yet insisted that it was wrong not to perform them.[12]

In his ceremony poems, Herrick typically mingles elements from classical, folk, Roman Catholic, and sometimes even Judaic traditions; thus it is difficult to separate these various traditions without violating the spirit of his poetry. Nevertheless, throughout *Hesperides* there are allusions to Roman Catholicism or, more frequently, to practices in the Anglican Church that were encouraged by Laud but that Puritans were condemning as actually Roman Catholic. In his trial, Laud was accused of importing various "Popish" things into the English Church—the wearing of surplices and other clerical vestments; the use of incense, candles, and holy water; making the sign of the cross; kneeling at the sacrament and bowing before the altar (his enemies called these gestures "Ducking" and "Cringing").[13] In *Hesperides* tapers burn (H 604), and holy water and incense abound (H 974, 1069, 898).

> Offer thy gift; but first the Law commands
> Thee *Julia,* first, to *sanctifie* thy hands:
> Doe that my *Julia* which the rites require,
> Then boldly give thine incense to the fire.
> ("*To* Julia," H 957)

Where Puritans objected to special vestments, preferring a "naked," unadorned service, Herrick gives instructions for the proper wearing of religious clothing. For her "Churching," Julia must put on *"Holy Fillitings"* and the *"Pious Priest"* will wear a white "Stole" (H 898). In another poem, both Julia and Herrick don "pure Surplices" according to the "commands" of "Old Religion" (H 957). Behind poems like these is the High Anglican assumption that worship should involve the body as well as the soul, that the physical can properly be used in the service of the spiritual, an assumption especially evident in Herrick's poem *"Mattens, or morning Prayer"* (H 320):

> When with the Virgin morning thou do'st rise,
> Crossing thy selfe; come thus to sacrifice:
> First wash thy heart in innocence, then bring
> Pure hands, pure habits, pure, pure every thing.
> Next to the Altar humbly kneele, and thence,
> Give up thy soule in clouds of frankinsence.
> Thy golden Censors fil'd with odours sweet,
> Shall make thy actions with their ends to meet.

12. On attitudes toward ceremony in worship, see Charles H. and Katherine George, *The Protestant Mind of the English Reformation 1570–1640* (Princeton: Princeton University Press, 1961), 348–63, and Horton Davies, *Worship and Theology in England* (Princeton: Princeton University Press, 1975), vol. 1, chap. 5.

13. See William Laud, *The History of the Troubles and Tryall of . . . William Laud,* ed. Henry Wharton (London, 1695), 340.

The offer of incense symbolizes and thus is the proper accompaniment for the sweet offer of the soul to God.

In this poem Herrick pointedly instructs his worshipers to kneel to the altar—a practice of the Laudian prelates that Puritans harshly criticized as a mark of idolatry, the worship of a material object. Indeed, throughout *Hesperides* "altars" appear with striking frequency (see H 251, 320, 366, 417, 657, 870, 874). Herrick's many altars gain added significance when we remember how much antagonism Laud aroused when he replaced the old communion "Tables" with new "Altars." Laud's "setting up of *Altars,* with all their *Service* and *Ceremonies*" was seen as a heinous reversion to heathen idolatry, for as Henry Burton said, "*Iesus Christ* [is] our *onely Altar.*" Prynne insisted that God's instructions to the Israelites "*not to follow the customes of the Cananites . . . to destroy their Altars, pull downe their Temples . . . abandon their ceremonies . . . utterly to abhorre, and detest them,*" should provide a pattern for our actions.[14] Turning divine instructions into human law, parliament on 26 August 1643 ordered that all altars in English churches "be utterly taken away and demolished."[15] And during the 1640s iconoclastic Puritans enthusiastically carried out these orders.

As if Herrick's altars were not enough, his emphasis on the performance of literal, physical sacrifices in *Hesperides* would have struck Puritans as barbarous, smacking of the "Heathenisme" and "Judaisme" that they associated with Roman Catholicism.[16]

> *Herr.* Come and let's in solemn wise
>   Both address to sacrifice:
>   Old Religion first commands
>   That we wash our hearts, and hands.
>   Is the beast exempt from staine,
>   Altar cleane, no fire prophane?
>   Are the Garlands, Is the Nard
> *Jul.* Ready here? All well prepar'd,
>   With the Wine that must be shed
>   (Twixt the hornes) upon the head
>   Of the holy Beast we bring
>   For our Trespasse-offering.
> *Herr.* All is well; now next to these
>   Put we on pure Surplices;
>   And with Chaplets crown'd, we'l rost
>   With perfumes the Holocaust:

---

14. Burton, *Replie,* sig. C2v; Prynne, *Histriomastix,* 32–33.

15. See *Acts and Ordinances of the Interregnum,* ed. C. H. Firth and R. S. Rait (Abingdon: Professional Books, 1978), 1:265. The quotation is from p. 425.

16. On the pagan-Jewish-Papist association, see, e.g., Burton, *Replie,* 32, and *For God and King,* 14.

And (while we the gods invoke)
Reade acceptance by the smoake.
(*"The Sacrifice, by way of Discourse betwixt
himselfe and* Julia," H 870)

As it details the preparations for this ritual, Herrick's poem insists that the sacrifice will be an actual, physical one (the "Beast" must be anointed with wine between his horns); and it demonstrates, indeed exaggerates, the very mingling of pagan, Jewish, and Christian that the Puritans abhorred and that they found in Laud's Anglican churches. For Puritans, the very word *Altar* conjured up both the idea of pagan / Jewish sacrifice and the "Popish" doctrine of transubstantiation, which was rejected by the reformed churches (including the Church of England). Prynne thought that Laud's addition of the words *sacrifice* and *offer up* in the directions for communion were evidence that his "maine end . . . was the introducing amongst us of Transubstantiation, and the Romish sacrifice of the Masse, with the very Masse-Booke it self."[17] In their mingling of religions and in the specificity and detail with which they recall classical ceremonies, Herrick's "sacrifice" poems often play with and exploit these Puritan views of Laudian and Roman Catholic worship.

Laud's introduction of "Romish" things was seen as a contamination of "pure" primitive Christianity. It is significant that the mingling of religious rites, words, and practices—so characteristic of Herrick's poetry—was one of the crimes with which Laud was charged. At the trial, Prynne brought as evidence against Laud a book of private devotions, seized when Prynne searched the Archbishop's study, in which Laud had included "passages from the *Roman Missal, Breviary,* and *Howers of our Lady.*"[18] For Prynne, that Laud used the words or prayers of Catholics was enough to convict him of being a Papist, a traitor to the English Church. Laud's defense of his use of Roman Catholic language or prayers in both the Book of Common Prayer and his private devotions makes explicit the position that also lies behind Herrick's eclectically religious poetry:

> I would have them remember, that we live in a Church *Reformed;* not in one made *New.* Now all *Reformation,* that is good and orderly, takes away nothing from the old, but that which is Faulty and Erroneous. If any thing be good, it leaves that standing. So that if these Changes from the *Book* of England be good, 'tis no matter whence they be taken. For every line in the *mass-Book, or* other *Popish Rituals,* are not all Evil and Corruptions. There are many good Prayers in them; nor is any thing Evil in them, only because 'tis there. Nay, the less alteration, is made in the Public Ancient *Service* of the Church, the better it is.[19]

If Herrick, like Laud, erects altars, introduces Roman superstition, and restores ancient ceremonies, he also fills his *"Temple"* with *"eternall Images"* and

17. *Hidden Workes of Darknes* (London, 1645), 160–62.
18. Prynne, *Canterburies Doome,* 67.
19. *History of the Tryall,* 113.

"Statues"—much as Laud did in the English churches. In a sermon in 1636, Burton expressed his outrage at the "setting up of Images" and statues in churches and cathedrals,[20] and at Laud's trial much was made of these images as well as of his repairing the stained-glass windows at Lambeth and other chapels (windows supposedly drawn in imitation of the Roman Missal). Laud's Puritan opponents insisted that it was "against Gods law & Commandment" for Christians to "make Images, and publickly to set them up in the Temples and Churches."[21]

When Herrick announces his role as a maker of images in the poem to his kinsman Richard Stone, his language not only puns on Stone's name but also evokes these contemporary controversies about the legitimacy of images and monuments in the church:

> To this *white Temple* of my *Heroes,* here
> Beset with stately Figures (every where)
> Of such rare *Saint-ships,* who did here consume
> Their lives in sweets, and left in death perfume.
> Come thou *Brave man!*
> (*"To his Honoured Kinsman, Sir* Richard Stone," H 496)

In 1643 and 1644 parliament passed two ordinances for destroying altars, monuments, and other relics of "Idolatry and Superstition." The second ordinance of May 1644 most closely speaks to the subject of Herrick's poem to Richard Stone, for it declares, "All Representations of any Persons of the Trinity, or of any Angel or Saint, in or about any Cathedral, Collegiate or Parish Church, or Chapell, or in any open place within this kingdome, shall be taken away, defaced, and utterly demolished; And that no such shall hereafter be set up."[22] Parliament commissioned men like William Dowsing to purge churches and cathedrals. Dowsing's *Journal* coldly records his many iconoclastic activities in Suffolk county.[23] In addition to such acts by parliamentary commissioners, during the 1640s many churches were ransacked by parliamentary soldiers. The propagandistic *Mercurius Rusticus* in 1646, written by an outraged Royalist and Anglican, provides vivid (if exaggerated) descriptions of these acts of desecration, noting how the soldiers would sometimes, as a final insult, "defile each part and corner both of Church and Chancell with their own excrements."[24]

Such iconoclasm provides an essential context for understanding Herrick's

---

20. *For God and King,* 159-63.
21. Prynne, *Canterburies Doome,* 104.
22. See *Acts and Ordinances,* 1:425.
23. See *The Journal of William Dowsing A. D. 1643-44,* ed. J. Charles Wall (London: Talbot, 18—).
24. [Bruno Ryves], *Mercurius Rusticus: Or the Countries Complaint of the barbarous Outrages Committed by the Sectaries of the late flourishing Kingdome* (London, 1646), 58. See also John Phillips, *The Reformation of Images: Destruction of Art in England, 1535-1660* (Berkeley: University of California Press, 1973).

poem to Richard Stone and *Hesperides* more generally. At a time when churches, altars, and images were being destroyed, Herrick published his temple of *Hesperides,* in which he consecrates its holy space and objects, performs rites, and erects altars and images. We do not know when he wrote *"To his Honoured Kinsman, Sir* Richard Stone," but, since Stone was not knighted until 1642,[25] it was almost certainly during the 1640s, when Puritan iconoclasm was at its height. Indeed, it is not impossible that Herrick wrote the poem in part as response to this 1644 parliamentary ordinance against "Representations." Herrick claims that his "Statues" are "High" and "no lesse / Strong then the Heavens for everlastingnesse." He proudly asserts his faith that his volume of poetry, though seemingly fragile, will in fact last "tho Kingdoms fal" (H 1129). Herrick is, of course, following Jonson and the classical poets in his celebration of the immortalizing power of poetry, but we see how the imitation of literary conventions can take on nonliterary polemical significance. Herrick's Jonsonian "classicism," his invocation of the commonplace of poetic immortality, has become charged with anti-Puritan meaning. His language vividly insists on the very things the Puritans were attacking. As he erects his *"eternall Images"* of virtue (H 496), Herrick declares his faith in the efficacy of poetry and supports the position of the Laudian church.

This, I think, helps to explain why Herrick so frequently describes the immortalizing power of poetry and the poet in distinctly biblical terms. As he invests supposedly classical traditions with Judeo-Christian sanctions and significance, he draws an analogy between poetic immortality and Christian salvation. Alluding to the Old Testament as well as to the Roman Catholic practice of canonization, Herrick "inscribe[s]" his kinsman Stephen Soame, "one of my righteous Tribe," in his book of life, his "eternall Calender" of Saints (H 545). Penelope Wheeler will also be "a Saint . . . In Chiefe" (there is a hierarchy) in Herrick's "Poetick Liturgie" (H 510). He separates "the Generation of my Just" (H 664; cf. Psalms 14:5), the "saints" he canonizes and blesses with immortal life, from the unregenerate, the "bastard Slips" that will "droop and die" (H 859)—a category that presumably includes many of what Richard Montague had mockingly called "our purer *Brethren."*[26] Herrick's appropriation of biblical language suggests his confidence that the people whom he, as poet-priest, has chosen for poetic immortality are also the ones that God has marked for salvation.

Laud's Puritan opponents were upset by attempts to reinstitute and encourage the Roman Catholic practices of preserving the "Reliques of Saints" and, even worse, commemorating and praying to these saints.[27] And what is Herrick doing but insisting that his worthies should be reverenced and remembered as he

---

25. As J. Max Patrick observes in his note to the poem, p. 247.
26. *Apello Caesarem* (London, 1625), 6.
27. Prynne, *Canterburies Doome,* 211, and *Hidden Workes,* 159; Burton, *For God and King,* 67.

preserves their "reliques" in his poetry. He even prays to his special patron saint, Ben Jonson, in a poem that, like so much of *Hesperides,* is characterized by a mixture of playfulness and seriousness.

> When I a Verse shall make,
> Know I have praid thee,
> For old *Religions* sake,
> Saint *Ben* to aide me.
> 2. Make the way smooth for me,
> When I, thy *Herrick,*
> Honouring thee, on my knee
> Offer my *Lyrick.*
> 3. Candles Ile give to thee,
> And a new Altar:
> And thou Saint *Ben,* shalt be
> Writ in my *Psalter.*
> ("*His Prayer to* Ben. Johnson," H 604)

Herrick was no more a secret Roman Catholic than Laud, though there was much in his poetry to encourage Puritans to bring this charge against him. This poem, in its witty adaptation of the Roman Catholic practice of praying to saints, is an appropriate tribute to Herrick's poetic mentor, himself a convert to Roman Catholicism for part of his life. But the poem goes beyond compliment as Herrick prays to Jonson for "old *Religions* sake," a term that refers not only to "the ancient form of *pietas*" (as J. Max Patrick observes in his notes to the poem) and to the religion of poetry to which Jonson, too, was dedicated, but also to the ancient Roman Catholic religion with which the Laudian Church of England claimed historical continuity. I can think of no better gloss for Herrick's poem than the comment of William Perkins that Roman Catholicism "makes the Saints in heaven idols. For it teacheth man to kneele downe to them, and to make praier to them, being absent from vs, as farre as heaven is from earth. And by praying to them, men doe acknowledge that they have power to heare and help in all places, & at all times, and that they know the secret mindes and hearts of men."[28] Herrick credits Jonson with the power to "heare and help" him; his "honouring thee, on my knee," insists on the physical demonstration of reverence that the Puritans abhorred; and he promises to give "Candles" and "a new Altar" to Ben. As reverential as the poem is toward Jonson, it ends with Herrick asserting his own powers as a poet as he offers to inscribe Jonson in "my *Psalter.*" In this deceptively simple poem, Herrick immortalizes Jonson; pays his poetic debts; defies the Puritan position on the invocation of saints, altars, and candles; and suggests the presence of a divine inspiration and authority in his poetry.

In 1644 the Puritan parliament tried and executed Laud as a traitor for his

---

28. Perkins, *A Warning Against . . . Idolatrie,* 679.

"innovations" in the Church of England. Given this climate and the strong links between Herrick's poetry and the Laudian practices of the Anglican Church, Herrick's publication of *Hesperides* in 1648 should, I think, be seen as a daring, imaginative declaration of religious as well as political and poetical allegiance. Herrick's volume of poetry, appearing the year after he was ousted from his parish by the Puritans, reaffirms and re-presents a Laudian ideal of worship, which he could no longer publicly perform. With this in mind, we should look again at the concluding epigram of *Hesperides*—"To his Book's end this last line he'd have plac't, / *Jocund his Muse was; but his Life was chast.*" For it serves not only as a conventional apology, exonerating the poet for lascivious poems seemingly unbefitting an unmarried priest, but also, more importantly, as a protective excuse for any poems that might have offended unsympathetic readers during a time when the very values and practices that *Hesperides* poetically legitimizes had been declared illegal and "treasonous" by parliament. The poems, he implies, are "only" art and thus, like the poet, innocent and harmless. Perhaps Herrick's ejection itself gave him a reason finally to publish his poems. In a time of Puritan ascendancy when parliament had even forbidden the use of the Anglican liturgy, Herrick could through his poetry continue his priestly role, singing his "Poetick Liturgie" safe in a *"Temple"* that he hoped would be impervious to destruction until the end of time.

Paul A. Parrish

11. The Feminizing of Power: Crashaw's Life and Art

This devout Poet, the Darling of the *Muses*, whose delight was the fruitful Mount *Sion*, more than the barren Mount *Pernassus*, was Fellow first of *Pembrook-Hall*, after of St. *Peters-Colledge* in *Cambridge*; a religious pourer forth of his divine Raptures and Meditations, in smooth and pathetick Verse. . . . He was much given to a religious Solitude, and love of a recluse Life, which made him spend much of his time, and even lodge many Nights under *Tertullian's* roof of Angels, in St. *Mary's* Church in *Cambridge*. —William Winstanley, "Mr. Richard Crashaw," *The Lives of the Most Famous English Poets* (1687)[1]

Master *Crawshaw* (Son to the *London* Divine) and sometimes Fellow of St. *Peter* house in *Cambridge* is another slip of the times, that is, transplanted to *Rome*. This peevish sillie Seeker glided away from his Principles in a Poetical vein of fancy, and impertinent curiosity; and finding that Verses, and measur'd flattery took, and much pleas'd some female wits, *Crawshaw* crept by degrees into favour and acquaintance with some Court-Ladies, and with the gross commendations of their parts and beauties (burnisht and varnish with some other agreeable adulations) he got first the estimation of an innocent, harmless Convert; and, a purse being made by some deluded, vain-glorious Ladies, and their friends, the Poet was dispatch'd in a Pilgrimage to *Rome*. —[William Prynne,] *Legenda lignea* (1653)[2]

William Winstanley's brief but sympathetic portrait of Richard Crashaw and William Prynne's snarling denigration are admittedly an odd coupling, yet each points to a dimension of Crashaw we have long accepted as characteristic: his love for privacy and the quiet, contemplative life and his remarkable attachment (in his poetry, at least) to women. A rehearsal of the life and a review of the poetry confirm an essential truth in each of these observations. Furthermore, it might be argued that these characteristics are only two facets of a "feminine" personality type, one that prefers privacy and intimacy to more public arenas, and prefers more gentle, tender, or emotional virtues to more physical, bolder, or logical "masculine" ones.[3] This association, suggesting a consistency and har-

1. From a Facsimile Reproduction with an Introduction by William Riley Parker (Gainesville: Scholars' Facsimiles & Reprints, 1963), 161–62.
2. Quoted in L. C. Martin, ed. *The Poems English Latin and Greek of Richard Crashaw*, 2d ed. (Oxford: Clarendon Press, 1957), xxxvi.
3. Marilyn French's feminist study, *Shakespeare's Division of Experience* (New York: Summit, 1981), sometimes criticized for its ideological and polemical aim, nonetheless offers a clear the-

148

mony between Crashaw's life and art, is revealing because it points to numerous occasions in the life and in the poetry that demonstrate Crashaw's allegiance to private, feminine virtues; it is inadequate, however, because it fails to acknowledge the complex relationship between these values and their antitheses. Preferring a life of solitude, Crashaw nonetheless was a committed Royalist who paid dearly for that public stance; his poetry, demonstrating his extraordinary devotion to femininity, also confronts the language and expectations of masculine conduct in which power, courage, and aggression are virtues. My aim is to reconsider Crashaw's life and art in terms of their allegiance to private and public virtues and, particularly in the poetry, to those virtues and values conventionally aligned with gender roles. His life points us to the double-sidedness of his interests; his poetry demonstrates that a commitment to feminine virtues in a world dominated by masculine conduct and language can be achieved only through subversion and transformation.[4]

I

Crashaw's mother died before he was seven; his stepmother, who was said to have had a "singular motherly affection to the child of her predecessor," died in childbirth only a short time later, and the young Crashaw must have known much isolation, if not loneliness, in his early years.[5] Crashaw's father, William, an outspoken opponent of Rome, died when his son was thirteen or fourteen, leaving Richard in the hands of two lawyers, Sir Henry Yelverton and Sir Randolph Crew. Before he was admitted to Charterhouse School in 1629, Crashaw had therefore experienced the loss of three parents. Although life at Charter-

---

oretical construct for a discussion of gender roles. Dividing human experience into "masculine" and "feminine" principles, French argues that the masculine principle is "associated with prowess and ownership, with physical courage, assertiveness, authority, independence, and the right, rights, and legitimacy" (21). The idealized feminine principle is "an expression of the benevolent manifestations of nature . . . it includes qualities like nutritiveness, compassion, mercy, and the ability to create felicity. It requires volitional subordination, voluntary relinquishment of power-in-the-world" and exalts "feeling over action, sensation over thought" (24).

4. In *Childhood and Cultural Despair* (Pittsburgh: University of Pittsburgh Press, 1978), Leah Marcus argues that, in reaction to the deterioration of order in the religious and political world, Crashaw retreats "into the phantasmagoric world of baroque Catholic spirituality and the poetic role of infant" (139). She suggests, as I do, that Crashaw's poetry responds to political developments in ways we would not immediately identify as "political." But she also sees the response as more narrow and more extreme than I do, viewing it as a "retreat" and "refuge" (139–42). She argues that Crashaw has a "need for absolute withdrawal from the tempestuous controversies of the time" (139–40) and that "in his religious verse he succeeded" (140). Noting his attention to women figures, she sees him identifying with the infant of the feminine; thus, "Crashaw's Christianity is a giant projection of the forms and processes of motherhood" (150).

5. The quoted passage is from the Bodleian Library copy (Malone 297) of a commemorative volume on Elizabeth Crashaw, Richard's stepmother, titled *The Honour of Vertue or The Monument erected by the sorowfull Husband*. Elizabeth and William Crashaw married in 1619, and she died in 1620. The biographical information in this essay is, unless otherwise noted, developed from my *Richard Crashaw* (Boston: Twayne, 1980).

house was rigorous and demanding, Crashaw later characterized the master, Robert Brooke, in gentle terms, as a kind of surrogate father. In a Latin poem accompanying Crashaw's 1634 *Epigrammatum Sacrorum Liber,* Brooke is described as one who was not quick to use the rod but who established instead a milder authority ("mitia jura").[6]

Crashaw was elected to a Fellowship at Peterhouse in 1635, proceeded M.A. in 1638, and continued at Peterhouse and Little St. Mary's church as catechist and curate. Life at Peterhouse was ideal for one who valued both isolation and humane communal virtues. Crashaw apparently had only three students under his tutorship, and in general his duties were not demanding. Furthermore, he had ready access to the extraordinary community at Little Gidding, established in 1626 by Nicholas Ferrar and his mother as a religious retreat.

Little Gidding existed as an alternative to the public life that had once typified the Ferrars. Nicholas was elected to parliament in 1624, the same year that his mother purchased the property at Little Gidding. Having previously rejected two other sites as too public, the Ferrars found Little Gidding an ideal setting where each occupant could realize Nicholas's goal: "to devote myself to God, and to go into a religious retirement."[7] Crashaw's poem "Description of a Religious House" may reveal some of the characteristics of Little Gidding, for we know he was a frequent visitor. The poem emphasizes the virtues of privacy, obedience, and peace:

> reverent discipline, and religious fear,
> And soft obedience, find sweet biding here;
> Silence, and sacred rest; peace and pure joyes;
> Kind loves keep house, ly close, and make no noise,
> And room enough for Monarchs, while none swells
> Beyond the kingdomes of contentfull Cells.

(30–35)

In a letter he wrote to one of the Ferrars from his exile in Leyden after parliamentary forces invaded Cambridge, Crashaw echoed that last line when he remarked that he feared he might never be able to return to his "little contentfull kingdom" at Cambridge.[8]

Evidence from Crashaw's life up to the time of his forced departure from Cambridge suggests that he valued the privacy and solitariness indicated in his vow: "I would be married, but I'de have no Wife, / I would be married to a single Life." There is no reason to doubt that Crashaw remained loyal to private

6. The poem is "Ornatissimo viro Praeceptori sue colendissimo, Magistro Brook." As the text of Crashaw's poems, I am citing George Walton Williams, ed., *The Complete Poetry of Richard Crashaw* (1970; rpt. New York: Norton, 1974).

7. Cited in Peter Peckard, *A Life of Nicholas Ferrar* (London: Joseph Masters, 1852), 94. The *Life* is an abridgment of Peckard's *Memoirs of the Life of Mr. Nicholas Ferrar* (1790).

8. Cited in Austin Warren, *Richard Crashaw: A Study in Baroque Sensibility* (University: Louisiana State University Press, 1939), 48.

virtues that would have been denied someone committed to the life of the court and state. But it is just as apparent that most of Crashaw's important associations, from Charterhouse onward, placed him in the midst of the political and religious controversies gripping England and made it impossible for him to stand apart from decisions with profound political implications.

While we have little evidence of Crashaw's responses to life at Charterhouse, we do have evidence that life before his entry into Cambridge was not without its political side. Robert Brooke, to whom Crashaw was clearly devoted, was expelled from his position by parliament. The historian of Charterhouse, Gerald Davies, notes, "Brooke's misdemeanour was his avowed adherence to the Royalist cause, and his having impressed his views upon his pupils, two of whom were the poets Richard Crashaw and Richard Lovelace."[9]

When Crashaw moved on to Cambridge, his allegiances and associations were even more obviously subject to political influence and interpretation. Pembroke College was characterized by its royalist loyalties and its High Anglican sentiments from the time of Lancelot Andrewes, and that spirit continued during Crashaw's years under the mastership of Benjamin Laney. A number of poems written during this period confirm Crashaw's allegiance to the religious, which is also to say political, position of his college. He praises Laney for his Laudian views and defends Robert Shelford, who was accused of having supported a Roman position on matters of faith and love.

Even more unequivocal are the political implications of Peterhouse and Little Gidding, the environments in which Crashaw spent his final years at Cambridge. Austin Warren remarks that Crashaw "had little taste for controversy" and thus sought out such "shrines of pious devotion" as Little Gidding.[10] This view is only partially true; indeed, by associating with Little Gidding, Crashaw did not at all escape controversy. Little Gidding was regarded with suspicion by both Puritans and Papists, but there is little doubt that it was cited most conspicuously for its associations with Laud and the king. It was attacked by Puritans as "the Arminian Nunnery" and was shown favor by King Charles on at least two occasions. There is no ambiguity in the action of Puritan forces in 1647, for they destroyed the house, church, and grounds at Little Gidding.

Peterhouse was the most Laudian and royalist of colleges at Cambridge, and Crashaw was singled out for attack when Puritan leaders mounted their investigation of the practices of Peterhouse. In a document written about 1641, Crashaw is accused of worshiping the Virgin, of engaging in "superstitious" practices at Little St. Mary's, and of following "the popish doctrine of private masses." We are also told of "other practices . . . of the like nature."[11]

9. *Charterhouse in London* (London: J. Murray, 1921), 232–33.
10. *Richard Crashaw*, 36.
11. From *Innovations in Religion & Abuses in Government in [the] University of Cambridge* (British Museum MS. Harley 7019, fol. 73). See also Allan Pritchard's discussion in "Puritan Charges against Crashaw and Beaumont," *TLS*, 2 July 1964, 578.

The extent of Crashaw's political commitment is suggested by his participation in a loan to the king and by his willingness to give up his "little contentfull kingdom" rather than renounce the king and the religious practice to which he was devoted and about which he had written with approval and praise. The private poet thus committed himself publicly, both pronouncing his loyalties in occasional verse and exemplifying them more decisively through his actions.

II

Crashaw's poetry has characteristically been regarded with grudging or qualified praise, and there are three principal reasons for the depreciation of his work. First, Crashaw is judged to be more Continental than his contemporaries; thus, when measured against the more "English" quality of Donne or Herbert, Crashaw typically suffers. Second, his poetry is seen as too obsessed with a limited range of experiences and images, especially images of liquefaction—water, milk, blood—and thus as unusual, strange, or grotesque. In the 1950s Robert M. Adams made perhaps the most damning assessment of Crashaw in finding some of his poetry representative of "bad taste" and in viewing some ill-chosen images as revolting and grotesque.[12] The third reason is not so openly acknowledged. We find Crashaw's poetry discomforting because it so obviously focuses on feminine figures and feminine qualities. Over and over we read of soft breasts, of milk-white doves, of well-fledged nests and winged loves. Such concerns fail to be tough, concise, direct, and precise—in a word, manly.

Mario Praz, for example, commenting on Crashaw's paraphrases of the Psalms, remarks that a "study of Crashaw's versions shows how incapable he is of a concise style, of rendering severe and manly feelings in a few strokes; how, on the contrary, he makes capital out of whatever lends itself to florid divagations and to description of tender and delicate emotions. Grace is not denied to him, but Strength is beyond his reach."[13] Praz's evaluation of the "Hymn to the Name of Jesus" is less pejorative, but Crashaw's achievement is again seen in terms of its feminine qualities, its "feminine tenderness," which is contrasted to the "heroic note" of which Crashaw is only rarely capable.[14] Warren, remarking on the sacred verse of Donne, Herbert, and Crashaw, observes that Donne's "Divine Poems have more passion, more intensity, than Herbert's; but their masculinity, their dialectic, their abrupt rhythms, their range of figures, separate them from Crashaw."[15]

To say it simply, we have at times clearly brought a masculine bias to our

---

12. "Taste and Bad Taste in Metaphysical Poetry: Richard Crashaw and Dylan Thomas," *Hudson Review* 8 (1955): 60–77. A useful corrective to Adams's view is R. V. Young's *Richard Crashaw and the Spanish Golden Age* (New Haven: Yale University Press, 1982), chap. 2, esp. p. 25.
13. *The Flaming Heart* (1958; rpt. New York: Norton, 1973), 245.
14. Ibid., 258.
15. *Richard Crashaw*, 113.

reading of Crashaw's poetry, and when it fails to meet the implicit criteria, it is judged to fail, or to succeed only occasionally. Taking this stance, however, we are critically begging the question and, more significantly, neglecting the quality of Crashaw's achievement that will be more apparent if we look at his poetry anew, with an eye toward its attention to power and gender roles. Intensely concerned about power and submission, activity and passivity, masculinity and femininity, Crashaw nonetheless is unwilling to accept conventional alignments and traditional expectations. In the poetry I will examine here—which includes occasional and more private verse, both secular and sacred—he charac-teristically acknowledges the virtues usually associated with the two sides of the human dialectic—the masculine figure of power, strength, and courage, the feminine figure of grace, emotion, and passivity—but also challenges and sub-verts those conventional roles and audience expectations, achieving in some of his most powerful poems a "cultural androgyny" that denies easy conceptions of the masculine and the feminine.[16]

III

Crashaw's "Panegyricke" is the royal poem most apt for this study and, sig-nificantly, it focuses on the queen. Among the other poems discussed here two important features are evident: in each there is an open or implicit contest be-tween masculinity and femininity, and each encourages a revaluation of what masculinity and femininity, power and courage, activity and passivity, finally mean. Just as Crashaw's life calls into question easy choices between contem-plative and active modes, so his poetry reveals a constant effort to rethink and to transform conventional assumptions about meaningful action and gender roles.

Crashaw's "Panegyricke" was printed in two versions, the first celebrating the birth of the Duke of York in October 1633 and the second a longer celebration of the royal family with attention to several of the children and the queen. The second version, which I will discuss here, was published in a volume of poems celebrating the birth of Prince Henry and published at Cambridge; that version was later printed in the 1648 edition of *Delights of the Muses*. The poem re-minds us of the parentage of the children celebrated and, in particular, of the two "Grandsires," Henry IV of France and James I of England. Henry was a warrior and is called Mars in the poem; James is associated with softer virtues

16. Cf. Cheri Register, "American Feminist Literary Criticism: A Bibliographical Introduc-tion," in *Feminist Literary Criticism,* ed. Josephine Donovan (Lexington: University Press of Ken-tucky, 1975), 19–20. Carolyn Heilbrun's *Toward a Recognition of Androgyny* (New York: Knopf, 1973) sets the tone for other studies that argue for the vitality of the androgynous impulse. Gayle Greene and Coppelia Kahn discuss the "productive" tension that exists in feminist criticism "between the celebration of the 'female' and the advocation of 'androgyny'" ("Feminist Schol-arship and the Social Construction of Woman," in *Making a Difference: Feminist Literary Criti-cism* [London: Methuen, 1985], 24).

and is Phoebus, "Wisdomes God." The young prince Charles is praised as a descendant of both and thus as a "full mixture of those mighty souls / Whose vast intelligences tun'd the Poles / Of peace and warre" (39–41). Later, the youngest child, newborn prince Henry, is portrayed as one whose presence frightens away the manly virtues imaged as war, blood, and death:

> Rebellion, stand thou by; Mischief, make room:
> Warre, Bloud, and Death (Names all averse from Joy)
> Heare this, We have another bright-ey'd Boy:
> That word's a warrant, by whose vertue I
> Have full authoritie to bid you Dy.
>
> (ll. 83–87)

While neither ignoring the conventional flattery involved in this occasional tribute nor arguing for Crashaw's originality in seeing a royal prince as one who will overcome the forces of rebellion and war, I would emphasize the language and values evident at this point, where a male heir is in opposition to traditional masculine virtues and where *his* virtues are those of peace and calm and felicity. Crashaw leaves his portrayal of the newest of Charles's progeny by reiterating his strengths—and they are feminine ones—in contrast to the qualities recognizably associated with the political world of power and conquest. The prince, a "sweet supernumerary Starre," is urged to

> Shine forth; nor fear the threats of boyst'rous Warre.
> The face of things has therefore frown'd a while
> On purpose, that to thee and thy pure smile
> The world might ow an universall calm;
> While thou, fair Halcyon, on a sea of balm
> Shalt flote; where while thou layst thy lovely head,
> The angry billows shall but make thy bed:
> Storms, when they look on thee, shall straight relent;
> And Tempests, when they tast thy breath, repent
> To whispers soft as thine own slumbers be,
> Or souls of Virgins which shall sigh for thee.
>   Shine then, sweet supernumerary Starre;
> Nor feare the boysterous names of Bloud and Warre:
> Thy Birthday is their Death's Nativitie;
> They've here no other businesse but to die.
>
> (ll. 99–114)

The considerable attention to the queen over the final section of the poem adds to its emphasis on feminine virtues, as the queen is praised for her fruitfulness and her chastity. In a poem that on one level is overtly political, the principal values enumerated stand in contrast to power and authority and war.

The male is strong and triumphant in Crashaw's "Epithalamium," written in celebration of the marriage of Sir John Branston and Alice Abdy in 1635, but in that poem winning and losing, being powerful and being passive become more complex and point us toward the more androgynous roles of later poems. Opening stanzas mildly denigrate the independence and aloofness of the woman about to be married, and she is figured through the "matchlesse maydenhead / that now is dead" (ll. 11-12). Virginity and independence are a "fine thin negative thing," "a nothing with a dainty name," "a selfe crownd King," and a "froward flower" with "peevish pride." Further imaged as a phoenix "chaced by loves revengefull arrowes," the feminine figure, in her independence, is said to oppose nature by freezing "the fruite of faire desire / which flourisheth in mutuall fire, / 'gainst nature."

Finding contentment and "rest" in the "soft breast" of Alice Abdy, the phoenix-maidenhead is nonetheless eventually won over by the forces of love "in noble Brampstons eyes," and the catalog of responses of the feminine suggests the uneasy vacillation of the conquered:

> With many pretty peevish tryalls
>   of angry yeelding, faint denyings
> melting No's, and milde denyalls
>   dying lives, and short lived dyings;
>   with doubtful eyes,
>   halfe smiles, halfe teares,
>   with trembling joyes,
>   and jocund feares;
> Twixt the pretty twylight strife
> of dying maide and dawning wife;
> twixt raine, and sunshine, this sweet maydenhead
>   alas is dead.
>
> (st. 7)

These images are not remarkable, nor are the portraits of the two participants in the premarital contest. More interesting are the images associated with the couple newly married. The male is the "faire oake" being embraced by the "Vine" of the female, but the stanza in which these conventional images are conveyed leaves ambiguous the relative strength of each:

> Nor may thy Vine, faire oake, embrace thee
>   with ivy armes, and empty wishes,
> but with full bosome enterlace thee,
>   and reach her Clusters to thy kisses;
>   safe may she rest
>   her laden boughes,
>   on thy firme breast,
>   and fill thy vowes,
> up to the brimm, till she make even
> their full topps with the faire eyed heaven,

And heaven to guild those glorious Hero's birth
stoope and kisse earth.

(st. 10)

The feminine figure is, if not the agent of power, at least the agent of opportunity and possibility, and the opening priority given the "faire oake" in contrast
to the "Vine" is mitigated through the full and circuitous entwining of the "laden
boughs." Active verbs are associated with the feminine, as she is seen to "embrace," "enterlace," "reach," "fill," and "make even" in her association with the
masculine figure. Attention to this dominant activity of the feminine largely
subverts our initial acceptance of the strength and authority of the masculine.

"Epithalamium" evolves from conventional portraits of masculine strength
and feminine softness but also encourages rethinking of conventional associations. Crashaw's poems addressed to women work even more decisively to
reveal the poet's allegiance to the feminine and the strength and control the
feminine ultimately exercises. Two epigrams Crashaw wrote on the woman of
Canaan as recorded in Matthew 15:21-28 (in Williams's edition, poems 182 and
183) provide fitting headnotes to the discussion that follows. In the biblical
account the woman engages in a verbal contest with Jesus, asking him to heal
her sick daughter. The disciples urge his refusal, and Jesus reminds the woman
that his mission is to the house of Israel, not Canaan. Her steadfast pleas win
him over, however, and the daughter is healed. Crashaw's two Latin poems on
the episode reveal that through passivity and surrender there may be victory, and
in the feminine there is strength. The first is exemplified not by the woman but
by Jesus, who, in yielding to the strength ("vires") of the woman, actually gains a
greater victory by seeing faith spread. The woman's strength, in turn, demonstrates the power of the feminine. Crashaw plays on the feminine gender of the
Latin "fides," remarking, "A woman, and of such strong faith? now I believe
that faith is / more than grammatically of the *feminine gender*" (Phyllis S. Bow-
man's translation in Williams's edition).

These controlling images, strength through yielding and strength in the feminine, find their principal display in Crashaw's poems addressed to contemporary women and to St. Teresa. The "Ode on a Prayer-booke Sent to Mrs. M.
R.," "To the Same Party Councel concerning her Choise," and the Letter to the
Countess of Denbigh all argue for decisiveness, for control, and for strength, but
in each instance these are to be realized through submission to a "dearer Lord."

The poem to Mrs. M. R. "concerning her Choise" and the Letter to the
Countess of Denbigh develop from similar situations, with the poet as friendly
counselor advising the woman to choose an eternal mate and thereby reject "the
Sonnes of Men." Mrs. M. R. has apparently been unfortunate in love, and
Crashaw takes advantage of the occasion to counsel her on behalf of his "dearer
LORD." The poem unites secular marriage and sacred commitment but does
not explore the erotic potential of that linkage. Mrs. M. R. is urged to avoid the
"painted shapes, / Peacocks and Apes, / Illustrious flyes, / Guilded dunghills"

and "glorious LYES" of this world in favor of a "braver love," "a farre more worthy SPOUSE / Then this world of Lyes can give ye." Indeed, the poet suggests that this "Mighty lover" has had a hand in the failure of worldly love so that he might woo her for himself. In view of more active roles assigned feminine figures in other poems, the role of Mrs. M. R. here is strikingly static. She is still suffering from crossed love, is unable or unwilling to act, and is receiving—happily or not we do not know—advice from one who knows her. The final lines suggest that in this poem the feminine is inactive, not because of gender but because of a sense of momentary defeat:

> Your first choyce failes, o when you choose agen
> May it not be amongst the sonnes of Men.

The Letter to the Countess of Denbigh is in two versions, the first of which is more personal and more directly challenges the woman addressed. Apparently unsettled about her ecclesiastical commitment, she is encouraged, as the first version has it, "to render her selfe without further delay into the Communion of the Catholick Church." To be decisive is, in this instance, to forego refusal and to give up what seems to be the strength of independence but is in fact "peevish strength / Of weaknes" (1652, ll. 41–42). Genuine strength results from a decision to yield:

> Raise this tall Trophee of thy Powre;
> Come once the conquering way; not to confute
> But kill this rebell-word, IRRESOLUTE
> That so, in spite of all this peevish strength
> Of weakness, she may write RESOLV'D AT LENGTH.
> (1652, ll. 38–42)

The second version of the poem urges yielding on impersonal, philosophical grounds, in less intimate language than the first version. The "Dart of love" and, contrastingly, the "well-meaning Wounds" of "Allmighty LOVE" will be aimed at the feminine heart that should yield to its force. But yielding is itself strength, and both versions of the poem close with that crucial paradox:

> Disband dull Feares, give Faith the day:
> To save your Life, kill your Delay.
> 'Tis Cowardise that keeps this Field;
> And want of Courage not to Yield.
>   Yield then, O yield, that Love may win
> The Fort at last, and let Life in.
> (1653, ll. 81–86)

The "Ode on a Prayer-booke," also in two versions, is the longest and most provocative of the three, and it most fully mingles imagery of love, war, and religion in its invitation to a young woman to be steadfast in love.[17] Stead-

---

17. I will be quoting from the second (1652) version, substantially the same as the version printed in 1648 but different from the first (1646) version.

fastness in love means resisting earthly lovers and keeping oneself pure for Christ, the "noble BRIDEGROOM." The prayer book serves as "love's great artillery" (l. 15) in defense against those who would storm "the hold of your chast heart" (l. 20). The heart, duly admonished by the words of the prayer book, is sufficient to stand and "be strong" (39). Avoiding "the gay mates of the god of flyes" (51) and forsaking the temptation of the "devill's holyday," the pure soul will be a fitting mate for the eternal spouse. As we would expect, the woman is to receive the advances of her spiritual lover, who will "poure abroad / His pretious sweets / On the fair soul whom first he meets" (ll. 93–95). But it is also left to the woman to assert her independence from the world and to seek aggressively the alliance that will empower her. She must "meet," "Seize," "tast," "rifle and deflour," and "discover" in her determination to be victorious through yielding. The final twenty lines of the poem focus on the aggressive action of the feminine in acquiring the pleasures and sweets of the masculine. Indeed, the almost startling fusion of influences as diverse as the Song of Songs, St. Teresa, and Thomas Carew's erotic poem "A Rapture" results in a near reversal of conventional gender roles, as the feminine figure forcefully acquires the "delicious dew of spices" yielded by "her sweet prey." The closing stanza and a half make clear the reversal of values and the consequent portrayal of the feminine as the aggressor, the masculine as the passive yielder. The "thrice happy" soul

> Makes hast to meet her morning spouse
> And close with his immortall kisses.
> Happy indeed, who never misses
> To improve that pretious hour,
>> And every day
>> Seize her sweet *prey*
> All fresh and fragrant as he rises
> Dropping with a baulmy Showr
> A delicious dew of spices;
>
> O let the blissfull heart hold fast
> Her heavnly arm-full, she shall *tast*
> At once ten thousand paradises;
>> She shall have *power*
>> To *rifle* and *deflour*
> The rich and roseall spring of those rare sweets
> Which with a swelling bosome there she meets
>> Boundles and infinite
>> Bottomles treasures
> Of pure inebriating pleasures
> Happy proof! she shall *discover*
>> What joy, what blisse,
> How many Heav'ns at once it is
> To have her GOD become her LOVER.
>> (ll. 102–24 italics added)

The poems discussed thus far suggest Crashaw's interest in exploring and transforming conventional views of victory and strength, of masculine and feminine, of activity and passivity. They also point to an ultimately androgynous portrait of humanity that has its fullest treatment in the poems on St. Teresa.[18] Perhaps in part because the historical Spanish saint so easily yielded such a portrait—though certainly a woman, St. Teresa was strong, aggressive, and powerful—and no doubt because he was personally and emotionally comfortable with such a portrait, Crashaw paints a Teresa who is gloriously free from the restrictions of being solely masculine or solely feminine.

The Hymn to St. Teresa rejects the conventional roles of both gender and age, as St. Teresa is both masculine and feminine, a child and mature. The full title announces these paradoxes: "A Hymn to the Name and Honor of the Admirable Sainte Teresa, Foundresse of the Reformation of the Discalced Carmelites, both men and Women; A Woman for Angelicall heigth of speculation, for Masculine courage of performance, more then a woman. Who Yet a child, out ran maturity, and durst plott a Martyrdome." The poem rejects traditional martyrdom with its masculine features in favor of a softer martyrdom embodied in a woman-child. Gone are the "old Souldiers, Great and tall, / Ripe Men of Martyrdom, that could reach down / With strong armes, their triumphant crown, / Such as could with lusty breath / Speak lowd into the face of death / Their Great LORD'S glorious name" (ll. 4–9). "Spare blood and sweat," Crashaw urges, and see instead love make "his mansion in the mild / And milky soul of a soft child" (ll. 13–14).

Throughout the poem Teresa is the feminine child embodying extraordinary power, never abandoning her femininity, never limited by it. Her heart is touched and burns with "brave heates" (l. 36); "she breathes All fire" (l. 39); and "Her weake brest heaves with strong desire" for something more than "her MOTHER'S kisses" (ll. 40–42). Her determination to be a martyr leads her to "travail," to "labor" as would a woman and to "travel" as would a man to realize that goal. The "milder MARTYRDOM" (l. 68) that she is called to embrace is not that of conventional victims but one more apt for a victim of love. The "death more mysticall and high" is both the experience of religious ecstacy and the image of sexual union, and the description fits one who receives and who is strengthened in that reception:

O how oft shalt thou complain
Of a sweet and subtle PAIN.
Of intolerable JOYES;

18. Two studies of the Teresa poems that bear on my interpretation here are Marc F. Bertonasco, "A Jungian Reading of Crashaw's 'The Flaming Heart,'" in Robert M. Cooper, ed. *Essays on Richard Crashaw* (Salzburg: Universitat Salzburg, 1979), 224–64, and Sandra K. Fischer, "Crashaw, St. Teresa, and the Icon of Mystical Ravishment," *Journal of Evolutionary Psychology* 4, 3&4 (1983): 182–95.

> Of a DEATH, in which who dyes
> Loves his death, and dyes again.
> And would for ever so be slain.
> And lives, and dyes; and knowes not why
> To live, But that he thus may never leave to DY.
> How kindly will thy gentle HEART
> Kisse the sweetly-killing DART!
> And close in his embraces keep
> Those delicious wounds, that weep
> Balsom to heal themselves with.
>
> (ll. 97–109)

The power of the saint is apparent as Crashaw anticipates the physical death of Teresa and her admission into heaven. There, all her works and all those "Thousands of crown'd Soules" (l. 166) whom she has made will greet her and bless her, as will the "soveraign spouse" who has, the poet says, "Made fruitfull thy fair soul" (ll. 168–69).

The Hymn to St. Teresa announces its androgynous aim at the beginning, but the interest in the inadequacy of conventional human gender roles is abandoned halfway through the poem in favor of a setting in heaven where gender designations are matters of language and convenience, not predictive or authoritative, where there would be, as St. Paul says, "neither male nor female." "The Flaming Heart" is similarly concerned with "manliness" and femininity but maintains that focus until the final twenty lines, where the poet's desire for religious ecstasy supersedes his determination to understand the true nature of the saint who is his subject. Here, as in the earlier Hymn to St. Teresa, Crashaw is unwilling to accept conventional gender roles and turns St. Teresa into a figure at once feminine and masculine, passive and active, submissive and powerful. "The Flaming Heart" challenges our understanding of masculine and feminine qualities and argues against the usual portrayal of Teresa as a "weak, inferiour, woman saint" (l. 26). Rather, she is the aggressor and the wielder of power. For Crashaw, of course, the source of such power is spiritual, and it flows from private experience, as the closing lines of the poem confirm.

The poem is a reaction to one or more paintings of Teresa and the angel who brought the flaming arrow (the "Dart") that inflamed the heart of the ecstatic woman. In traditional portrayals, Teresa is the submissive recipient, the angel the active provider. Crashaw urges a reversal of roles in language that confronts both power and sexuality.

> Give her the DART for it is she
> (Fair youth) shootes both thy shaft and THEE
> Say, all ye wise and well-peirc't hearts
> That live and dy amidst her darts,
> What is't your tastful spirits doe prove
> In that rare life of Her, and love?

Say and bear wittnes. Sends she not
A SERAPHIM at every shott?
What magazins of immortall ARMES there shine!
Heavn's great artillery in each love-spun line.
Give then the dart to her who gives the flame;
Give him the veil, who kindly takes the shame.

(ll. 47–58)

The "flaming heart," the most visible symbol of the private experience of ecstasy, is imaged in terms drawn from both sexual and military conquest and in language that challenges, indeed subverts, conventional notions about femininity and masculinity, the passive and the active, the submissive and the conquering. Love and devotion and ecstasy—"feminine" qualities that Teresa so vividly displays—are shown to be powerful and transforming virtues in the poem. As Crashaw puts it, "Love's passives are his activ'st part" (l. 73), and the "great HEART," which, true to the private, emotional experience of the poem, loves, dies, bleeds and yields, is nonetheless a powerful and evident influence over others, as Crashaw's litany of the heart's achievements makes clear:

Live here, great HEART; and love and dy and *kill;*
And bleed and *wound,* and yeild and *conquer* still.

(ll. 79–80, italics added)

IV

Much that we read about Richard Crashaw's friends, activities, and professed values would lead us to believe that he was apolitical, giving his time and attention to more private pursuits and more gentle ambitions. This is, of course, only a partial truth, for the political and religious allegiances of Crashaw can be confirmed and documented. Few of his contemporaries were turned more starkly—and more desperately—into political exiles because of their unwavering beliefs. These public and private sides of Crashaw are revealed in his poetry, though in ways that are subtle and transforming.

The poetry confirms his commitment to the private, "feminine" virtues of love, compassion, and feeling and his simultaneous recognition of the worldly attraction of power, conquest, and might. Indeed, one of the obvious ironies in Crashaw's subversion of conventional power is that the world of masculine, public conduct, though dispraised and rejected, inevitably yields the language through which the usually secondary feminine virtues can be elevated to primacy. Unwilling to be no more than a distant observer in the ongoing political and religious skirmishes, Crashaw was incapable of endorsing many of the conventional values associated with the political life. His answer was to moderate the prominence of power and force in a poem such as the "Panegyricke," where they might have been expected, and to heighten those same images in his poems on contemporary women and St. Teresa, where they would be least expected.

Both poetic strategies reveal his deep allegiance to feminine virtues. In the public world of religious controversy and political warfare, masculine qualities are, in Crashaw's hands, minimized and subdued; in the imaginative world of saints and idealized feminine figures these same qualities function as images—forceful, original, provocative and disturbing—to remind us that devotion and loyalty and love are also powerful and conquering.

M. L. Donnelly

12. Caroline Royalist Panegyric and the Disintegration of a Symbolic Mode

Is't not enough thy Dignity's in thrall,
But thou'lt transcribe it in thy shape and all?
(Cleveland, *The Kings Disguise*)

Panegyric has not enjoyed much favorable critical attention in this post-Romantic world, from either new criticism or old. It is usually dismissed as base flattery and insincerity, couched in an empty rhetoric of personification, allusion, and mythological embellishment. Few traditional studies have taken the form seriously—Warren Chernaik's treatment of Waller in *The Poetry of Limitation* and Ruth Nevo's *Dial of Virtue* are notable exceptions.[1] However, the recent emergence of a new historical criticism suggests approaches that confer on the form new interest and significance. Asserting the status of literature as product and expression of ideology, new historical studies highlight the pressures of social and cultural, as well as generic and "literary," contexts. They postulate a reciprocal influence: literature reflects the pressures of its context and also reacts upon it. The new historicists explore the social function of literary texts, the "work" texts do. Applying to Renaissance literature a "hermeneutics of suspicion" and employing modern psychological and anthropological concepts to elucidate literature's intertextual relations, recent criticism has drawn into the center of our focus what had previously been marginalized or suppressed.[2] Such critical approaches seem made to order for analysis of panegyric, a form highly conventionalized, embedded in social contexts and hierarchies, and full of potential ambivalence between avowal and actual purpose, formal and contextual demands.

Panegyric is a mode of praise representing the virtues and achievements of its object, or rather an idealized version of that object's aspirations or self-image. It is written by an admirer, adherent, or would-be client. The tone is enthusiastic

1. Chernaik, *The Poetry of Limitation* (New Haven: Yale University Press, 1968); Nevo, *The Dial of Virtue* (Princeton: Princeton University Press, 1963).
2. For a survey of the central tenets of new historicism, together with sketches of the work of some of its leading practitioners, see Jonathan Goldberg's "The Politics of Renaissance Literature: A Review Essay," *ELH* 49 (1982): 514–42, which also affords a sample of the polemical manner that has sometimes accompanied the assertion of hegemonic claims by adherents of the approach.

and warmly approving; a gesture toward objective, even-handed judgment is not ordinarily to be looked for from the form. This tone is in keeping with the panegyric's usual function and context: panegyrics might be pronounced in public on ceremonial occasions (the form's original scene), or appear in published collections celebrating a public occasion of rejoicing. Always the form voices an ideology and places its subject and event in a larger context, conferring significance at the same time that it affirms its author's participation in the circle or society that shares that significance. Panegyric reflects the way its object would like to be represented, but it also augments and elaborates that representation. Thus, the panegyrist validates power by reflecting and disseminating the image power would like to project.

By affirming its author's acceptance and approval of that image, and serving as testimony to his complicity in its construction and projection, the panegyric avows its author's assent to the terms and forms of the power he is courting. Ultimately, of course, the panegyrist may hope that his literary offering will be reciprocated with real power or privilege or reward. But surely not every panegyric produced by college fellows for their university's collection or circulated in manuscript among friends and connections can have been written with the expectation of such material reward. It must be stressed that one function of panegyric is the self-affirmation of the author's right-mindedness, his participation in the mythos to which his representation contributes. In other words, as I hope the following examination will demonstrate, these supposedly inherently insincere and empty literary performances could have a credal value, a virtually liturgical function, for their authors and the community for which they were written.

The nature of that credo, a consistent ideology or mythos voiced by many different participants, emerges from an examination of the strategies of representation characteristic of Caroline royalist panegyric. The poems of this genre written for royal personages between about 1624 and 1641 largely suppress narrative mappings of historical incident; they also generally lack dialectical or expository thrust. Instead, these royalist poems of praise tend to rely on a static manipulation of a series of givens—personifications, types, hierarchically ordered icons that repress or triumph over one another in accord with a fixed allegorical program. While some of the typical identifications are part of a conventional grammar of praise, recent scholars have shown how a specific iconography of adulation attaches to a particular monarch. For example, while images of Diana, petrarchan mistresses, and Astraea were appropriate to and therefore appropriated by Elizabeth, James, for whom a different style was obviously required, cultivated representation through allusions to Solomon, Augustus and a Roman imperial style, and such classical figures of harmonizing power as Orpheus, Amphion, Arion, Mercury, and even Hercules. Charles, succeeding to the throne, inherited some of these representations. He likewise seems to have inherited from his favored elder brother, Prince Henry, dead at eighteen, the burden of a certain set of military and chivalric expectations. These roles and images, with his delight in connoisseurship and his native inclination toward piety and a rather solemn religiosity, established the iconography of representation peculiar to his person and reign, enunciating his aspirations and program.[3]

In both the content of panegyric images and the manner in which they are mobilized for imaginative effect, affinities with the Stuart court masque are obvious. Like the court masque, Caroline panegyric is the art of a debased Platonism. It creates icastic images, that is, sensible imitations of the real, including those realities apprehensible to intellect alone. To its practitioners, perhaps the formulation of Jacopo Mazzoni describing the Song of Solomon would have seemed the most appropriate characterization of Caroline panegyric: it is of a kind "which under the husk of the literal sense conceals pure and complex truth. Hence it can be called phantastic with respect to the literal sense, but icastic with respect to the allegorical sense."[4] These images are calculated to elicit from the audience emotional assent and aspiration to the values they embody. Like the court masque, panegyric is a Machiavellian art whose "idealizations are designed to justify the power they celebrate."[5] As in the masque, a unique relation subsists between the person represented and the image or figure that represents: a transference coalesces the individual with the images that represent him or her. For Caroline panegyric, not only is history timeless, but royal roles and gestures "repeat eternal truths."[6] The concept of *figura* is apropos here, not precisely in the Christian sense Warren Chernaik suggested, but as that ancient and fundamental "notion of the new manifestation, the changing aspect, of the permanent" that, Erich Auerbach asserts, "runs through the whole history of the word."[7]

As significant as the content of royal representations is their ordonnance and mobilization. Typically, the royal personages and their types and attributes exercise a hegemonic power over the field of praise, displacing other persons and deeds. As a consequence, elaborated contemporary historical reference is generally absent from these texts, and subsidiary, nonroyal persons disappear from

3. See especially Graham Parry, *The Golden Age Restored: The Culture of the Stuart Court, 1603–1642* (New York: St. Martin's, 1981), esp. chaps. 1, 3, 6, 9, and 10. On the transfer of hopes and interests from Prince Henry to Charles, see also Pauline Gregg, *King Charles I* (Berkeley: University of California Press, 1981), 32–37.

4. Cited in Allan H. Gilbert, *Literary Criticism: Plato to Dryden* (1940; rpt. Detroit: Wayne State University Press, 1962), 390.

5. Stephen Orgel, *The Illusion of Power: Political Theater in the English Renaissance* (Berkeley: University of California Press, 1975), 40. I would qualify the application of Orgel's description to panegyric by observing that as long as the masque-programs were in the hands of Jonson, the educational function of the spectacles remained a prominent motive; it is precisely my point that in the poets and poems I am concerned with here, that function is minimal if not absent entirely.

6. Cf. Goldberg, "Politics of Renaissance Literature," 541.

7. Chernaik, *Poetry of Limitation,* 126; Auerbach, "Figura," from *Scenes from the Drama of European Literature* (1959; rpt. Gloucester, Mass.: Peter Smith, 1973), 12.

the textual commemoration of events in which their actual role was, in fact, significant.[8] Another characteristic representational strategy might be described as the transcendence of categories. The most striking of these images, oxymoronic and paradoxical couplings of unlike or even contradictory qualities, present the king's nature, like God's, as embracing contraries; another set may be grouped around assertions of the positively magnetic power of the royal person and the royal virtues, operating effortlessly as an ontological given. Waller and Denham afford notable instances.[9]

The concepts that sustain the imagery and representational devices of literary encomium developed easily in the adulatory atmosphere of the court. Even without the processes of literary and artistic transformation and validation, the customs, practices, rules, and decorum of the court conspired to turn the king into a power larger than life, an icon, a heroic, quasi-divine being. But the Caroline panegyric articulates a mythos that does more than justify a code or ritual of personal conduct relating to royalty within the narrow circle of the courtier's daily life. Its tropes and modes of presentation actually embody the language of politics as postulated by Charles I, following in his father's footsteps.[10]

The Stuart monarchical style was already present in James's entry into London. Jonathan Goldberg summarizes the contrast to Elizabeth's reception into the city forty-five years before: "Unlike Elizabeth, James said nothing throughout his entrance. . . . As he arrived, like the sun giving life, like the groom entering the bride, like a king in court, the city sprang alive, acting in word and deed to show what the royal presence contains in itself and gives merely by being present and being seen. . . . Unmoved, he is yet the animating force, the model of an unattainable power and unapproachable virtues to be copied but never achieved."[11] James affirmed repeatedly the power of his own words to annihilate any opposing discourse or argument. But he preferred that such opposition not

---

8. Compare Waller's "Of the Danger his Majesty [Being Prince] Escaped in the Road at St. Andrews" (written by spring, 1624?), "Of his Majesty's Receiving the News of the Duke of Buckingham's Death" (August 23, 1628), "To My Lady Morton, on New-Year's Day, 1650," "To the King, on his Navy" (1627? 1636?), and "Of Salle" (fall 1637), all found in *The Poems of Edmund Waller*, ed. G. Thorn Drury, 2 vols. (London: A. H. Bullen, 1901); note the lack of specificity in Cartwright's references to "Heate of Businesse," and "such State-throng / Disputing Right and Wrong" in his panegyric celebrating the marriage 2 May 1641 of Charles I's daughter to the son of the Prince of Orange (*The Plays and Poems of William Cartwright*, ed. G. Blakemore Evans [Madison: University of Wisconsin Press, 1951], 539-41), and the elusive and allegorical manner of allusion to Strafford's fall in *Cooper's Hill* (*The Poetical Works of Sir John Denham*, ed. Theodore Howard Banks, Jr. [New Haven: Yale University Press, 1928], 80-85), for the last of which, admittedly, reasons of tact also exist.

9. Waller, speaking of Charles's restoration of St. Paul's, avers, "Two distant virtues in one act we find, / The modesty and greatness of his mind" (*Poems*, 1:17.29-30). Denham develops such combinations of virtuous traits at some length in the 1642 edition of *Cooper's Hill*.

10. Cf. Parry, *The Golden Age Restored*, esp. chaps. 9 and 11. Once again, I would stress that besides the persistence of specific symbols and associations, the identity of mode is what unites the attempt of the two Stuart kings to control the agenda and terms of political discourse.

11. *James I and the Politics of Literature* (Baltimore: Johns Hopkins University Press, 1983), 31, 32.

be articulated in the first place; in any case, he quelled presumptuous inquiry and speech by his personal authority and prerogative, not by exposing his *arcana imperii* as arguments for vulgar ears. Goldberg observes, "The language of mysteries continued to the end of James's reign, and in a 1621 letter to Parliament, James tells them not to 'presume . . . to meddle with any thing concerning our Government, or deep matters of State' . . . ; in a second letter, James glosses this sentence as alluding to 'mysteries of state.'"[12]

Charles echoes the paternal style in a letter also cited by Goldberg, written from Spain on 17 March 1623, informing his father of the progress of negotiations relating to the match with the Infanta: "I beseech your Mtie advyse as littell with your Counsell in thease businesses as you can."[13] Laud's sermon opening Charles's first parliament asserted in James's own terms his son's concurrence with the view that parliament's power in the kingdom, and the law's force, derived from the king and was to be employed in support of his authority. The body need not deliberate to enact the directives of its head and soul. When he acted against the publication of religious controversy that kept the commonwealth in a stir, Charles threatened that "if controversial preaching and printing continued he would take action that would make the perpetrators wish 'they had never thought upon these needless controversies.'" He opened the parliament of 1628–1629 with an attempt to silence debate and elicit immediate action giving him a vote of supply: "'These times are for Action', he said, 'wherefore, for Example Sake, I mean not to spend much Time in Words; expecting accordingly, that your . . . good Resolutions will be speedy, not spending Time unnecessarily or (that I may better say) dangerously; for tedious Consultations at this Conjecture of Time is as hurtful as ill Resolutions.'. . . If the situation was not clear, he said, 'no Eloquence of Men or Angels will prevail. . . . Take not this as Threatening for I scorn to threaten any but my equals.'"[14] The reign of Charles, like that of his father, is marked by continuous efforts to silence debate by emphasizing the distance between crown and subject, and the consequent incapacity of the latter to "meddle" in the former's "state secrets." The Stuart monarchs strive to preempt the field of discourse, not with their own words, but with silence, with their presence and gesture asserting their will as God's will.

Unfortunately for its larger social efficacy, of course, the process only possessed complete imaginative authority within the increasingly isolated world of the court. It was worse than useless as an "art of regiment." Beyond its lessened force outside the circle of those whose daily lives and fortunes were immersed in the ritual order of the court, this process of heroic metamorphosis and apotheosis of royal power is fundamentally flawed as a way of dealing with the exigencies and demands of political power and social tensions. It exalts ontology over

12. Ibid., 251, n. 1, citing John Rushworth, *Historical Collections of Private Passages of State* (London: 1721), 1:43, 51.
13. Ibid., citing British Library, Harl. Ms. 6987, fol. 33.
14. Gregg, *King Charles I*, 127, 185, 171.

process, hypostatizing unchanging qualities and hierarchical relations as immune to the operations of intellect, action, or that other potent hypostasis, history. In the royalist mythos as presented in panegyric and masque alike, even those virtues made so much of by "personalist patterns of thinking"[15] seem to have revealed themselves (already possessed) as if in some gorgeously costumed tableau, rather than to have actually enacted anything, ventured into trial, conflict, agonistic drama. This mythos and its mode of representation were especially unsuited to contend with an increasingly articulate, critically self-conscious, active, and self-confident opposition. Arrayed against the Stuart monarchical style of representation were potent discourses speaking for energetic and restless interests that would not be silenced, preempted, or marginalized: the dialectical and rhetorical styles of parliamentary procedure and committee deliberation; religious and political polemic; the disputes and precedents of lawyers; and the exegetical, hortatory, and suasive modes of homiletics, among others.

Reactions to the disruption of the royalist decorum of representation validate our thesis that, far from being casual poetic ornament or servile flattery, its devices were deeply rooted in a profoundly felt belief-system. Although participants in the mythos could ignore the alternative discourses, the events of the Civil War decisively disrupted the royalist semiotics of hierarchy and power, and a new order ultimately inscribed its meaning on the king's very body. While supporters of the king seem to have been utterly disoriented by these events, even the new order's apologists were confronted with urgent issues concerning the legitimation of power and the representation of authority. A wide variety of strategies of literary accommodation appeared in response as writers tried to adjust their old belief-systems and the imagery and iconography they entailed to the new state of affairs. Some tried to carry across the terms of Caroline royalist panegyric to the praise of the new order—an expedient clearly unsatisfactory because of the contrasting origins and sanctions for their power. The hollowness of the old terms when applied to the fallen dynasty was equally obvious and forced various adjustments. Some developed and adapted concepts merely implicit or present though not dominant in the earlier strategies, and some invented new tropes and allusions contingent on silencing the old.

By the spring of 1646, military resistance to his enemies had become virtually impossible for the king. The encirclement of Oxford, his headquarters, was ensured, and it was clear the city would not be able to stand a long siege. Early in the morning of Monday, 27 April 1646, King Charles, his hair and beard trimmed, and dressed in the clothes of a serving man, slipped out of Oxford and, after eight days of wandering with two companions, delivered himself into the hands of the Scots. Two poems presumably written soon after these events reveal through their images and allusions the profound psychological impact, not

15. Nevo, *The Dial of Virtue*, 84.

just of the failure of royal military and political power, but more importantly of the inversions, disjunctions, and alienation of self embodied in the king's self-divestiture.

In Henry Vaughan's "The King Disguis'd," the rhetoric veers from imperatives to wishes, exclamation to apostrophe; the wit sounds hysterical and desperate. Shifts of hypotheses straining to encompass the incident in a net of conventional, accustomed assumptions are marked by a trail of "buts" and abrupt alternation of predications. However, while the content of the tropes and allusions alters with the king's altered circumstances, for Vaughan the strategies remained largely those of earlier panegyric. The oxymora are now simply more frantic ("A King and no King! Is he gone from us, / And stoln alive into his Coffin thus?"), and his attribute is a "(now spotted) spottles Majestie."[16] The paradoxes here *really* cancel each other out.

Charles's piety was always a ground of praise, but Vaughan's use of imagery based on that virtue prepares the way to later encomium on the royal martyr: he is a "Royal Saint" who has "put off thy self a while, / To serve as Prophet to this sinful Isle." In "Of Salle" (1637), Waller had compared Charles to Samuel slaying Agag, king of the Amakelites, but now Vaughan compares him to Samuel earlier in the same story, when he pronounced God's judgment on Saul for rebellion against God's commandments ("for rebellion is as the sinne of witchcraft," 1 Samuel 15:23), and Saul, seizing the hem of his robe as Samuel turned away, tore the garment. As Samuel told Saul that the tearing of his garment figured the tearing of the kingdom of Israel from Saul, because he had cast away the commandment of God, and hence was cast away himself, so Vaughan interprets Charles's disrobing as an event that does "figure out anothers Punishment." As the disordering of the prophet's garment signified the divine punishment of the bad king, the royalist poet makes the disordering of the good king's garment a sign of the impending punishment of the bad "prophets" of sectarianism.

As Charles's fortunes suffered eclipse in the revolution, the dominant iconography associated with his person shifted from the classical, mythical, and heroic, or these mixed with religious allusions, to the biblical, presenting him as prophet, saint, martyr, and sacrificial victim. All the allusions in Vaughan's "The King Disguis'd" are scriptural.[17] Of course, pagan classical literature provides fewer great examples of "the better fortitude of patience and heroic martyrdom"; but also, in a death-struggle, one's frame of reference shrinks to the essential. The texts alluded to concern God's warnings and punishments for rebellion as denying providential guidance and also threats to true worship rooted in a commercial culture. Both would have seemed to royalists to have immediate application to their opponents. Still, as in prewar panegyric, the

16. *Works of Henry Vaughan,* ed. L. C. Martin, 2d ed. (Oxford: Clarendon Press, 1957), 625–26.

17. Ezekiel 2:1–3:3 and 21:1; the driving of the scapegoat into the wilderness; the mysteries and visions of the books of Esdras; and the money changers in the temple.

work of the poem is done by types and figures, by the allegorical interpretation of the homologies laid out by the poet, not by narrative action, the working out of character and thought, or the battery of argument.

Vaughan's poem tells us by its jagged questioning and exclamatory accents that the poet was "vext" even before the poet says so. Likewise, real emotional distress and psychological confusion seem to shape John Cleveland's "The King's Disguise," written at about the same time in response to the same incident. Again it is not the failures and miscalculations of the king's policies, the defeats in the field, the weakness and vacillation of Charles's leadership that provoke this relentlessly rhymed, desperately epigrammatized anguish. As in Vaughan's poem, the "disguise" of Charles's royal person, his donning clothes and a persona inappropriate to his divinely ordained role, administers the shock that the poet tries to diffuse or denature through new representations of the king arrived at in witty conceits and elaborate rationalization. Cleveland's is the response of one who assents emotionally *and intellectually* to the role and imagery of the royal masque. Charles is "coffin'd in this vile disguise"; "who but sees blasphemes thee with his eyes."[18] It is allegiance not to look at him, as he usurps himself. The central modality of the poem is a trial of interpretations—the frenetic attempt to find a simile, a trope, an allusion that will allow comprehension of the impossible inversion and traduction that has taken place. For once, the intense personal loyalty that has always been a prominent feature of the royalist ethos wavers as Cleveland tries to drive a wedge between "the king's two bodies," separating the object of loyalty and veneration from the person who at the moment seemed inadequate to the role history had called him to play:

> Oh for a State-distinction to arraigne
> *Charles* of high Treason 'gainst my Soveraigne.
> What an usurper to his Prince is wont,
> Cloyster and shave him, he himself hath don't.
>
> (ll. 5–8)

"And Majesty defac'd the Royall stamp," that is, the king himself has marred or altered the royal visage, which (as the royal face is the image stamped on coin of the realm making it legal tender) would be treason in anyone else. "This Priviechamber of thy shape would be / But the Close mourner to thy Royaltie," that is, his disguise has removed him from his public role as head of the state and made him a mere private man; but in doing so (with a pun on "close," "clothes," "closet") his disguise as a private person becomes secretly next of kin (as near as the clothes on his back) surviving his royalty, which is symbolically deceased when its appropriate garments, perquisites, and the etiquette they demand are laid aside.

---

18. *Poems of John Cleveland,* ed. Brian Morris and Eleanor Withington (Oxford: Clarendon Press, 1967), 6.

Is't not enough thy Dignity's in thrall,
But thou'lt transcribe it in thy shape and all?

(ll. 13-14)

As God's vice-regent, divinely appointed to his place, he is responsible for its maintenance, and open now to penalties for irresponsibility: "Heaven, which the Minster of thy Person owns, / Will fine thee for Dilapidations." He has done to himself what reforming and Puritan frenzy did to the old religious houses and collegiate centers of learning, or worse; his attire is "prophanation" and "sacriledge."

From this violently witty and accusatory attack, Cleveland modulates to milder paradoxes, echoing but transmuting the language and assumptions about the king's emblematic associations characteristic of the preceding two decades of court panegyric. Oxymoronic couplings of the king's attributes have been thrown into violent opposition; he is

Angell of light, and darknesse too, I doubt,
Inspir'd within, and yet posses'd without.

(ll. 39-40)

Charles is still the divinely chosen king, though hidden under the darkness of his humble costume, and bears the mind God gave him, though his person is prisoner to his enemies. But the telling confession, "I doubt," now hangs suspended, grammatically and semantically, over the whole process of paradoxical predications. The imagery of earlier panegyric identifying the king with the sun and life-giving light is eclipsed:

Majestik twilight in the state of grace,
Yet with an excommunicated face.
. . . .
The Sun wears Midnight, Day is Beetle-brow'd,
And Lightning is in Keldar of a cloud.

(ll. 45-46)[19]

Cleveland touches on, without attempting a solution to, the problem of providence and fate:

Oh the accurst Stenographie of fate!
The Princely Eagle shrunke into a Bat.
What charme, what Magick vapour can it be
That checkes his rayes to this Apostasie?

(ll. 47-50)

The poet seeks in witchcraft and spells the solution to a problem that simply did not arise in earlier panegyric. The earlier poetry's sublime indifference to pro-

---

19. "Keldar" is Dutch for womb, but means also "cellar"; the world's turned upside down. Ibid., 89, note on l. 46.

cess and its comfortable espousal of unchanging truths permitted it to ignore the possibility of conflict in that which is coming-into-being rather than metaphysically given. Cleveland is undecided whether to blame Charles for having undone himself or curse his enemies for undoing him. How could a divinely ordained king, God's deputy, be brought to such a pass that he must turn disloyal to the respect and honor due his own person, so that by his attire he is "halfe depos'd," and "look'st like one / Whose looks are under Sequestration"? To be sure, all the language hits indirectly at the king's enemies, who have done or tried to do these very things to him and to his loyal followers; but opprobrium sticks to Charles, himself, too. "Y'are not i'th'presence, though the King be there." Like some of the imperfect types to which he was once favorably compared in figurative tropes, Charles has fallen short of the figure he was called upon to fulfill.

Cleveland's treatment of his subject consists of almost hysterical attempts to lay hold of the situation in language whose conventional meanings have been given the lie by the unnatural course of events. With the discrediting of the old, self-confident royalist hermeneutics that forthrightly identified power and virtue with the fixed iconography of their symbols and trappings, the correct interpretation of the inverted signs and mysteries shown by the face of things becomes a necessity. Finally, Cleveland hits upon the conceit of the king's disguise as a "puzling Pourtraiture, to shew that there / Riddles inhabited," and he has a new key to turn in the lock of interpretation. The king in disguise is a type, *figura,* showing forth not sovereignty but Religion; Cleveland suggests that Solomon, conventionally a type of Christ, in his gnomic proverbs was a similar "Text Royall," "array'd" in "so obscure a shade" and requiring interpretation just as does Charles in disguise.[20] The poet flouts "all ye brats of this expounding age, / To whom the spirit is in pupillage," saying they will never get keys for this cipher/cabinet, the king's disguise. The "opening" of that receptacle of mysteries depends on two senses of "to open," both of which are responsive only to "St. Peter's keys." The cipher may be "opened" as Scripture is "opened" by exposition; in another, even more urgent sense, the king's person as cabinet is "opened" in the sense that it is "released" or freed from the aspersion of his disguise (as the soul under its carnal disguise is released from its bondage to sin). In either case, the opening is possible only with the keys of St. Peter, which symbolize ecclesiastical authority, and therefore the support of orthodox belief. With that emblem of ecclesiastical authority, of course, the king's foes would have nothing to do, choosing instead to pursue secular force. Hence, to the keys as the badge symbolizing the spiritual power to bind and loose given by Christ to his Church, they have no claim. Right interpretation still depends on right-mindedness.

The concluding lines of the poem sound almost like a transposition of the

20. Ibid., 9, ll. 93–8; see p. 91, note on l. 98.

rhetoric and imagery of royal panegyric into a minor key: the true nature beneath the cypher/character/disguise presents

> an aspect would benight
> Critick spectators with redundant light.
> A Prince most seen, is least: What Scriptures call
> The Revelation, is most mysticall.
>
> (ll. 111–14)

But if mystical interpretation by displacements and inversions suggests a means to save the appearances and retain the mythos, the poem nevertheless ends with an exclamation of figurative identification at once bitterly satiric and truly distressed. Reflecting on the king's putting himself into the power of his former enemies, the Scots, notorious to Englishmen like Cleveland both for poverty and perfidy, the poet cries,

> But oh! he goes to *Gibeon,* and renewes
> A league with mouldy bread, and clouted shooes.
>
> (ll. 123–4)

The original league between the Gibeonites and Israel was obtained from Joshua by the Gibeonites' fraudulent pretense that they were not neighbors and residents in the promised land, but from a country so distant that their shoes had worn out and their provision gone stale and moldy in the journey (Joshua 9:3–27). But Cleveland's figure seems to refer to David's renewal of the league with Gibeon after Saul, in his zeal, broke it and slew them. That association helps account for the anxiety and bitterness of Cleveland's concluding couplet: the Gibeonites exacted from David as the price of their renewed league the lives of seven of Saul's sons and kinsmen, whom they "hanged . . . in the hill before the Lord: and they fell all seven together, and were put to death in the days of harvest, in the first days, in the beginning of barley harvest" (2 Samuel 21:9). The Anglican Cleveland obviously dreads in advance the price the Scots will exact for their alliance from the English Church and the royalist faithful. Identification of the king with religion may attempt to compensate emotionally for the loss of sovereignty, but this figure covertly confesses that the royal person neither commands nor controls the historical situation.

The assumption of the centrality of the king's person to all value, beauty, and good possessed enormous emotional power and persistence. Cleveland's poem reflects the verbal contortions and sense of unfathomable duplicity produced by the derangement or effacement of even the external paraphernalia of that system of belief. Of course, given the strong transference of emotion and value from the things signified to the signs in that system, no disordering of the signs would be possible without profound derangement of the signified. One response, a desperate one, pursues the transcendence of categories to its ultimate mystification, identifying the martyred king inextricably with Christ. No better example could be adduced than an elegiac epode by Richard Lovelace to the evanescence of loved and valued worldly things. In "To Lucasta. From Prison. An Epode," references to "the KING" who is sacred light and whose dwelling is the "glorious Starry Waine" achieve almost perfect ambiguity, or bivalence.[21] One feels the true weight and places the sentiment rightly, hearing under the diction and rhythm of the final stanza the analogous cadences of such poems of world-weary religious aspiration as Vaughan's "They are all gone into the world of light" and "Cock-crowing." In the end, the deification of the sovereign, the identification of Charles as figure and type of the divine, the yearning after a fixed, eternal, static order where all things are beneficently good and beautiful, and everything is in its place, have reduced loyalty to the martyred king, anticipation of the heavenly Jerusalem, and longing for a release from the clouds and cares of this life to one and the same thing. Such a response, however, while sufficient to fuel an emotional elegy or an act of self-immolation, proves difficult to sustain and an inadequate motive for rational action in the world, especially as months and years go by without the eagerly desired sign from a heaven suddenly inscrutable.

In response to the actual course of affairs unredeemed by divine signs, some poets, like Cowley, developed imagery that suggests growing skepticism about the power or validity of the kinds of representation we have been examining. In his poem "Upon the Death of the Earl of Balcarres," Cowley voices a puzzlement, a sense of the enigmatic obscurity of God's design. This note is foreign to earlier articulations of the royalist mythos. God "for good and righteous ends" that he nevertheless does not intend that "erroneous mankind should . . . understand" has not permitted Balcarres to complete "his distracted Nations Cure."[22] However, he has taken the earl's soul to dwell with him in Heaven. In this, God acts like kings, who "for secret causes known / Sometimes, but to themselves alone," send their ablest ministers "abroad to Treaties, which th'intend / Shall never take effect." But even so, the master rewards his faithful, though deluded, servant, with "some honorable room" "near himself" at home; and Cowley calls this inscrutable royal master, with his dissimulation and reserved intentions, "just and righteous" when he completes the reward of "the happy agent." Lost in the dark experience of petition and delay, suit and verbal promises and bearings in hand, dark plots and obscure counterschemes that constituted the world of

---

21. *The Poems of Richard Lovelace,* ed. C. H. Wilkinson (Oxford: Clarendon Press, 1930), 48–51. Though Manfred Weidhorn (*Richard Lovelace* [New York: Twayne, 1970], 71) followed Margoliouth in dating this poem 1642, not only the whole tone but specifically line 24 and the last stanza seem to me convincing evidence that it cannot have been written before the execution of the king, as Thomas Clayton, in his recent edition of *Cavalier Poets: Selected Poems* (Oxford: Oxford University Press, 1978) asserts (p. 264, note).

22. Abraham Cowley, *Poems,* ed. A. R. Waller (Cambridge: Cambridge University Press, 1903), 413–16. On Alexander Lindsay, second baron Balcarres and first earl of Balcarres (1618–1659), whose career suggests the breakdown of simplistic categories for religious and political alignments during the civil war, see *DNB,* 11, s.v. "Lindsay, Alexander."

royalist intrigue in exile, Cowley reasons himself into a stance of acceptance somewhere between Stoicism ("Thus far the greedy Sea may reach, / All outward things are but the [beach]") and a Miltonic "All is best, though we oft doubt, / What th'unsearchable dispose / Of highest wisdom brings about." Though a congruity is still asserted between the dealings of God and those of kings with their servants, the providential order must now be deciphered through shadowy types, and signs may mean their opposites. To the royalist poet, an easy affirmation of the existing order of things is no longer possible.

Since one cannot judge the world by its appearances, the only real greatness and quality must be always inward—and therefore at any given moment perhaps apprehensible only by God or angels. This position, of course, denies a cardinal principle of Caroline panegyric. Reflecting on the mystery, Cowley even pens a kind of retraction of "The King's Disguise" poems. In hindsight, welcoming Charles II back to his heritage in 1660, he reflects on how

> To *Angels* and their *Brethren Spirits* above,
> No show on Earth can sure so pleasant prove,
>   As when they *great misfortunes* see
>   With *Courage* born and *Decency.*
> . . . .
> So were they born when no *Disguises clowd*
> His *inward Royalty* could *shrowd*[.]

So much is inward worth to be preferred to outward pomps, Cowley assures his royal audience, that one of the angels sent by God to guard the Black Boy in his flight and exile had confirmed

>   in a *Vision* th'other night,
> That *He* (and who could better judge than *He?*)
>   Did then more *Greatnesse* in him see,
>   More *Lustre* and more *Majesty,*
> Than all his *Coronation Pomp* can shew to *Human Eye.*[23]

Cowley has come to see in Charles II that the only true value is inward value, which may be hidden. Likewise, Balcarres shows that the only safe and finally gratifying aspiration in this world is personal salvation, not the successful achievement by human effort and worth of communal good, or the satisfaction of cooperating with providence in securing a national end. The necessity of substituting inward quality for external signs and shows, recognizing a dichotomy between appearance and true nature impossible before the cataclysm of revolution and defeat, shows how far we have come from the confident identification of the Stuart divine-king with the established order of things.

In this "Ode. Upon His Majesties Restoration and Return" Cowley indeed tries to revive the rhetoric and attitudes of the prewar court, but his effort shows

23. Ibid., 429, stanza 14.

the strain involved, and what he inscribes is no longer what it once was. Significantly, the imagery and allusion of the poem, like that of the distressed royalist poems of defeat, is almost entirely confined to biblical, rather than classical, mythical, or historical figures. Moreover, these figures are not generally warrior-heroes and Davidic or Solomonic kings, but patient victims of heroic martyrdoms. Apocalyptic imagery is applied to the restored Stuart line, rising to a climactic allusion to the three holy children in the furnace, and a messianic apostrophe. Climactic, but not conclusive. For, unlike the Caroline panegyrics that centered on the royal person, this Carolean one goes on. The Queen Mother is depicted as a kind of *mater dolorosa*, transcending categories in an oxymoronic blend of bliss and bale, "wisely managing the wide *Extreams* / Of great *Affliction*, great *Felicity*," "*Daughter* of *Triumphs*, *Wife* of *Martyrdom*." General Monck is honored as "Their great *Zerubbabel*" (a forerunner and type of Christ who restored the second temple and helped recall Judah from its rebellion and apostasy). This new model royalist panegyric concludes at last with an unprecedented distribution of acknowledgments to those who had not figured in the charmed circle of such praise in any of the poems written by Caroline panegyrists before the war: those *"great Patriots"* and *"Worthies,"* "Who have redeem'd from *hatred* and from *shame* / A *Parliaments* once *venerable* name" by ratifying the restoration.[24]

After more than a decade of exile and dependency, the attitudes supporting Stuart royal power have undergone a bitter chastening. Gone are the assurance, the easy assumption that royal pomps and prerogatives figure the divine and natural order of things, by their mere appearance and role guaranteed an easy and masque-like triumph over the personified grotesques of an antimasque of follies, vices, ridiculous enthusiasm, and rebellious passions. Other poets, like the tough-minded Marvell, learned quickly from events the irresistible imperatives of history and began to postulate the centrality of discursive reason, calculation, and Machiavellian virtù, rather than Platonic virtue, in ordering reality and giving it comprehensible form; in their verse, the adulatory imagery of transformation and revelation characteristic of royalist panegyric disappeared, or was demoted to an ornamental role, to be supplanted by the exaltation of foresight, policy, and cooperation with an unpredictable destiny that favors, not the sons of kings, but the bold, the resolute, and the wise. After the Restoration, Waller and Dryden, among others, attempted to revive the transfiguring language of Caroline panegyric. But the attitudes that had sustained that grammar of praise were effectively dead, extinguished on 30 January 1649, but drastically eroded by events even before that day.

24. Ibid., 431–32, stanzas 17–19.

Stella P. Revard

13. Building the Foundations of a Good Commonwealth: Marvell, Pindar, and the Power of Music

In 470 B.C. when the tyrant Hieron of Sicily was about to dedicate the new city of Aetna, he called on the poet Pindar to compose an ode celebrating the city's founding. Pindar struck the lyre, invoked the Muses, and created Pythia 1, a poem that praised both the power of music and the ideal of good government on earth. In 1654 at the end of the first year of the protectorate, Cromwell of England also needed a poem that would commemorate the success of the new protectorate and would defend the principles on which it was founded. Like his Greek predecessor, the poet Andrew Marvell answered the ruler's call. Striking his metaphoric lyre and likening the building of a sound state to Amphion's raising of the Theban walls with his music, Marvell demonstrated in "The First Anniversary of the Government Under His Highness, the Lord Protector" that poetry still possessed the power to address the subject of the ideal state and to create through its harmonies an image of how a free commonwealth might flourish on earth.

The concurrence in Pythia 1 and in "The First Anniversary" of occasion, subject, and thematic treatment is not, I think, accidental. Marvell was an expert classicist who knew Pindar well; he probably studied him in either Erasmus Schmid's 1616 or Johannes Benedictus's 1620 edition, both of which contain copious notes, commentary, and rhetorical analyses. Further, as an accomplished Latin poet, who had himself composed Latin verses for ceremonial occasions,[1] he was well aware that both Latin and vernacular poets had been composing odes and encomia modeled on Pindar's odes to rulers of government for over 150 years. Having modeled his ode on Cromwell's return from Ireland on Horace's political poems, Marvell might logically have turned only a few years later to Pindar, Horace's master, for a longer, more formal public poem, and in many ways a more ambitious one.

The political pindaric had been introduced into Europe at the end of the

1. Marvell's first published works were a pair of poems, one in Latin, the other in Greek, written to Charles I on the the birth of Princess Anne and published at Cambridge in 1637 in a collection of university verse. See *The Poems and Letters of Andrew Marvell*, ed. H. M. Margoliouth, 3d ed., rev. by Pierre Legouis with E. E. Duncan-Jones (Oxford: Oxford University Press, 1971). Marvell's poems are cited from this edition.

fifteenth century by the minor Italian poet Francesco Filelfo, who composed five books of Latin odes, written in a variety of meters, none of which attempts to approximate Pindar's strophes.[2] Imitating here and there Pindaric language and devices and adopting the mode Pindar had used for cultivating the Sicilian tyrants Hieron and Theron, Filelfo addressed his odes to Italian dukes and princes whose favor he was courting. His poems served as examples to the next generation of Italian and French poets of a medium they might espouse for praise of such diverse rulers as Ferdinand of Aragon, the Emperor Charles V, François I, and Henry the Eighth of England.[3] Following in this tradition, Ronsard adapted Pindaric ode to the vernacular, addressing odes and hymns to Henri II and figures of the French court.[4] Ronsard undoubtedly gave the encomiastic ode in the style of Pindar international popularity, provoking imitations in French and Latin in his own country and inspiring the minor Elizabethan poet John Soowthern to laud his own patron, the earl of Oxford, and to boast in addition that he was the first in English to pindarize.[5] Drayton and Jonson, following in this tradition, celebrated the nobles of the Jacobean and Caroline court with their odes.[6] While the vernacular ode was solidly established after Ronsard, Latin pindarics continued to be written well into the seventeenth century. One of the most popular of these neo-Latin imitators was Casimire Sarbiewski, dubbed by his admirers the Polish Pindar, whose odes on Horatian and Pindaric models became popular after their first appearance in the 1620s. Casimire was certainly known to Marvell in the original and probably also in the volume of selected odes that G. Hils published in 1646 with facing English translations. While he composed many familiar odes, Casimire also addressed political leaders on issues of state, adopting the vatic authority of Pindar to speak for truth and against public wrong.[7]

The political pindaric runs the gauntlet from pure panegyric, in which little is attempted but flattering praise of the ruler, to poems of pointed if sometimes veiled advice and commentary. Some Pindaric poetry is related to Pindar only

2. Francescus Philelfus (Francesco Filelfo), *Odae* (Brescia, 1497).

3. Petrus Crinitus sings the praises of Ferdinand of Aragon (see *Poematon* [Leiden, 1543], esp. II.1); Johannes Secundus and Antonio Minturno both praise Charles V (see Ioannes Secundus, *Poetae Elegantissimi Opera* [Paris, 1561], especially Odes I and VI); Antonio Minturno (Sebastiani) (*Epigrammata, et Elegiae* [Venice, 1564]) wrote Odes I and II to celebrate Charles V's victories in Africa; Luigi Alamanni (*Opere Toscane* [Florence, 1532]) wrote Hymn I and II to François I; Benedetto Lampridio (*Carmina* [Venice, 1550]) addresses an ode to Henry VIII of England as well as to the Medicis. All the poets above wrote in Latin except for Luigi Alamanni, whose odes in Italian to François I may have served as models for Ronsard's in French to Henri II, François's successor.

4. Pierre de Ronsard, *Odes* (Paris, 1550); *Le Cinquième Livres des Odes* (Paris, 1552).

5. John Soowtherne, *Pandora* (London, 1584).

6. Drayton's "To the Virginian Voyage" in *Odes with other Lyrick Poesies* (London, 1619) celebrates the nobles of James's court who set off for America, just as Jonson's Cary-Morison ode celebrates Charles's noblemen.

7. Matthias Casimire Sarbiewski, *Lyricorum Libri IV* (Antwerp, 1632); *The Odes of Casimire*, trans. G. H. (G. Hils) (London, 1646).

casually by its adoption of poetic form, technique, subject, or allusive language. While poets such as Lampridio, Alamanni, and Minturno attempt to approximate Pindar's triads, others do not. Ronsard in his odes uses triads; in his hymns, where Pindaric material is just as fully exploited, he uses hexameters. Jonson's Cary-Morison ode is triadic; his earlier ode to Desmond is not.[8] Casimire himself makes no attempt to imitate Pindaric meters; Hils uses couplets in his translations of Casimire. Abraham Cowley, whose *Pindariques,* printed in 1656, just one year after "The First Anniversary," include two translations and a group of occasional odes, chooses irregular stanzas rather than triads. Clearly, in the middle of the seventeenth century, a poet was free to use stanzas, couplets, or any other verse form he deemed appropriate for Pindaric imitation.

When a seventeenth-century poet undertook Pindaric imitation, then, his primary aim was something other than duplicating in English the orderly march of strophe, antistrophe, and epode. Abraham Cowley in the preface to his *Pindariques* indicates that he was attempting both to experiment with some of Pindar's well-known stylistic devices and to capture Pindar's spirit.[9] Marvell's aim as a poet is not, I think, dissimilar. Surely he wished, in writing a long, complicated political poem, to profit from Pindar's methods in handling complex poetical material; he also aspired to catch Pindar's spirit. For he saw in Pindar's approach to political situations and his use of subtle political analysis methods and a mind congenial to his own. Critics have often remarked on not only the stylistic eccentricities of "The First Anniversary" but also its ambiguous political approach.[10] If we look at Marvell's poem as a political pindaric, we may better understand both the strategy of Marvell's poetical design and the complexity of his political statement.

Stylistic imitation is the easier of the two to deal with, although it must be said that in Marvell, as in all good poets, style and content are hardly separable. Yet, looking at the overall structure of "The First Anniversary," we can observe many resemblances to Pindaric ode. First of all, Marvell's poem opens, as do Pythia 1 and a good many other odes by Pindar, with a highly developed poetic figure. It

8. Jonson's ode to James Fitzgerald, earl of Desmond (in "The Under-wood") is not in triads, even though Jonson therein invokes Pindaric inspiration. Ronsard's *Hymnes* in hexameters or vers Héroiques use Pindaric techniques, references, and myths. See *Les Hymnes de P. de Ronsard* (Paris, 1555), 5-37.

9. "Preface," *Pindarique Odes* (London, 1656).

10. See, e.g., Annabel Patterson, *Marvell and the Civic Crown* (Princeton: Princeton University Press, 1978), 68; John Klause, *The Unfortunate Fall: Theodicy and the Moral Imagination of Andrew Marvell* (Hamden, Conn.: Archon Books, 1983), 67; Barbara Everett, "The Shooting of the Bears: Poetry and Politics in Andrew Marvell," in *Andrew Marvell: Essays on the Tercentenary of His Death,* ed. R. L. Brett (Oxford: Oxford University Press for the University of Hull, 1979), 91-92; John M. Wallace, *Destiny His Choice* (Cambridge: Cambridge University Press, 1968), 106-44; J. A. Mazzeo, *Renaissance and Seventeenth-Century Studies* (New York: Columbia University Press, 1964), 185-206; Steven Zwicker, "Models of Governance in Marvell's 'The First Anniversary,'" *Criticism* 16 (1974): 1-12; and Derek Hirst, "'That Sober Liberty': Marvell's Cromwell in 1654," in *The Golden and the Brazen World,* ed. John M. Wallace (Berkeley: University of California Press, 1985), 17-53.

proceeds, as do most Pindaric odes, by episodic unfoldment, using, when appropriate, a digression featuring a figure from classical myth or from history. It shifts suddenly, perhaps abruptly, from section to section, using material for poetic effect and not adhering to chronological order. This kind of poetic structure with these types of rhetorical effects was classified by Renaissance critics as Pindaric. A century and a half of Renaissance scholarship on Pindar had preceded the writing of Marvell's poem. Commentators such as Portus and Aretius, editors such as Benedictus and Schmid, had analyzed the structure of all Pindar's odes, dividing them into rhetorical parts. Schmid, for example, lists four rhetorical parts for Olympia 1: exordium, confirmation, digression, and epilogue, all united by Pindar through the theme of Hieron's excellence. Portus poses a seven-part rhetorical structure for Pythia 1, in which the poet begins with the praise of poetry and moving through six successive stages comes at last to the praise of Hieron.[11] Although Renaissance critics conceded that Pindar is a difficult and sometimes obscure poet, their commentaries emphasize the orderliness and control that underlie his brilliant virtuosity and intricate poetic structure. This rhetorical approach, which Portus and Schmid used to analyze Pindar's Pythia 1 or Olympia 1, the modern critic John Wallace employs to similar effect to dissect Marvell's "The First Anniversary." Arguing like Portus and Schmid that a poem can be divided into rhetorical parts, Wallace posits seven sections to Marvell's poem, corresponding to the following rhetorical divisions: exordium, narratio, divisio, confirmatio, refutatio, digression, conclusion.[12] Though he never mentions Pindaric analysis, he has discerned independently in Marvell exactly the same structure that Schmid and Portus discerned in Pindar. Hence, the seven rhetorical parts of "The First Anniversary" neatly complement those of Pythia 1, just as the seven gates of London those of seven-gated Thebes.

Interesting as these structural correspondences are, they would hardly be more than empty architecture were they not supported by intellectual correspondences. When Marvell wrote his ode on Cromwell's return from Ireland on a Horatian model, he did so because he was interested in the way in which Horace had dealt with the problems of Caesar's ascent to power. When he turned to Pindar for his anniversary poem, he was seeking a model that is both an encomium to an enlightened dictator and an investigation of the problem he faces in wielding absolute power. Of all Pindar's odes to kings and tyrants, Pythia 1 most nearly fits the requirement, for it was composed for Hieron of Syracuse near the end of his reign to celebrate a particular occasion and to praise the accomplishments of that reign, composed to praise while recognizing the difficulties faced by the man and the government.

---

11. See the following editions of Pindar's odes: Erasmus Schmid (Wittenburg, 1616) and Johannes Benedictus (Saumur, 1620). See also Benedictus Aretius, *Commentarii Absolutissimi in Pindari* (Geneva, 1587); Franciscus Portus, *Commentarii in Pindari Olympia, Pythia, Nemea, Isthmia* (Geneva, 1583).

12. *Destiny His Choice*, 137. Also see Patterson, *Marvell and the Civic Crown*, 68.

Pindar's Sicilian odes, even as they commemorate the victories won by athletes supported by the powerful tyrants of Syracuse and Acragas, Hieron and Theron, all contain subtle political commentary and advice. Pindar never fails to laud his patrons, but he also has other ends in mind. As a servant of Apollo and the Muses, as a celebrator of Zeus as well as of the kings and tyrants who reign through Zeus' permission, the poet exalts these first and never tires of reminding rulers that they are mortal men who have responsibilities to the gods and to the subjects they rule. Why else, while celebrating in Olympia 1 and Pythia 2 Hieron's splendid horse-racing and chariot victories, does Pindar introduce the cautionary myths of Tantalus and Ixion, rulers who forgot that they were human beings and committed crimes against gods and men? Pindar's astute analyses of the contemporary scene in Sicily were not undetected by Renaissance writers. Roger Ascham comments that Pindar promoted "stoutnes in warre, and just government in peace," and Sir Philip Sidney remarks that Pindar had such influence through his verse that he made the tyrants Hieron and Theron wise and just princes.[13]

Pindar was connected with Sicilian politics and the Sicilian tyrants for over twenty years, visiting Sicily during the 470s (probably in 476 B.C.) and writing some of his most elaborate odes during that era. It was a brilliant but turbulent time, marked on the Greek mainland with the repulse of the Persian invaders and in Sicily with the defeat of the Carthaginians, events inextricably linked in the Greek mind. Theron, joined by Gelon, Hieron, and Polyzelus, won a stunning military victory in 481 B.C. against the Carthaginians at Himera, an event that, though it occurred somewhat earlier, Pindar presents in Pythia 1 as paralleling the Athenian victory at Salamis and the Spartan victory at Plataea over the Persians in 480 and 479 B.C. respectively. Following the victory at Himera was a period of expansionism in both Syracuse and Acragas. On the one hand, the tyrants swiftly executed their foes and amassed vast wealth from the spoils of war; on the other, they used that wealth to encourage the arts, to build temples, to colonize new cities (notably Aetna, celebrated in Pythia 1), and to spread their fame abroad by competing at Olympia and Delphi in the prestigious chariot and horse races and by making offerings to the sanctuaries of the gods there. Although both Theron and Hieron achieved and maintained their positions with military power, both were benevolent, sympathetic to democratic regimes, and opposed to harsh tyrannies in southern Italy and Sicily. Theron had expelled the tyrant Terillus from Himera; Hieron had helped the Sybarites against Croton and had deterred Anaxilas of Rhegium from attacking the Locri. Hieron, moreover, organized the new city of Aetna as a limited monarchy with a democratic constitution and overthrew Thrasydaios, Theron's son, and appointed democ-

---

13. Ascham, "The Scholemaster" in *Elizabethan Critical Essays*, ed. C. Gregory Smith (Oxford, 1904), 1:8; Sidney, "The Defence of Poesie," *The Prose Works*, ed. Albert Feuillerat (Cambridge, 1963), 33.

racies in Acragas and Himera when Thrasydaios did not follow the mild rule of his father.[14] While holding his own power by force, Hieron was attentive to the rights of those he ruled and eager to win their approval.

That Marvell should see a resemblance between Hieron's enlightened dictatorship and Cromwell's is not surprising. Like Hieron, Cromwell came to power suddenly, was a nonhereditary leader, and ruled briefly—how briefly, Marvell did not yet know. If Hieron had continually to intervene in the affairs of Sicilian and Italian city states, Cromwell had the rebellion of the Irish to crush and the revolt of the Scots to deal with. If Hieron faced the threat of the Carthaginians to the South, the Phoenicians and Persians to the East, and the Etruscans to the North (whom he fought in a savage sea battle off Cumae in 477 B.C.), Cromwell had the Catholic monarchies of Europe to contend with, as well as the sea power of the Dutch in the naval wars with Holland. Internally, Hieron was continually on guard, as was Cromwell, who faced not only dissident royalists but also anarchic libertarians dissatisfied with the very liberties with which he had sought to endow the Protectorate.

Pythia 1 was one of the last odes Pindar composed for Hieron. Hieron was at the height of his power, having won the prestigious chariot race at Delphi and having dedicated the city of Aetna, which he had founded some years earlier; at the same time, his future was uncertain. Pindar catches a sense of both exultation and uncertainty in the ode, praising the accomplishments of Hieron's relatively few years in power but acknowledging that every mortal man's days are numbered. Pythia 1 was widely admired in the Renaissance. Ronsard echoed it several times and modeled the second of his hymns to Henri II on it, alluding to Pindar's celebration of Jupiter's victory over Typhon while lauding Henri's prowess in arms and his recent victories over the English and the Italians, and praising Henri's liberality, as Pindar had praised Hieron's. Yet while he used Pythia 1 as a model, Ronsard hardly penetrated into the meaning of the poem, echoing its encomiastic praise without considering that praise in relationship to the other aspects of the poem. He was happy simply to identify himself with Apollo, who strikes his lyre in service to his father, as Ronsard does in service to Henri. Yet for Pindar the relationship of the poet to Apollo and that of the ruler to Zeus are integral to the meaning of the poem, not mere complimentary flourishes. For the responsibilities of the poet to Apollo and the ruler to Zeus are essential to the way in which the poet rules his art and the ruler his state. When Andrew Marvell came to Pythia 1, he understood these relationships and responsibilities.

For Marvell, as for Pindar, government comes from God and is part of the cosmic ordering of things. A true governor is the deity's power on earth—vir-

---

14. Pindar wrote Olympia 2 and 3 for Theron; Olympia 1 and Pythia 1, 2, 3 for Hieron, as well as a number of other odes for Sicilian victors connected with one or the other of the tyrants. See Pindar, *The Olympian and Pythian Odes*, ed. Basil L. Gildersleeve (London: Macmillan, 1908).

tuous, high-minded, godly in his purpose, omnipotent like God, because like God he wields his power righteously and commands respect for his iron hand and for the justice of his ways. Both Zeus and Jehovah establish government through ordinance, after putting down brutish enemies through their thunderbolt. Zeus has to defeat Typhon, the monstrous cipher of pure physical power, who would rule by force alone. Imprisoning him under Aetna, Zeus becomes the lord of the mountain and creates government through dispensation. As both dispenser of Hieron's authority and example to him, Zeus teaches the ruler that he must keep his own enemies in check; if he does not control the brutish hordes of Africa, Asia, and northern Italy that threaten Sicily, then no free and enlightened government will be possible on earth. Paradoxically, Pindar pleads that force must be used to guarantee freedom, for unless the strong and just wield force for good ends, the unjust will use force to enslave them. Thus he provides Marvell with the argument that underlies "The First Anniversary." Adapting Pindar's historico-religious tradition to his own, Marvell argues that Jehovah's establishment of patriarchal law grants to Cromwell the right to resist by force dissenters at home and enemies abroad. Like Hieron, Cromwell as just ruler holds his dispensation from a god, who has defeated his own foes through force and imprisoned them underground. The God of "The First Anniversary" controls the Locusts from the pit and dispenses justice against the Great Dragon. He authorizes "angelic" Cromwell to defend England against the brutish enemies at home and on the Continent that attempt to deprive her of her freedom, resist them with the might that paradoxically will keep her free.

> 'Tis not a Freedome, that where All command;
> Nor Tyrannie, where One does them withstand.
>
> (ll. 279–80)

To argue that force is justified when wielded by the deity's deputy on earth is not an original position for a poet apologist to take. What Pindar says of Hieron and Marvell of Cromwell, Pindar's sixteenth-century royalist imitators say of Ferdinand and Charles and Francis and the two Henrys of France and England. Why then is Pindar's treatment of the issue or Marvell's imitation of Pindar different or in any way more persuasive? Partly it is, I think, that Pindar, and following him Marvell, connects the enlightened autocrat not merely with God, be it Zeus or Jehovah, but also with the poet-musician. Both Pythia 1 and "The First Anniversary" begin with musical metaphors that define what the good governor and good government are. In the process the ruler becomes the cosmic musician who moves in harmony with the very nature of things and tunes his state accordingly. Hence, Pindar's opening address to the golden lyre, held in common right by Apollo and the Muses, is more than a graceful compliment to the affective powers of music. It is a leading concept of the poem:

> Χρυσέα φόρμιγξ, Ἀπόλλωνος καὶ ἰοπλοκάμων
> σύνδικον Μοισᾶν κτέανον· τᾶς ἀκούει

μὲν βάσις ἀγλαίας ἀρχά,
πείθονται δ᾽ ἀοιδοὶ σάμασιν
ἀγησιχόρων ὁπόταν προοιμίων
ἀμβολὰς τεύχῃς ἐλελιζομένα.

(ll. 1–4)

Golden lyre, possession in common right
Of Apollo and the violet-tressed Muses, which
The step, the onset of revelry heeds;
The singers obey the signals,
Whenever you with your quivering sound
Lead the chorus with your prelude
To lift up their dancing feet.[15]

As the chorus moves in response to the lyre the poet strikes, the lyre "rules" the chorus; the poet-composer who metaphorically or actually strikes the lyre rules it, giving it its earthly voice; he himself is ruled by the divine force within him—Apollo and the Muses—that inspires his poetry. Thus the poet too is the deity's power on earth, the one who controls the many, a "ruler" through the god Apollo, just as the prince or tyrant is a ruler through Zeus. The lyre itself is a cosmic symbol; the phorminx or lyre was a constellation of the Greek sky, itself made up of a group of stars that move in consort with other stars in the heavens. It is a continual reminder of the cosmic or divine power of music; it moves within the spheres of heaven and orders or rules them, as the harmonies of music (Pindar was well acquainted with Pythagorean theory) order both heaven and earth. Music like the good governor has the power not only to order but also to control, to subdue violence and to bring all under a beneficent rule. Pindar tells us, therefore, that music's charms can quench the thunderbolt, can keep the powerful eagle subdued, and can even make the warlike Ares drop his arms. All respond to the music—all, that is, but those who reject the principle of law and social contract, such as Typhon, who in refusing Zeus's rightful authority as divine ruler also rejects the power and beauty of music.

In the first long section of "The First Anniversary," Marvell develops the notion of time, as Pindar has developed music, as a symbol of good rule. As the poet in Pythia 1 controls the lyre and the prince the instrument of government, so Cromwell controls time, bringing its forces under his hand and creating through it a cosmic harmony comparable to that the poet-ruler creates. Like Pindar, Marvell employs a highly developed figure to convey his argument. While the opening image of the stone dropped in water does not directly imitate Pindar's struck lyre, its intellectual transformations in the verse paragraph that follows betray a debt to Pindaric poetics. By likening the passage of time to the circles of water that form about a dropped object, Marvell suggests that the just

15. The text for Pindar's Odes is *Carmina*, ed. C. M. Bowra (Oxford: Oxford University Press, 1935). All translations are mine.

ruler, such as Cromwell, controls these "vain Curlings of the Watry maze" (l. 1), while others are merely overwhelmed by them. Like the reverberations of sound that proceed from the struck lyre, the circlings of time are an earthly pattern of a cosmic design. Time moves in an orderly circuit, a sequence of days, months, years controlled by the orbiting of the spheres that move the universe, move it musically as the creator God ordains. Cromwell, the poet-musician in tune with God's purposes, "tunes" these spheres; he "cuts his way still nearer to the Skyes, / Learning a Musique in the region clear, / To tune this lower to that higher Sphere" (ll. 45–48). The ordering of time, then, effected by the musicianly Cromwell, is analogous to the ordering of the chorus by the poet in Pythia 1. Musical references so permeate the first section of Marvell's poem that time almost becomes music. Cromwell's orbit is not dull and saturnine; the "Jewell of the yearly Ring," he contracts the "force of scatter'd Time," producing in one year "the work of Ages" (ll. 12–14). Unlike the heavy monarchs governed by malignant Saturn, who have no musical instinct and are only like the "wooden Heads unto the Violls strings" (l. 44), Cromwell commands music within the state. Marvell compares his construction of a good government to Amphion's raising of the walls of Thebes with the playing of his lyre. (In an ode to the rulers of Poland [IV.26], Casimire had also alluded to Amphion's feat.)

> And still new Stopps to various Time apply'd:
> Now through the Strings a Martial rage he throws,
> And joyning streight the *Theban* Tow'r arose;
>
> . . . .
> But, for he most the graver Notes did try,
> Therefore the Temples rear'd their Columns high:
> Thus, ere he ceas'd his sacred Lute creates
> Th' harmonious City of the seven Gates.
>
> (ll. 58–66)

Marvell likens Cromwell's tuning of the ruling Instrument with "wondrous Order and Consent" (ll. 67–68) to Amphion's raising of Thebes, Pindar's native city, by the injunction of the gods. The poet, prompted by the god, creates with his sacred Lute, whether it is a well-ordered city or a well-ordered ode. In so doing he imitates the archetypal creation of God himself. The divinely ordained ruler, in turn, creates order within the state, the state being as much his creation as the ode is the poet's or the world is God's. Music for the poet, the ruler, the god is the ultimate civilizing force, and for that reason Marvell likens Cromwell's accomplishments as state-builder to those of the builder-poet. Further, as the millennium approaches, there is still greater need for a ruler who can bring the discordant elements that strive against harmony into a final concord and consent. At this point the earthly poet-musician-architect becomes heavenly, and the music we hear is not just creative but apocalyptic. Cromwell becomes "angelic Cromwell," "Michael," the punisher of the dragon and the herald of the last age.

In Pythia 1, the dragon Typhon represents the primeval anarchy that resists the establishment of justice (diké) not only at the beginning but also at the end of things. Pindar inherited the figure of Typhon from Hesiod's *Theogony*. This monster child of Earth and irreconcilable foe of Zeus cannot be civilized and made a part of Zeus's commonwealth. Though overthrown and pinioned under Aetna, he is never entirely silenced. Pindar describes him at the beginning of the first epode—a hundred-headed beast, sprawled full length under the mountain, the pillar of Aetna piercing his spine and causing him to bellow in pain and send forth clouds of smoke and rivers of fire. This monster enemy of Zeus is also an enemy of the Muses, whose beauty and harmony he hates. The new city of Aetna, an emblem of the new age, cannot flourish unless such enemies as Typhon are kept in check. Pindar includes in Pythia 1 a prayer of blessing on Aetna; he implores the Zeus that conquered Typhon that the Carthaginians stay at home and that the battle cry of the Etruscans not be heard in the land. Hoping that the force Hieron evinced at Cumae will dissuade his enemies from pursuing warfare, Pindar rejoices not only in the prowess of the Syracusan leader but also in that of the Athenians and the Spartans, who scattered the hundred-headed Persian galleys in the sea at Salamis and defeated the Persian army at Plataea, preserving good government and a home for the Muses in Greece as in Sicily.

Like the ancient Sicilian ruler, Cromwell takes a firm stance toward his enemies, reconciling those he can, strongly resisting the others. Some opponents may be useful to the government, their opposition serving to make the fabric of the state stronger, as opposing pressure in an arch serves to uphold the single center stone.

> The crossest Spirits here do take their part,
> Fast'ning the Contignation which they thwart:
> (ll. 89–90)

Other antagonists, however, must be more strictly dealt with, or their dissonant voices will drown all harmony: they "sing Hosanna to the Whore, / And her whom they should Massacre adore" (ll. 113–14). Neither the Romish Whore nor the Dragon is friend to the Muses. Well-known analogues to the serpentine Typhon of Hesiod and Pindar, the "Romish Whore" and the Dragon, described in Revelation, also oppose God, religion, and government. "Angelique *Cromwell*," like the biblical Michael or the heroic Zeus, must pursue "the Monster thorough every Throne: / Which shrinking to her *Roman* Denn impure, / Gnashes her Goary teeth: nor there secure" (ll. 128–30). Further, her partner, the dragonish Satan, though defeated and dispossessed of the kingdom of Heaven, like Typhon, remains a menace: "Stars still fall, and still the Dragons Tail / Swindges the Volumes of its horrid Flail" (ll. 151–52). Satan controls the thrones on earth and attempts through Rome to topple those states headed by just, god-like rulers; like Hieron, Cromwell cannot relax his guard. At home, Cromwell faces still more paganish foes, the dissident sects that, drawing another biblical parallel, Marvell describes as "Accursed Locusts" from the pit.

With such enemies, Cromwell must steer cautiously and hold the reins securely. As the "Peoples Charioteer" (l. 224), he guides the government for the people but holds the reins from God. The image of Cromwell as charioteer once more has Pindaric affinities. Pindar so described Hieron, perhaps in compliment to his chariot victory at Delphi, perhaps because the image of the steersman or charioteer was one of Pindar's favorites. The poet prays that he steer his own course straight, that he hit the mark; for Hieron, he prays that he steer his people with a just tiller (l. 86), keeping Sicily free and plotting a course for his son, as king of Aetna, to follow. Marvell's portrayal of Cromwell as the steersman for a democratic state makes him a leader superior to the mere king: "For to be *Cromwell* was a greater thing, / Than ought below, or yet above a King" (ll. 224–25). Cromwell is a man of destiny, whose fate has been plotted by God himself, one at "whose happy birth / A Mold was chosen out of better Earth" (ll. 159–60). With the millennium imminent, Cromwell "knowing not where Heavens choice may light, / Girds yet his Sword, and ready stands to fight" (ll. 147–48). Angel-like, he guards England, prepared for Christ's ultimate coming.

In the first part of Pythia 1, Pindar argues Hieron's right by connecting him with the divine musician and with Zeus himself; in the second, he alludes to types closer to the ruler—human leaders who justly or unjustly discharge their rule. The effect in one sense is to bring Hieron down to earth, to remind him he is a man, not a god, and to urge him to rule generously and justly. The first of these types is a hero of the Trojan War—not Achilles or Ajax, whom elsewhere in the odes Pindar cites as supreme heroes, but the archer Philoctetes, a man mortal and limited, afflicted with a foul and grievous wound, who, nonetheless, was courted by the Greek leaders, since his presence was necessary to effect Troy's final capitulation. Of Philoctetes, Pindar says: ἀσθενεῖ μὲν χρωτὶ βαίνων, ἀλλὰ μοιρίδιον ἦν· Though he walked on feeble flesh, he was a thing governed by fate (l. 55). Some commentators believe that in comparing Hieron to Philoctetes, Pindar was commending Hieron's courage in persevering despite illness. Yet, it also seems to me that he is reminding the tyrant and his audience that though governed by destiny, Hieron is still a man, subject to human limitation.

Marvell's controversial allusion to Cromwell's coaching accident, like the Philoctetes reference, looks two ways. On the one hand Marvell can rejoice that providence saved Cromwell's life; on the other, he can read in the episode the inexorable truth that as a mortal man Cromwell must one day die. No ruler, however angel- or god-like, may escape the human destiny. Both he and his accomplishments must be measured by a human yardstick.

In the final sections of Pythia 1 and "The First Anniversary" this human yardstick is applied yet more rigorously. Although the poets still offer words of praise, they begin to assess for posterity how the still-living rulers have fulfilled the requirements of good leadership. By setting up types, by introducing still more digressive material, they measure their own good governors, Hieron and Cromwell, against human models drawn by Pindar from Greek, by Marvell from Hebraic history. The ideal of the good leader may be laid up in Heaven, but its fulfillment must be on earth by mortal men. Pindar prays that Deinomenes, Hieron's son, may follow his father's example and be a constitutional monarch in the Dorian tradition, a leader attentive to the needs and views of his people, who steers his course with justice, having forged his tongue, as Pindar says, on an unlying anvil. He should be a faithful steward, who does not seek his own profit, but is generous to his people. They in turn will testify to his worth, a testimony that the poet echoes with his praise. For Pindar the poet is the custodian of the future, who will decide whether a ruler will be remembered as a Croesus, the most generous of kings, or a Phalaris, the most hated of tyrants (a final counterpart in this poem of the monstrous Typhon). "The generous-hearted virtue of Croesus does not fade," comments Pindar, "but hateful report everywhere holds down Phalaris, and neither lyres nor youthful choruses welcome him" (ll. 94–98). Through the divine power of music, the poet, the lord of the lyre, has the last words in this poem as he had the first. Addressing his parting words to Hieron, he declares,

> τὸ δὲ παθεῖν εὖπρῶτον ἀέθλων·
> εὖδ᾽ ἀκούειν δευτέρα μοῖρ᾽· ἀμφοτέροισι δ᾽ ἀνὴρ
> ὃς ἂν ἐγκύρσῃ καὶ ἕλῃ,
> στέφανον ὕψιστον δέδεκται.
>
> (ll. 99a-100b)

The first of prizes is to fare well,
But the second to be well praised;
He who meets with both and grasps them
Has won the highest garland.

Pindar's treatment of the contrasting rulers—Croesus and Phalaris—is not a device merely for praising Hieron. Though Pindar identifies Hieron by implication with Croesus and urges him to be openhanded and kind to his subjects, he is also cautioning him about the sting to future fame in less magnanimous behavior.

Marvell's use of types is yet more cautionary. Some critics have remarked that Marvell refrains from connecting Cromwell with David the king, even though such a connection was almost proverbial for the good Christian ruler, Puritan or royalist. Instead, he alludes to different Old Testament figures: the prophet Elijah, the soldier Gideon, the patriarch Noah. Steven Zwicker has argued that these allusions to pre-Davidic judges of Israel, rather than to kings, affirm Marvell's approval of Cromwell's having refused the title of king.[16] This may be so.

---

16. "Models of Governance in 'The First Anniversary.'" Also see Hirst, "'That Sober Liberty.'"

Yet prophet, soldier, and patriarch are presented in episodes that both illustrate their successful leadership and comment on its sometimes problematical consequences. Elijah the prophet refreshed a thirsty land but, like Cromwell, brought on a storm that wet a king. Gideon defeated two kings with a small band of followers yet lost the support of the elders. Noah survived the deluge and as a husbandman planted the vine of liberty but, as he brought the ark to safety, caused unwittingly the division among the sons who saw his nakedness. The heroes of history earned praise despite actions that, like Cromwell's, made them unpopular with some. Marvell's allusions to these episodes indicate how aware he was of the difficulty a strong leader has in ruling with equity and with praise. The voice of the future, which the poet in one sense looks forward to, may not be a chorus of approval.

For this reason, perhaps, Marvell puts the final praise of Cromwell's accomplishments into the mouths of his adversaries, the grudging choir of European kings who collectively complain of the virtues of the Lord Protector and the accomplishments of the infant Commonwealth. The encomium of the good leader is spoken by his enemies, who recall his feats as Captain of the Wars, razing and rebuilding the state, and who praise his reconstruction of the British navies to take command of the Oceans:

> The Nation had been ours, but his one Soule
> Moves the great Bulk, and animates the whole.
> He Secrecy with Number hath inchas'd,
> Courage with Age, Maturity with Haste:
> The Valiants Terror, Riddle of the Wise;
> And still his Fauchion all our Knots unties.
>
> (ll. 379–84)

Ironically, it is these foreign kings who acknowledge that Cromwell possesses qualities of a "King-like" ruler, while he maintains a constitutional equality granted him by the respect of his people.

> He seems a King by long Succesion born,
> And yet the same to be a King does scorn,
> Abroad a King he seems, and something more,
> At Home a Subject on an equall Floor.
>
> (ll. 387–90)

Marvell was aware of the irony of rendering praise to Cromwell by recording the Fear and Spite of his enemies, rather than the Love and Duty of his people. Yet, of this Fear and Spite, he could have said, as Pindar did in urging Hieron to persevere despite criticism: "envy is better than pity" (Pythia 1, l. 85).

With Pindar's example, Marvell has written a poem of celebration that does not shrink from grappling with hard issues, that looks at Cromwell, wart and all, and, while praising him as a man of destiny, acknowledges that he walks, like all human beings, in mortal flesh. While he may deny him the Davidic crown,

Marvell has given Cromwell something more kingly—the Davidic lyre, which associates him not only with the greatest Hebraic hero-poet but also with the Greek heroic bard, Pindar, whom the Renaissance often associated with David. For the poet-prophet is ultimately the only one who masters time and melody, who like the angel of the apocalypse can announce the last age or who like the angel of Bethesda pool, to whom Marvell compares Cromwell in the last lines of the poem, can both move the waters and make them heal.

Marshall Grossman

14. Authoring the Boundary: Allegory, Irony, and the Rebus in "Upon Appleton House"

In the seventeenth century, a growing mastery of "second causes" reformed agriculture and, together with the development of a European "market economy," transformed and redistributed economic power.[1] By 1688, a rhetoric of progress and accumulation had displaced a rentier ideology that no longer answered to the material organization of social life.[2] In the transition, traditional views of the social and political world were challenged by the incipient perspectives of an emerging alternative order. However, the ideological competition that occurs during such a transition is not, by its nature, perceived or recorded as such. The civil wars fought across England were also fought within individuals, who experienced the division of their social world as an inward division of the self.

As a modern developer of the land and a general of the parliamentary army, Marvell's patron, Thomas Fairfax, epitomizes the seventeenth-century modernizer caught between a temperamental and intellectual attachment to the rising class on the one hand and a historical attachment to the traditions of the landed gentry on the other.[3] As an English loyalist who may have, for a time, supported the king and flirted with the Roman church, but would later represent the merchants of Hull in Parliament, Marvell too may have felt himself suspended between a dying past and an immature future.[4] In "Upon Appleton House," he

---

1. See Christopher Hill, "The Agrarian Legislation of the Revolution," in *Puritanism and Revolution: Studies in Interpretation of the English Revolution* (New York: Schocken, 1964), 153–96, and Lawrence Stone, *The Causes of the English Revolution, 1529–1642* (New York: Harper & Row, 1972), 66–67.

2. On the development of the rhetoric of the market economy, see Joyce Oldham Appleby, *Economic Thought and Ideology in Seventeenth-Century England* (Princeton: Princeton University Press, 1978).

3. See Raymond Williams, *The Country and the City* (New York: Oxford University Press, 1973), 54–59. For a useful discussion of the Fairfaxes' social position and expectations, see also Lee Erickson, "Marvell's 'Upon Appleton House' and the Fairfax Family," *English Literary Renaissance* 9 (1979): 158–68.

4. For the characterization of Marvell as a "loyalist," see John M. Wallace, *Destiny His Choice: The Loyalism of Andrew Marvell* (Cambridge: Cambridge University Press, 1968), and R. I. V. Hodge, *Foreshortened Time: Andrew Marvell and Seventeenth Century Revolutions* (Ipswich: D. S. Brewer, 1978), esp. 117–31. Contra, see Warren L. Chernaik, *The Poet's Time: Politics and*

obliquely treats Fairfax's decision to resign his command rather than lead Parliament's expedition against the Scots, by embedding a parallel moment of choice in an evocation of Fairfax's estate and a recapitulation of his family history.

With Fairfax's military career suspended, and without a male heir to extend the family tradition, the Fairfaxes broke the entail on Nun Appleton and Bolton Percy so that the inheritance would pass to the children of their young daughter, Mary. The choice of a husband for Mary would then settle the destiny of the Fairfax family in a new line and a new name.⁵ Thomas Fairfax's decision to end his military service to Parliament and the settlement of the Nun Appleton estate on his daughter's heirs may thus be viewed as paired choices. Marvell's narrative of the Fairfax's family and political affairs mirrors these mirror-image choices with a lyric evocation of the poet as he moves between the poles of social engagement—celebrating his patron, tutoring Fairfax's daughter, commenting on his master's decision to withdraw to his estate to sit out the remainder of the civil wars—and contemplative withdrawal at Nun Appleton.

I should like to examine the rhetoric through which Marvell pairs the historical narrative of the Fairfax family and the contemplative lyric of the poet-tutor and to suggest that the organizing tropes of "Upon Appleton House" constitute a seventeenth-century effort to represent an inward division of the self as a discontinuity in the relationship of individual action to providential design, choice to destiny, during a period of material historical change. My formal analysis of "Upon Appleton House" seeks to describe the articulation of politics on and in poetic form, to show how the political choices of Fairfax and Marvell presuppose relations of self to history—the realization of individual acts in and as the destiny of England—that are at once formed in and reflected by literature, so that historical and literary experience each become the other's mirror and the distinction between the original and its image is rendered moot.

Men in the seventeenth-century still expected to find nature's nature reflected in the literary mirror, but as the social consensus decays, the image found in the literary mirror becomes blurred, doubled, and unstable. The world of innocent speculation that gives Mary Fairfax "for a Glass the limpid Brook / Where *She* may all her *Beautyes* look" (ll. 701-2) coexists, in the poet's more sophisticated experience, with a flowing river whose serpentine folds are "a *Chrystal Mirrour* slick; / Where all things gaze themselves, and doubt / If they be in it or without" (ll. 636-38).⁶ The formal accommodation of these newly tendentious "reflec-

Religion in the Work of Andrew Marvell (Cambridge: Cambridge University Press, 1983), 6-7. Michael Wilding provides an explication of Marvell's political environment, with particular attention to the possibility of a position at once conservative and Cromwellian, in "Marvell's 'An Horation Ode Upon Cromwell's Return from Ireland,' The Levellers, and The Junta," *The Modern Language Review* 82 (1987): 1-14.

5. Erickson, "Marvell's 'Upon Appleton House,'" 159-60.

6. All citations of Marvell's poetry refer to H. M. Margoliouth, ed., *The Poems and Letters of Andrew Marvell*, 3d ed., rev. by Pierre Legouis and E. E. Duncan-Jones (Oxford: Clarendon, 1971).

tions" is a problem at once political and literary, and the peculiar engrafting of narrative and lyric in Marvell's poem thus records a struggle to refigure the self as a historical actor by refiguring its relations to received literary traditions.

"Upon Appleton House" joins innocent to experienced speculation through a dialectical mediation of allegory and irony. By allegory I mean a continuing reference to a specified precedent text. Allegory locates meaning in a time or place other than that of the narration itself, and the interpreter of an allegorical text must pass through the narrated events to discover a prior truth concealed behind or beneath them. Allegory thus reduces history to signification.[7] By irony I understand the momentary dismantling of the illusion of continuity between world and representation. Allegory conducts its reader to a realm of universal and atemporal truth, while irony makes present the moment of representation itself, calling attention to itself as a *figure* by denying the *literal* truth of what it says. Thus irony reverses allegory by reducing signification to the inscription of a historically present voice.[8]

Allegory projects the world of innocent speculation. In its mirror, the marriage of Isabel Thwaites to the first Lord Fairfax and the consequent rise of Appleton House and the Fairfax line out of the ruins of the nunnery specify a precedent text that glosses the meaning of the impending marriage of Mary Fairfax as the founding of a new and, at least, equally illustrious line. We do not

7. I have defined allegory here with respect to the peculiar temporality it develops in "Upon Appleton House." In *The Language of Allegory: Defining the Genre* (Ithaca: Cornell University Press, 1979), Maureen Quilligan argues against the assumption that allegory and *allegoresis* (the allegorical interpretation of nonallegorical texts) are identical procedures. Rejecting the traditional understanding of allegory as a "vertical" system that uses narrated actions to imply and conceal an allegorical truth, she argues that "all allegorical narrative unfolds as action designed to comment on the verbal implications of the words used to describe the imaginary action" (p. 53). This conversion of allegory from a "vertical" to a "horizontal" procedure has tricky implications for the kind of temporal classification I am here proposing, since it moves allegory away from any aspiration toward iconic representation and makes verbal representation its theme and essence. As my argument develops it will become clear that Marvell does indeed allegorize in Quilligan's sense at some points—developing narrative sections of the poem as commentaries on the puns and etymologies employed in his own text (see note 30, below). It is also true, however, that Marvell is thematically, even parodically, engaged with *allegoresis* as a general method of articulating the eternal and the temporal and that any generic classification of the poem along the lines suggested by Quilligan's definition would have to contend with this sophisticated and ambivalent inmixing. In advancing the definition given in my text, I am concerned not with allegory as a genre but as a trope, a manipulation of the text that encodes a specifiable relation of verbal representation to historical time. (I am indebted to Heather Dubrow for drawing my attention to this issue.)

8. Cf. Paul de Man's argument that the textual features of allegory and irony are antithetical codings of "a truly temporal predicament," in "The Rhetoric of Temporality," in Charles S. Singleton, ed., *Interpretation: Theory and Practice* (Baltimore: Johns Hopkins University Press, 1969), 173–209; the quoted phrase appears on p. 203. (This essay is also available in the revised edition of *Blindness and Insight: Essays in the Rhetoric of Contemporary Criticism* [Minneapolis: University of Minnesota Press, 1983], 187–228.) My argument departs from de Man's by demonstrating a dialectical linkage of allegory and irony in Marvell's poem, while de Man believes these two tropes to be historically distinct and incapable of mediation. In response to de Man's claim that irony supersedes allegory at a given literary historical moment, I seek to demonstrate the mutual implication of these two rhetorical codings of time at the moment of the inception of a narrative subject whose temporal predicament each, in its way, represents.

know whether Mary's 1657 marriage to the odious George Villiers, second duke of Buckingham, was anticipated when Marvell wrote his poem, but if any major aristocratic marriage was envisioned, the new line would certainly have invited thoughts of a reinvigoration of England through the marriage of the best of the old and new orders. The allegory of "Appleton House" thus defeats time and historical change by asserting an eternal cycle of Fairfacian fair doings. However, the poet's ironic self-presentation disrupts this timeless story and makes present the historical and contingent scene of its writing; it reverses the temporality of allegory and suggests that the family's future will determine the significance of its past. Displacing meaning from an originary act to its eventual consequence, Marvell's oscillation from allegory to irony projects character alternately as the iteration of an a priori essence and as the result of accumulated historical experiences. The allegorical character expresses his inborn essence in varied situations; the ironic character discovers and revises his meaning through such situations: He is the prototypical self-made man. Where allegory tends to be iconic, irony, depending as it does on the perceived difference between represented and representation, is ostentatiously verbal.

Marvell mediates iconic representation and verbal allusion by a variety of the rebus, which Geoffrey Hartman defines as "a special form of the emblem representing words by things . . . [in which] the text is projected by the picture or action of a particular stanza."[9] I use the term *rebus* to refer not only to a pictorial pun on the sound of a word but also, more broadly, to a general class of figures, the comprehension of which requires an intermediary pictorial step.[10] The rebus uses words to evoke a picture, which, at the moment of perception, refers itself to a second verbal text. This second text provides a necessary gloss according to which the meaning of the figure's occurrence in the poem is revised. The rebus, then, requires a double reading in which the developing narrative of the poem is juxtaposed to and reread within an alternative context through the device of a pictorial mediation.[11]

9. "Marvell, St. Paul and the Body of Hope" in *Beyond Formalism* (New Haven: Yale University Press, 1970), 164.

10. Hartman's use of the term *rebus* for Marvell's figure is opposed by Ann Berthoff in *The Resolved Soul: A Study of Marvell's Major Poems* (Princeton: Princeton University Press, 1970): "A rebus is a visual pun . . . , wordplay made visible. The semantics of the rebus is absolutely different from that of the emblem, which always has a temporal ambience" (p. 25, n. 16). Berthoff argues, "an emblem is a narrative moment from which the particular occasion has, to various degrees, been refined" (p. 24). But the figure with which I am concerned is not an emblem in Berthoff's sense. It does not "refine away" the "particular occasion." It effects a transfer or exchange of contexts so that the occasion represented in the poem may be read in the context of another occasion that is allegorically related to it. Rather than a visual moralization abstracted from a narrative context, as is the emblem, Marvell's rebus is the metonymy of a metaphor, the transfer of an analogy from one narrative context to another.

11. Cf. Harold Skulsky, "Upon Appleton House: Marvell's Comedy of Discourse," *ELH* 52 (1985): 603–4. Skulsky argues that the poet of "Appleton House" invites his auditor to "regard one notion as a representation or icon of another" (603), but he fails to consider the specific hermeneutic conventions at play in the poem, and consequently produces a curiously unhistorical reading that reduces what I see as a quite serious comic exploration of the nature of the self in the mid-seventeenth century to a celebration of the games language plays.

Paradigmatically, the second context to which the rebus points us and which it imposes as a gloss on the events narrated in the poem is a scriptural one. By alluding to scriptural texts in this way, Marvell transfers narrated events from their local, "historical" contexts to a providential narrative that subsumes and interprets them. Thus, the poem "contains great things in less" by progressively revealing that mundane, human actions are signs in a divine discourse. The movement from the historical to the providential demystifies the lived drama of human life by subsuming contingent and apparently meaningless events within a completed narrative that discloses their ultimate meaning.[12] The subsequent reading of the providential back into the historical discloses the divine intention in everyday life.[13] The rebus is, therefore, a particular, literary species of the scriptural type, and the term *rebus* may be taken with its Latin signification: The figure shows us that "Truth" is inscribed not only in the verbal revelation of Scripture but also *in the things* of this world—as illuminated by revelation. The same need to assert a renewed continuity of past and present and a new understanding of historical action during a period of radical social change underlies both the politics of the doctrinal ascendancy of typological hermeneutics in the Reformation and the poetics of the rebus.

The rebus is inherently unstable. Its perception as a rebus brings about its dissolution as a picture. Oscillating between a verbal decoding in which meaning is disclosed, in time, through reference to an absent, prior text, and a moment of pictorial presence that is not yet meaningful, it mediates between the allegorical and ironic responses to man's complex experience of time. The two phases of interpretation appear in Marvell's poem as a dialectical sequence of allegorical reference and ironic self-reference, promising but always deferring a synthesis of destiny and choice. The world of experience is negated yet preserved as significant in relation to an immortal and perfected design that is always present as design but whose material realization is perpetually deferred. It is from this complex temporal position that decisions such as Fairfax's must be made.

The characteristic oscillation of the rebus between ironic and allegorical speculation structures "Upon Appleton House" according to the relationship of meaning to visible or audible signs implied in the sixth stanza of the poem:

> *Humility* alone designs
> Those short but admirable Lines,
> By which, ungirt and unconstrain'd,
> Things greater are in less contain'd.
> Let others vainly strive t'immure

---

12. On the configuration of episodes within a narrative closure, see Louis O. Mink, "History and Fiction as Modes of Comprehension," *New Literary History* 1 (1970): 541–57.

13. Paul Ricoeur has written extensively on the notion of a double hermeneutic comprising an initial demystifying of the text followed by its restoration through a mythic interpretation. See for example, *Freud and Philosophy: An Essay on Interpretation,* trans. Denis Savage (New Haven: Yale University Press, 1970), esp. 20–36.

> The *Circle* in the *Quadrature*!
> These *holy Mathematicks* can
> In ev'ry Figure equal Man.
>
> (ll. 41–48)

The citation of short but admirable lines refers at once to the architectural moderation and grace of Appleton House and the octosyllabic couplets of "Upon Appleton House." The moment in which the signified of "Lines" slips from the estate to the poem is ironic because the word *Lines* at the same time asserts and cancels a historical referent, reminding us that we are not observing Appleton House but reading a verbal description of it.

Referring at once to Vitruvian architectural harmonies and the noble numbers of metrical composition, "holy Mathematicks" allows both poem and building to equal—let us say, to represent—man, to be the signature of poet or builder.[14] Thus, the famous Vitruvian figure of a man inscribed in a circle within a square succeeds where others "vainly strive t'immure / The *Circle* in the *Quadrature*."[15] Traditionally the circle stands for eternity and the square for earth or the world. Man, earth inhabited by soul, squares the circle and mediates the mundane and the divine.[16]

A similar route may be followed referring "Lines" to the poem itself rather than the architecture of the house. The poem's stanzas of eight lines of eight syllables each form the figure of the square that Puttenham associates with the earth and the *hominem quadratum* of Aristotle's *Ethics*.[17] The squares of the poem contain the humble spirit of the poet as the modest vault of Appleton

14. See Vitruvius, *On Architecture*, ed. from the Harleian MS 2767 and trans. by Frank Granger, in two volumes, The Loeb Classical Library (Cambridge: Harvard University Press, 1970), 1:7: "Both in general and especially in architecture are these two things found; that which signifies and that which is signified. That which is signified is the thing proposed about which we speak; that which signifies is the demonstration unfolded in systems of precepts."

15. Ibid., 1:161. The figure of the man circumscribed in a circle and square is also important in the construction of perspective pictures, whose anamorphic "now you see it; now you don't" reproduces the relationship of space and time given in Marvell's poem. See Ernest Gilman, *The Curious Perspective: Literary and Pictorial Wit in the Seventeenth-Century* (New Haven: Yale University Press, 1978), 22.

16. The literature on the Renaissance interpretation of the circle and the square is extensive. See, for example, Rudolph Wittkower, *Architectural Principles in the Age of Humanism* (London: A Tiranti, 1952), 15. Particularly useful on Marvell's use of the figure are Kitty W. Scoular, *Natural Magic: Strategies in the Presentation of Nature in English Poetry from Spenser to Marvell* (Oxford: Clarendon, 1965), 180, n. 2, and Maren-Sofie Røstvig, "'Upon Appleton House' and the Universal History of Man," *English Studies* 42 (1961): 342.

17. George (?) Puttenham, *The Arts of English Poesie: Continued into three Bookes: the first of Poets and Poesie, the second of Proportion, the third of Ornament* [1589], a facsimile reproduction, intro. by Baxter Hathaway (Kent: Kent State University Press, 1970), 113. The figure of the square in "Upon Appleton House" has been discussed by Wallace, *Destiny His Choice*, 237–38. Rosalie Colie cites Wither on the cube in this context in *"My Echoing Song": Andrew Marvell's Poetry of Criticism* (Princeton: Princeton University Press, 1970), 228, n. 25. It may also be noted that the sixteen syllables in each Marvellian couplet correspond to Vitruvius's diplomatic choice of a perfect number, *On Architecture*, 1:165.

House contains the spirit of Fairfax. Further, as Maren-Sofie Røstvig has shown, the square stanzas of "Upon Appleton House" are arranged into circles of numerologically significant repetitions.[18] The material presence of the poem may thus be seen as pictorially representing the mediation of earth and heaven, or, in narrative terms, of history and Providence.

The thematic circularity of the poem, which extends the microcosmic self-reference of the stanzaic structure to the narrative whole composed by the little squares, may be observed in the figure of the fishermen in the final stanza. The use of the epithet *"Tortoise-like"* (l. 773) for the "rational *Amphibii*" at the end of the poem sends the reader back to "the low-roof'd Tortoises [who] dwell / In cases fit of Tortoise-shell" (ll. 13–14) at the beginning and suggests that the meaning of this curious image is to be found endlessly replicated in the preceding text. The salmon fishers represented at the poem's close are amphibious because man belongs to both earth and heaven and because fishermen move between the elements of earth and water. Each visual representation—the squared circle, "the low roof'd Tortoise-shell," the salmon fishers—functions as a rebus to organize as pictorially present the truth that is revealed in the temporal unfolding of the poem, a truth that emerges, epiphanically, from the repeating patterns to be found *in the things* of Appleton House.

The allegorical narrative of the Fairfax estate is joined to the ironic lyric of the poet in the act of composition by the same holy mathematics that join the poem to the thing it describes through a common architecture. By obscuring the boundary between the verbal and the pictorial, the rebus represents a mediation of the boundary between the temporal and the eternal. The poet occupies this borderline or amphibious position when he retreats into the natural world of Fairfax's park, where *"Natures mystick Book"* appears as a *"Mosaick"* of light and shadow formed by the sun shining through the leaves (ll. 577–84). Given Marvell's fondness for using *light* as a vehicle for God's presence in his material creation, we may read "In this light *Mosaick*" as informed by the unmediated presence of the holy Spirit. Thus the poet reads the light in the light of the light.[19] But, while the celestial light makes the mosaic pattern on the trees and ground, it is the poet's "Phancy" that weaves the leaves into "Strange *Proph-*

18. "*In ordine di ruoto:* Circular Structure in 'The Unfortunate Lover' and 'Upon Appleton House,'" in K. Friedenreich, ed., *Tercentenary Essays in Honor of Andrew Marvell* (Hamden, Conn.: Archon Books, 1977), 245–65.

19. Against Skulsky's objection that "nothing in what precedes the phrase ['light Mosaick'] allows 'light' to be construed as a noun meaning illumination" ("Marvell's Comedy of Discourse," 619, n. 38), I offer his own substantial list of critics who have so read it. Against a theoretical restriction of semantic meaning to what is syntactically permitted stands the ample evidence that for many readers the resonances of the phrase exceed grammatical containment. Cf. Peter Schwenger, "'To Make his Saying true': Deceit in *Appleton House,*" *Studies in Philology* 77 (1980): 98–99: "[The Sibyl's leaves] are scattered to be recombined according to the poet's will rather than God's." But the point of Marvell's lines is that the poet's fancy, if properly schooled, can go on assembling innumerable and unexpected "leaves" in accord with the will of God, that it can read a divine meaning in *all things,* past, present and to come.

ecies." In doing this the fancy is informed by the light Mosaick of the Scriptures themselves, for it is only by calling on his previous knowledge of Moses's light that the poet can recognize in nature what "*Rome, Greece, Palestine,* ere said."[20] These earlier texts supply the meaning of nature and history by disclosing their ends, in both the logical and the temporal senses. In this way they contribute to one History that consumes, "Like *Mexique Paintings,* all the *Plumes*"; that is, the pens of all previous writers.

The rebus places the poet in a mediate position between what his senses perceive and what his intellect knows of a providential history conceived of as already completed. His fancy weaves the impressions of the moment into the already given design of scriptural history, and his poem, itself a light mosaic, represents the dialectical synthesis of sense and Scripture that lies at the center of eschatological thought. In this way the poetics of the rebus extend the restrained allegory of typological hermeneutics from biblical texts to the unfolding text of political choice.[21] Despite its theoretical neatness, in practice this process is tense and risky. For the poet on the borderline is at once a historical subject and the subject of history. He is enjoined to undertake historical acts, the rectitude of which is secured precisely by his insight into a transhistorical design. Like the reader of a rebus he must find truth as it emerges—fleetingly— from the midst of things.

The politics of Marvell's poetic practice may be understood in the light of Barbara Lewalski's observation that Protestant exegetes modified the medieval emphasis on Christ as "the antitype who fulfills all the types *forma perfectior,*" to shift the "emphasis from *quid agas* to God's activity in us [and] . . . assimilate the pattern of individual lives to the pervasive typological patterns discerned in

20. Wallace believes Marvell's source for these lines is Davenant's *Gondibert,* II.v.45: "Now they the *Hebrew, Greek,* and *Roman* spie; / Who for the Peoples ease, yoak'd them with Law; / Whom else, ungovern'd lusts would drive awrie; / And each his own way frowardly would draw" (cited from Wallace, *Destiny His Choice,* 250). The "Hebrew, Greek, and Roman" of Davenant refer to wise but pre-Christian writers. Adopting this reference for Marvell's poem makes the stanza invoke the superiority of the covenant of Love to that of Laws and the subsumption of the Old Testament in the New. Although *Gondibert* may indeed be Marvell's source, the fact that he reads in "the light Mosaick" argues that the Roman, Greek, and Hebrew texts in Marvell's poem are the principal linguistic representations of the Bible, all of which are enlightened by the Spirit of the Gospels, which fulfill and unify them. Taking these texts as translations rather than precedent essays in "natural theology" is not essential to my argument, but the advantage of doing so will be clarified by the discussion of typology below.

21. An important tradition of recent scholarship views typology as a Protestant hermeneutic opposed to the Thomistic allegory of the Jesuits and the even less restrained allegorical procedures of the neo-Platonists. See, for example, William Madsen, *From Shadowy Types to Truth: Studies in Milton's Symbolism* (New Haven: Yale University Press, 1968), esp. 83–85. Significantly different from these allegorical traditions though it may be, typology should be understood not as anti-allegorical but as a specific kind of allegorical procedure. The definition of allegory given at the beginning of this essay certainly includes it. For the relationship of typology to history, see Erich Auerbach, "Figura," in *Scenes from the Drama of European Literature* (New York: Meridan Books, 1959), 11–76.

Old and New Testament history."[22] Beyond and behind the doctrine of biblical literalism to which it is commonly attributed, this shift in hermeneutic practice bespeaks an understanding of the Christian subject as a narrative character who exists on the borderline of time and eternity and makes judgments and choices in time so as to actively fulfill his providential destiny.[23] Eschatological thought—with its articulation of prospective and retrospective points of view—is the doctrinal manifestation of a narrative conception of the subject. In "Upon Appleton House," the amphibious poet is situated on the borderline between his lived experience and a predestined Providence that interprets it. By relocating the meaning of temporally unfolding events in an eternally present design, the poet's fancy re-presents the perspective of pictorial presence and textual *differance* projected by the rebus as the point, moving in space and time, where the Christian ego is formed. The reader's progress from a diachronic series of episodes to a grasp of the synchronic design of the narrative reproduces within the representation the sublation of history into eternity that is the goal of the moral life.

Marvell's rebus, as the rhetorical shuttle of "fancy's" loom, thus performs a textual function analogous to the one called for by Hobbes in his description of Fancy as the faculty answerable at once to memory (history) and precept (design):

> Time and Education begets experience; Experience begets memory; Memory begets Judgment and Fancy: Judgment begets the strength and structure, and Fancy begets the ornaments of a Poem. The Ancients therefore fabled not absurdly in making memory the Mother of the Muses. For memory is the World *(though not really, yet so as in a looking glass)* in which the Judgment, the severer Sister, busieth her self in a grave and rigid examination of all the parts of Nature, and *in registring by Letters their order, causes, uses, differences, and resemblances;* Whereby the Fancy, when any work of Art is to be performed, findes her materials at hand and prepared for use, and needs no more then a swift motion over them, that what she wants, and is there to be had, may not lie too long unespied.[24]

Both fancy and judgment are grounded in memory, which is, itself, grounded in experience. Fancy, as a synthetic faculty, picks up the threads of experience and weaves them on the loom of judgment. The fabric thus woven assimilates new experience to the pattern of previous experience as threads might be added to a

---

22. *Protestant Poetics and the Seventeenth-Century Religious Lyric* (Princeton: Princeton University Press, 1979), 131–32.

23. Cf. Milton's description of Adam and Eve as "Authors to themselves in all / Both what they judge and what they choose" in *Paradise Lost* III. 122–23 and the discussion of typology in Marshall Grossman, *"Authors to Themselves": Milton and the Revelation of History* (Cambridge: Cambridge University Press, 1987), 12–21.

24. "Answer to Davenant's Preface to *Gondibert* 1650," in J. E. Spingarn, ed., *Critical Essays of the Seventeenth Century* (1909; rpt. Bloomington: Indiana University Press, 1968), 2:59 (italics added). Cf. Wallace, *Destiny His Choice*, 238–41.

cloth. Fancy's work is as good as the framework judgment supplies, as good as the design according to which new threads are incorporated into the fabric. Like Marvell, Hobbes identifies a historical failure of the precepts of "Moral vertue" as requiring a contemporary reliance on a specifically structural or architectural Fancy:

> But so far forth as the Fancy of man has traced the ways of true Philosophy, so far it hath produced very marvellous effects to the benefit of mankinde . . . Whatsoever commodity man receive from the observations of the Heavens, from the description of the Earth, from the account of Time, from walking on the Seas, and whatsoever distinguisheth the civility of *Europe* from the Barbarity of the *American* savages, is the workmanship of Fancy but guided by the Precepts of true Philosophy. But where these precepts fail, as they have hitherto failed in the doctrine of Moral vertue, there the Architect, *Fancy,* must take the Philosophers part upon herself.[25]

For Hobbes, the architect assembles materials out of experience, according to precepts supplied by philosophy, or discovers these precepts where philosophy has failed to provide them.[26] Similarly, Marvell's fancy creates a verbal architecture in accord with the precepts of the holy mathematics to join spirit to matter through the composite or amphibious nature of man. Fancy both discovers and constitutes a divine design, which is revealed at once in Scripture and in nature. That two such politically different figures as Hobbes and Marvell should inscribe the same set of ambivalences around "Moral vertue" suggests to me that we have reached the rhetorical substrate of the ideological conflicts between them, the boundary of what could be thought in and immediately after the English revolution.

The dialectic of allegory and irony conveyed by the rebus in Marvell's poem—which we may now understand as a figure of the dialectic of completed design and temporal sequence—represents the paradoxical temporality of eschatological thought, which determines present action not by prior cause but by subsequent fulfillment. The moments of pictorial fullness in the poem are also necessarily moments of linguistic transparency. The putative autonomy of the sensory image conceals the ongoing, constitutive activity of the poet's fancy and creates an emblem that becomes meaningful only when it is restored to the narrative. Thus the meaning of Appleton House cannot be indicated without the

25. Hobbes, "Answer to Davenant's Preface," 2:60.

26. Cf. Leone Battista Alberti; *Ten Books on Architecture,* trans. into Italian by Cosimo Bartoli and into English by James Leoni, Venetian Architect, 1755, ed., Joseph Ryhwert (London: A. Tiranti, 1955), preface, xi: "We consider that an Edifice is a Kind of Body consisting, like all other Bodies, of Design and of Matter; the first is produced by Thought, the other by Nature; so that the one is to be provided by the Application and Contrivance of the Mind, and the other by due Preparation and Choice. And we further reflected, that neither the one nor the other of itself was sufficient, without the Hand of an Experienced Artificer, that knew how to form his Materials after a just Design." Hobbes's *fancy* is to poetry what the architect is to building and, to a surprising degree, the language of the materialistic Hobbes remains in touch with that of the neo-Platonic tradition of the Renaissance.

excursion into the history of the estate and the Fairfax family on the one side and the prophecy of Mary Fairfax's future marriage on the other. As "Beasts are by their Denns exprest," Fairfax's moral character is expressed in Appleton House; reciprocally, Appleton House can speak only as an allegorical representation of the history of the Fairfax line. *Signans* and *signatum,* vehicle and tenor, are, in practice, reversed. While the tortoise's life is determined by his shell, the narrative of "Appleton House" confirms the easier belief that the Fairfax shell is determined by the family's character. The final cause of the tortoise's shell is not his ecological niche and certainly not his choice, but the choice the Creator has made, in advance, for the tortoise's participation in creation as a whole. Its role as a sign of the divine order is its destiny.

The reversal of sign and referent noted in Marvell's poetic practice playfully discloses the undecideability of destiny and choice and of man as creator and as creature within such a constitution of the subject. The serious implication of this playful design is the representation of a self that is known to be destined but is experienced as radically indeterminate. This oscillation of perspective between an indeterminate present and an anticipated destiny parallels the ironic and allegorical polarities of Marvell's poetics on the one hand and the context in which moral choices—such as Fairfax's withdrawal from his military command—must be made on the other. The very instability of the rebus affords a privileged view of the formation of a new political actor. Suspended between allegorically iconic and ironically verbal conceptions of the self, the poetics of the rebus superposes the newly emerging Cartesian subject, whose self-awareness is the arbiter of certainty within which all things are contained, and the older understanding of the subject as one who is under the authority of another.[27] Marvell's amphibious subject contains and creates his destiny by anticipating his role as a character in a narrative always already produced under the authority of a divine author.

The notion that history unfolds within a transcendent and wholly conceived Providence has specific implications for the individual attempting to evaluate the moral character of his acts. Marvell explores these implications as they pertain to the Fairfax family and, in more interesting ways, as they affect the poet in the act of composition.

The evaluation of Fairfax's withdrawal from his command waits upon the unfolding of consequent events. Since these events are already complete from the perspective of Providence, the ethics of the withdrawal are determined but

27. The OED records no uses of "subject" in the modern philosophical sense, "for the mind or ego considered as the subject of all knowledge," before the eighteenth century. Transitional uses are cited from 1682 and 1697. However, the late change in the use of the word *subject* is doubtless part of a general shift toward an experience of the mind as the center of the "cogito" that had been taking place for some time. On the development of an English vocabulary of inwardness to accompany the formation of free-standing subjectivity, see Anne Ferry, *The "Inward" Language: Sonnets of Wyatt, Sidney, Shakespeare, Donne* (Chicago: University of Chicago Press, 1983).

not yet fully knowable. A parallel case in the poem is the justification of the earlier Fairfax's violent "liberation" of Isabel Thwaites from the Cistercian nuns: "Yet, against Fate, his Spouse they kept; / And the great Race would intercept" (ll. 247–48). The weak justification of the legal warrant is given divine assent by a reading of posterior events. Moral validation is subsequent to the act; necessarily so, given the processes of eschatological thought.

But Marvell's ironic appreciation of the present moment does not allow the problems of eschatological ethics to escape unnoted. Consider the episode near the end of the poem when the Fairfaxes, by choosing a mate for Mary, will make "*Destiny* their *Choice*" (l. 744). The imagery is of sacrifice: "Whence, for some universal good, / The *Priest* shall cut the sacred Bud" (ll. 741–42). The indeterminacy of the future is emphasized by the linguistic indeterminacy of the vague "some universal good." The loss of possibility implicit in choice becomes, from a temporally reversed point of view, the achievement of destiny.

Like the shadowy patterns of the leaves that the poet read in the light mosaic, the still virgin Mary is a cipher of limitless potential meanings, subsuming, as do Mexique Paintings, all potential assemblies of the material at hand:

> *She* counts her Beauty to converse
> In all the Languages as *hers;*
> Nor yet in those *her self* imployes
> But for the *Wisdome,* not the Noyse;
> Nor yet the *Wisdome* would affect,
> But as 'tis *Heavens Dialect.*
>
> (ll. 707–12)

"Heavens Dialect," in this passage, remains meaning *in potentia* until time renders it readable: "Till Fate her worthily translates, / And find a *Fairfax* for our *Thwaites*" (ll. 747–48).

The depiction of the halcyon flying across the darkening horizon, with which Marvell marks Mary's entrance into the poem, provides a rebus of Mary's temporal predicament, which is, in turn, the predicament of the Marvellian subject, suspended between his own moment of moral choice and an always deferred higher authority:

> The viscous Air, wheres'ere She fly,
> Follows and sucks her Azure dy;
> The gellying Stream compacts below,
> If it might fix her shadow so;
> The stupid Fishes hang, as plain
> As *Flies* in *Chrystal* overt'ane;
> And Men the silent *Scene* assist,
> Charm'd with the *Saphir-winged Mist.*
>
> (ll. 673–80)

Like the halcyon, Mary moves along a borderline between light and dark, knowledge and ignorance. This border is now revealed to be the present, always moving yet, in a deeper sense, always still, always the single point between an irreversible past and an unpredictable future. Temporal "virginity" freezes the narrative and threatens, like Keats's Grecian Urn, to "tease us out of thought." An emblem, abstracted from its narrative context, leaves us hanging in the air, like stupefied fish, waiting for the inevitable and necessary splash back into temporality and narrative.

The identification of Mary and Isabel implies a corollary identification of the garden retreat with the nunnery and emphasizes the responsibility of the self to its historical context, the individual to the race.[28] The implicit comment on Fairfax's retirement is clear, if complex. The retirement itself is a historic act that will be revealed, at a later date, to have been either a humble recognition of and submission to Providence or a proud and vainglorious attempt to withdraw from God's already written narrative. Fairfax's action is at once freely taken and part of the plan, and his moral character will be disclosed in and through a subsequent history that extends to the apocalypse. Only then will the significance of any world historical episode be fixed. Moral virtue is the ability to recognize the pattern as it develops, to discover one's destiny in time to choose it, and thus to construct one's life as a narrative text. One might add, however, that insofar as Fairfax accepts this equation of his own ethos and the accumulating sum of his freely taken actions, he has already invested his destiny with the rising bourgeois class and broken with the rentier past that Appleton House might be taken to represent, a "predestination" through choice reflected in the poem by the emphasis on such modern agricultural practices as the flotation of the meadow.

The belief that one's present acts become legible only when understood as signs in an incompletely known text, existing in an impenetrably alien temporal matrix, engenders a sharp discontinuity between the self as subject of one's acts and the self as subjected to the transcendental script of Providence. This discontinuity is explored within "Upon Appleton House" in at least two episodes. In stanza 71, the poet's reading in the book of nature momentarily suggests a simple continuity between nature and its human observer. In the following stanza, the poet acquires the mute language of the natural world, and he and nature become fixed in a discourse that is likened to a trap: "And where I Language want, my Signs / The Bird upon the Bough divines; / And more attentive there doth sit / Then if She were with Lime-twigs knit" (ll. 571–74). The retreat into nature is also a retreat into a discourse of fixed gestures, a slippage from human

28. Cf. Don Cameron Allen, *Image and Meaning: Metaphoric Traditions in Renaissance Poetry* (Baltimore: Johns Hopkins University Press, 1960), 147: "[The Thwaites and Mary Fairfax episodes] are brought together as history and prophecy, as 'Scatter'd Sibyls Leaves' and the light 'Mosaick.'" Rosalie Colie sees Mary Fairfax as the typological fulfillment of the antitype, Isabel Thwaites (*"My Echoing Song,"* 252).

language to natural signs. Like bird song, these signs are limited to a timelessly repeated self-assertion. Unable to refer beyond the situation of their production, such signs recall the ironic reduction of meaning by the assertion of a here and now that cannot be identical with the present of the text but refuse the allegorical assertion of a meaning that is elsewhere than the text. The language of the retreat into nature recalls that of "The Garden," where the solitary nature-lover reduces the social and historical symbolism of "the Palm, the Oke, or Bayes" (l. 2) to literal self-reference: "Fair Trees: where s'eer your barkes I wound, / No Name shall but your own be found" (ll. 23–24). Nature's time, measured in "The Garden" by a sundial of flowers, is cyclical, an endless, seasonal succession. Such a temporality of repetition looks back to the agrarian world that supported the hegemony of landed aristocrats. But Marvell's Protestant poetics again silently "predestines" the reader to a representation of the self in which man's responsibility is to act within the linear time of irreversible events until history is subsumed in eternity.

By weaving together the observations of experienced life and the prophetic text of Scripture, man discovers the "holy Mathematicks" of divine architecture. Thus, in stanza 73, to which I have already alluded, "Phancy" begins to weave "strange" or new prophecies. The poet escapes the pictorial stasis of his "lime-twig" discourse with nature and, having recourse once more to human language, resumes his narrative. By assimilating the images of nature to the narrative patterns of revelatory verbal texts, the *"Prelate of the Grove"* preaches, in words, his own incarnation as a sign, not in Nature, but in a poem, a lesser thing in which the greater is contained. The rhetoric of his incarnation is the textual representation of a man whose actions make and are made by history as a poet's words make poems, by whose form they are constrained.

Man's amphibious nature as the producer and product of his own history, as the chooser of an already chosen destiny, and as the *image* of an *invisible* God is dramatized by the disjunction of the author *of* the poem and the author *in* the poem in the episode of the slain rail:

> But bloody *Thestylis,* that waites
> To bring the mowing Camp their Cates,
> Greedy as Kites has trust it up,
> And forthwith means on it to sup:
> When on another quick She lights,
> And cryes, he call'd us *Israelites;*
> But now, to make his saying true,
> Rails rain for Quails, for Manna Dew.
> (ll. 401–8)

Thestylis at once illustrates and parodies the use of typological metaphor: she supplies the reference to the biblical text, the extension of the biblical context to the historical present ("he call'd us Israelites"), and the typological substitution that fulfills the prophecy ("Rails rain for Quails, for Manna Dew"). The poem first presents the death of the rails as contingent, but Thestylis's comic typology re-presents it as destined.

Thestylis, moreover, addresses the poet in the act of composition, appropriating to her interpretation the authority to "make his saying true." This momentary representation of the struggle for authority between the intentions of an author and the seemingly independent life of his created world is the textual image of the tension between individual choice and providential destiny. In the moment that Thestylis asserts the literal truth of the poet's world, she reduces him to a figure in it, passing him through the looking glass of verbal speculation: "Where all things gaze themselves, and doubt / If they be in it or without" (ll. 637–38). When the fictionality of the poem's narrative surfaces in Thestylis's claim that her actions confirm rather than reflect the poet's characterization, the materiality of language represents the surplus of destiny over choice, as the typological fulfillment of the text takes place only on the level of the signifier, as a phonic play on words: "Rails rain for Quails, for Manna Dew."[29] The providential hand guiding this substitution is the attraction of a rhyme, and the difference between type and antitype is precisely the phonemic difference r / q.[30] The typological shuttle between diachronic experience and synchronic design— between history and providence—is mirrored in and by the linguistic shuttle between a diachronic series of sounds and a synchronic system of phonemic differences. Thus the oscillation between space and time, between pictorial and verbal text, between description and narration in Marvell's poem, can be seen as an (ironically) allegorical representation of the way the self both produces and is produced by its language on one level and its history on another.[31]

The escape of the writing self from the rebus of language that can never fully

29. Don Cameron Allen sees the episode of Thestylis and the rail as an allegory of the civil war, the rail representing the slain king (*Image and Meaning*, 135–37). The possibility of such a reading is another illustration of the typological pattern. The narrated events refer at once to a scriptural and a historical context. In this way the historical event is understood in light of its putative providential significance.

30. Cf. Augustine's more straightforward assertion that the anagrammatic pun on the Greek ΙΧΘΥΣ and the appellation of Christ is a divine inscription in the language and may serve as the basis of an allegorical reading of the blessing: "be fruitful and multiply." *Confessions*, XIII, xxii–xxiii. See also the relevant discussion in Marshall Grossman, "Augustine, Spenser, Milton and the Christian Ego," *New Orleans Review* 11 (1984): 9–17, and Quilligan's argument that "allegorical narrative unfolds as a series of punning commentaries, related to one another on the most literal of verbal levels—the sounds of words" (*Language of Allegory*, 22). Thestylis's paronomasic reproduction of Exodus surfaces as the ironic moment of *allegoresis* itself by foregrounding the dependence of typology itself on an association made only on the level of signifier. In effect, it puts in question the Augustinian institution of allegorical interpretation by repeating it as parody.

31. Cf. de Man, "Rhetoric of Temporality," 196: "The reflective disjunction [of the subject] not only occurs *by means of* language as a privileged category, but it transfers the self out of the empirical world into a world constituted of and in language, a language that it finds in the world like one entity among others, but that remains unique in being the only entity by means of which it can differentiate itself from the world. Language thus conceived divides the subject into an empirical self, immersed in the world, and a self that becomes like a sign in its attempt at differentiation and self-definition."

and "literally" contain it graphically depicts the problematic relationship of self to time that is the burden of much of Marvell's poetry. The dialectic of icon and sign, image and word, established in "Upon Appleton House" is the rhetorical strategy through which the poem contains the poet, but also, necessarily, allows him to escape. The image is rectified by the word, the word made full by the image. The poet creates the poem that includes but does not contain him, as God created a universe that includes but does not contain him. Man is an amphibium; *in* this world but not contained by it. But his existence beyond it must be read in a book whose time is irreducibly other; each of his actions in this world is a sign in the as yet unreadable portion of that book, to be judged retrospectively by whether or not it fits the rebus that joins him to eternity. The question of withdrawal from worldly affairs—of Fairfax's withdrawal from the Commonwealth government or the poet's withdrawal into the *locus amoenus* of the garden—is inscribed within this charmed (and charming) circle.

"Upon Appleton House" is neither a lyric nor a narrative poem, dedicated neither to the ironically textual presence of the poet's absent voice nor to the allegorical incorporation of that absent voice into a literary utopia in which its presence is ensured by its self-proclaimed atemporality. Similarly the subjectivity represented in the poem is neither that of a secure landholder in a rentier oligarchy nor that of a fully developed bourgeois. In fact the consolidation of bourgeois ideology will be marked by the concealment of that which Marvell's poem reveals, the social construction of the historical actor in relation to time and the modes of production. What will soon be absorbed within an ideology of nature is shown, like Appleton House itself, under (re)construction. But poems do not simply reflect ideological changes; they also participate in them, and it is this mutual reflection, this reading of the self as it is represented in its literary products, that I have been most concerned to show. The Marvellian subject wears his temporal and epistemological predicament as the tortoise wears his shell. Like a fisherman whose head is shod in his canoe, he exists along a horizon between day and night, past and future, light and darkness. Irremediably outside the sign of himself in history and Providence, he can only terminate his contemplation and act by identifying himself with that sign, as equivocally determined in two distinct narratives, one of earth and one of heaven, one ironic, the other allegorical. The actor who emerges from this identification crosses the boundary of the poem and enters the material text of history.

Richard Strier, Leah Marcus, Richard Helgerson,
and James G. Turner

15. Historicism, New and Old:
Excerpts from a Panel Discussion

[The panel discussion from which the following statements are excerpted was organized and chaired by Richard Strier and featured, in addition to Strier, Leah Marcus, Richard Helgerson, and James G. Turner. Intended to be informative but not polemical, the discussion sparked an energetic and positive response from the audience. The excerpts presented here have been edited and, in some cases, augmented by the panelists.]

Leah Marcus

The word *historicism* was never so monolithic as to connote one single all-embracing methodology. In the 1980s however, we are confronted with a historicism divided into two major camps marked by differences in method and purpose: there is the old historicism, not so called until the advent of the new historicism, a deliberate break with the old and a cohesive movement to supplant it. Here, I will argue that it is time (and past time) for the old and the new historicism to look beyond the rift between them in order to learn from each other's methodological strengths. We who consider ourselves historicists can profitably look to the new historicism for a whole range of new interdisciplinary approaches, an infusion of new theory and vitality; nevertheless, we need to continue to take much of our working methodology, our techniques for research and investigation, from that which is labeled "old."

Very generally, the old historicism operated according to narrative paradigms. It emphasizes *sequences* of events moving dynamically through time. It sees meaning as emerging from the shaping of events over time—in terms of progression and even progress, causality, or repetition. The new historicism tends to deny or erode causality and displays little interest in dealing with gradual cultural change. If we are to seek a paradigm for the new historicism—or "Cultural Poetics" as it is sometimes termed instead—we can find it more readily in the lyric poem. New historicist analyses characteristically begin with narrative: a brief anecdote that serves to introduce an alien cultural pattern that will be further elaborated in the body of the critical essay. But the emphasis in the new historicism is not on sequence but on simultaneity—the identification and analysis of structures that establish a common cultural language, echoing each other through various levels of a society at a given historical moment. While the old historicism tends to be linear in terms of its guiding metastructures, the new is more nearly cross-sectional—a mode of analysis that, like the formalist analysis of a lyric poem, captures a given moment in spatial rather than temporal terms by demonstrating connections among clusters of meaning that seem to occur together.

Given its predilection for narrative paradigms, it is not surprising that the old historicism is good at charting linear affiliations of various sorts—chains of political, economic, and social causality that allow us to talk about literature and history as developing over time according to identifiable patterns of influence. The new historicism has challenged many of the old historicism's filiative structures of interpretation. In the new historicism as a mode of literary analysis, lines of influence are replaced by more indefinite and unspecifiable intertextual relationships. Poets and playwrights are less writers than written, shaped by the culture that their own work simultaneously articulates. In the new historicism, what we used to call "the author's intent" usually gets lost or denied. Intentionality is, of course, a cultural construct itself, one that attained particular prominence in the late Renaissance. But as used by the old historicism, the idea of authorial intent allowed access to texts on a level that formed a fertile ground for other modes of analysis. It was a construct that performed for the old historicism several useful functions that are largely unavailable to the new.

For one thing, intentionality was an invaluable tool in dealing with matters of canonicity, particularly in the enlargement of that body of writing which is privileged with the name of Literature. The mechanism of intentionality worked something like this: a given text excluded from the canon on account of its seeming incoherence or irretrievably flawed aesthetics could be "redeemed" for Literature by an appeal to its historical context. By seeing a work as "authored," as trying to "make sense" and achieve coherence in terms of a given cultural situation, the old historicism was able to rehabilitate neglected texts by making them accessible and thus to enlarge the canon. By disallowing intentionalist analysis, even in the instrumental terms I have described here, the new historicism has lost a valuable tool for performing such acts of salvage. In fact, until very recently the new historicism has dealt almost exclusively with canonical texts. In terms of its own ideological agenda, it is far more likely to question the very concept of canonicity, and commit itself to the recovery of silenced voices than the old historicism. Yet, to the extent that it elides intentionality it deprives itself of a useful mechanism for making such voices audible by making them at least minimally intelligible, giving them the basic grounding in an ordered scheme for meaning that allows us to go on to probe their dissonances and contradictions.

It is arguable that the new historicism is, in covert ways, strongly dependent on the old historicism's capacity to bring a text that seems irretrievably "foreign," chaotic, and unintelligible into contact with our own systems for conferring meaning. That is a hidden continuity between the old and new historicism which needs to be more openly acknowledged. Moreover, the new historicism's abolition of the construct called authorial intent makes it harder for us to make useful distinctions between "authored" and "nonauthored" texts and the different codes of meaning by which contemporaries might have approached them. To be able to make that sort of distinction is extremely useful, at least if we are dealing with writings of the English Renaissance, in which the invocation and deconstruction of intentionalist modes of reading might turn out to be highly significant even within a single fascinating, problematic text.

Another area in which the new historicism has lost an interpretive technique available to the old is in its ability to mobilize different models for interaction among various forces active within a given culture. The overriding "cultural poetics" that tend to be favored by the new historicism can become a kind of prison, lead to an interpretive gridlock that, however profoundly anti-formalist in its insistence on literature's embeddedness in wider cultural patterns, can become a metaformalism of its own with no way of accounting for change and development, for the quirky, sometimes quasi-independent functioning of various sociocultural forces at any given time. There are instances when we need to be able to assign, at least temporarily and for explanatory purposes, a set of independent functions to one or another group or institution operating within a given cultural matrix. That is easy under the old historicism, much more problematic with the new.

All of this is not to suggest that the new historicism lacks its own set of strengths. If the old historicism excels at familiarizing the alien and the incomprehensible, the new is far more successful in dealing with the overly familiar—in exploring ruptures and discontinuities, in "Estranging the Renaissance," to borrow the title of the 1985 English Institute, in taking texts that have been worked over for generations to the point of stultification and making them suddenly seem fresh and unexplored. If the old historicism altered the canon by creating new contexts for intelligibility, the new historicism revitalizes the canon by giving us new ways of going beyond that intelligibility to reconceptualize texts that have become, over decades of interpretation, *too* orderly and predictable. The new historicist breakdown of the distinction between literature and other things enlarges the interpretive scope of our work by giving us access to anthropological, psychoanalytic, and poststructural methodologies on a level at which they were previously unavailable. At least potentially, the new historicism therefore has as useful a set of methodological resources for enlarging the canon as does the old historicism, along with a far more potent set of weapons for undermining the hegemonic force of the very concept of canonicity. But that potential remains largely unexplored in practice, in part because the major literature has seemed to offer challenge enough to the new methodologies, in part, I suspect, because the new historicism has been reluctant to draw upon resources of the old historicism that might compromise its sense of distinctness, its rift with what came before.

I am arguing, in brief, that the strength of each historicism is the weakness of the other. Each addresses with particular effectiveness an area in which the other is prone to deadness or rigidity. The new historicism revitalizes tired and overfamiliar texts; the old historicism, potentially at least, can creatively unsettle the new historicist tendency to spatialize analysis to the point that cultural change and the mechanisms by which it happens are lost. Rather than segregating ourselves defiantly and defensively in separate camps as old or new historicists, we should begin to think more dialectically about what each set of methods has to offer across the rift we ourselves have created. The two historicisms are interdependent in that each has been defined against—and to the exclusion of—the other.

If we are to draw on the strengths of each set of methods, we need first of all to cultivate more flexibility in interpretive practice. If old historicist methods are shaken free of some of the assumptions with which they have traditionally been bound up, they can offer us a whole new bag of tools that we can use in various combinations to do new things with texts. We need to be able to identify the area and purpose of our critical endeavor at any given point: sometimes we will find ourselves searching to articulate large cultural patterns, and at such times we may find new historicist methods most valuable; at other times, we may find ourselves needing to reconstruct highly detailed cultural transactions that are unrecoverable without old historicist techniques of research and causal interpretation. Old historicist microanalysis can contribute to our sense of the nuance and complexity of large cultural patterns, but it quickly becomes "mere" pedantry, empty antiquarianism, without the charge of dynamism that broader theoretical frameworks like those generated by the new historicism can bring to it. We need to localize our methods—vary them along with the materials we are working with, and according to the kinds of tasks we are trying to perform. If greater methodological eclecticism makes it harder for us to identify ourselves definitively as old or new historicists, perhaps that is an outcome we need neither fear nor avoid.

Richard Helgerson

After two days of lively and interesting papers on early seventeenth-century poetry and politics, it seems to me appropriate to turn the question we've been asking the past around and ask it of ourselves. What then is the politics of our own critical practice? More particularly, what is the politics of the new historicism that has in various ways, overtly and covertly, been at issue in this conference? *Has* the new historicism *a* politics? If so, is it, when once brought to the surface and fully articulated, a politics to which many of us would willingly subscribe?

First a brief definition—one that I've used before—of new-historicist practice. Its most obvious characteristic is a concern for the historical specificity of all forms of discourse, including literary discourse. A new historicist denies literature the iconic autonomy that had been claimed for it by formalist critics, denies literature its cultural transcendence. Instead he (or she) insists on the involvement of the literary in the mundane and conflict-ridden workings of power by which the social order is constituted and maintained. If a literary work survives the moment of its creation, it owes that survival, a new historicist would say, less to its universality than to its continual reinscription in ever-changing patterns of authority. It survives because it continues to serve powerful interests that have a stake in its survival.

Now, for all its talk of power and authority (favorite new-historicist buzz words), this definition doesn't sound especially political in any but an academic way. Clearly new historicism does oppose other sorts of literary criticism and thus claims for its adherents (as would any other movement) a larger share of the good things—publications, appointments, promotions, fellowships—that are the reward for academic success. But it doesn't seem to oblige one to take any particular stand on issues of public moment in the way the papers we have been hearing have seen Donne, Jonson, Herbert, Herrick, Marvell, Milton, and the rest doing. Was early seventeenth-century poetry political to a degree that late twentieth-century literary criticism isn't?

Probably so. Despite elaborate claims made during the last couple of centuries for poetic autonomy, it is probably true that poetry in the seventeenth century was a less autonomous discourse—a discourse less removed from the day-to-day pressures of ordinary political life—than literary criticism is today. Conflicts between Anglican and Puritan, between court and country, between king and Parliament impinged on poets as conflicts between, say, Democrats and Republicans don't impinge on us, at least not as critics.

Still, new-historicist theory itself would suggest that such autonomy is never complete, that no discourse is free from ideological commitment. And there is in the case of new historicism evidence that those commitments may be of a rather troubling sort. Most suggestive is the strong emergence in the last couple of years of a closely allied movement in Britain that calls itself "cultural materialism." Unlike American new historicists, the cultural materialists have no shyness about announcing their political allegiance. They are Marxists, committed to the radical political program of the British Labour party's left wing, and they obviously think that their critical methods, methods that are virtually indistinguishable from those of the new historicists, serve the cause of revolution. By discovering the historical specificity of even the greatest literary works (Shakespeare has been a favorite target lately), they expose the lie of universality and cultural transcendence from which, they suggest, our middle-class and capitalist social order derives its legitimacy. By bringing down its "monuments of unaging intellect," they hope to bring down the bourgeois state.

An unlikely project? Perhaps. Discussions of Renaissance literature take place too far from the great centers of power to have much effect on them. Neither Reagan nor Thatcher has ever expressed much worry about readings of Herrick, Marvell, or even Shakespeare. And bourgeois institutions, including the university, have shown a remarkable ability to co-opt their critics—particularly critics who owe their economic well-being to those very institutions. Still, the question remains: Are American new historicists engaged, however unknowingly and however futilely, in a similar project of radical subversion? Is even a sedate gathering like this an unsuspected nest of pinkos and fellow travelers?

In a very brief comment of this sort, I haven't time even to make a start at answering these questions. Much could, I'm sure, be said on both sides—and some of it will, I hope, be said in our discussion. But I do want to add that I find the current prospect both alarming (in a mild sort of way) and inescapable. The most unqualified defenses I've heard recently of the cultural values we are so busy undermining have come from a Russian émigré novelist, from Chinese survivors of the Maoist Cultural Revolution, and from an Eastern European opponent of Soviet hegemony—all concerned with defending *themselves* against the incursion of a totalitarian state. With people like this arguing the case for high art, and arguing it with such motivation, I feel a little uncomfortable being on the other side, especially when my comrades-in-arms identify as their chief villain a nasty ideological formation called "liberal humanism." In America liberal humanism has long been the *bête noire* of the fundamentalist far right. And most of us once thought ourselves both liberals and humanists.

But all the same, though the company is sometimes uncomfortable, a commitment to the set of assumptions I defined as characteristic of the new historicism seems to me, as I think it does to many of my contemporaries, inevitable. It fits our personal experience as members of the antiwar generation of the sixties and our professional experience as the heirs of a discredited and deconstructed formalism. We may have merely bought into another ideology, but it feels like truth. Whatever its political consequences, we can hardly do literary criticism any other way.

So where does that leave us? Manufacturing the shovels that will bury us? Maybe not. But if not, what else are those tools good for?

Richard Strier

Perhaps the first thing to say about "new historicism" is that the phrase itself is distractingly ambiguous. It means different things depending on which of the terms in it one emphasizes. In Jean Howard's essay on "The New Historicism in Renaissance Studies," which has attained an oddly canonical status, the emphasis is on the second term, new *historicism,* so that "historicism" is what is "new" as opposed to a previously dominant formalism. This is the understanding of the phrase that is prevalent in other (non-Renaissance) fields of English literary study, especially Romanticism, but not in American studies. This understanding of the phrase makes sense with regard to the general history of English studies since its institutionalization, and with regard to a general shift away from the new formalism of "deconstruction" very recently, but it does not make sense with regard to English Renaissance studies. English Renaissance studies has always, despite the prominence of Donne and Marvell in new critical theory and practice, been dominated by historical scholarship. Tuve, wrongly taken as a model historicist, has always been taken (wrongly) to have won her battle with Empson, wrongly conceived as anti-historicist. In English Renaissance as in American studies, the point of the phrase is the adjective, a new as opposed to an "old" type of historical study.

The trouble with this polemical edge is that it often relies on a parodic view of "old" historicism. Most of us, especially those of the "new" persuasion, would readily agree that "the simplicities of Burckhardt seem a long way behind us." As Gordon Braden has recently pointed out, this happy agreement is extremely unfortunate and unearned (although it seems a necessary structural delusion for every field to believe that it is somehow constantly transcending its founding figures); Braden rightly describes Burckhardt's *Civilization of the Renaissance in Italy* as itself engaged in the ("new historicist"?) enterprise of "reading a particular culture as a unified whole, of integrating political, social and material history together with our continuing response to the art and literature of the time."[1]

The "new historicism" is not primarily an archival movement. Its triumphs are not discoveries of new documents but stunning and suggestive reinterpretations and reconfigurings of existing materials, of materials in fact discovered by the "old" historicists, the nineteenth- and twentieth-century scholars and antiquarians who put together the variorum editions, collected accounts of popular pastimes, edited the old books as historical curiosities, and found the textual and historical sources for the works of Shakespeare and others. I do not wish to deny that Stephen Greenblatt does something new with the relation of Samuel Harsnet and *Lear* or that Louis Montrose does something new with Simon Forman's Journals; what I do wish to deny is that these scholars need to be antagonistic or condescending to their forebears (forbearance to forebears seems to be my theme). At times, "new" history is simply "old" history rephrased. I see no fundamental difference between Foucault's "Renaissance episteme" and Tillyard's "Renaissance world picture"—they present the same (misleading) view and base themselves on many of the same texts. "Epistemes," however, have a different ring to them. Finally, it should be acknowledged that the "old" historicism is neither, as the Burckhardt example suggests, a simple thing nor a single thing. Many different sorts of historical inquiry are lumped under the label *old*—political history, intellectual history, descriptions of customs, etc.—just as the conception of a single "new" historicism may well be misleading.[2]

1. "It's Not the Years, It's the Mileage," *New Literary History* 14 (1983): 673.
2. This paragraph draws on some points in Heather Dubrow and Richard Strier, "The Historical Renaissance," the introduction to Dubrow and Strier, eds., *The Historical Renaissance: New Essays in Tudor and Stuart Literature and Culture* (Chicago: University of Chicago Press, 1988).

As Leah Marcus has pointed out, the "new" historicism has its weaknesses as well as its undoubted strengths. Much of the strength of the "new historicism" comes from its adoption of terms and assumptions from contemporary cultural anthropology, from the work of Clifford Geertz and others. The key and enabling assumption is that art is a cultural practice that is to be seen in relation to the other cultural practices of a society. As Geertz explains, "what this implies, among other things, is that the definition of art in any society is never wholly intra-aesthetic. . . . The chief problem presented by the sheer phenomenon of aesthetic force, in whatever form and in result of whatever skill it may come, is how to place it within the other modes of social activity, how to incorporate it into the texture of a particular pattern of life."[3] This premise allows for the striking juxtapositions of works of art with other practices that are such a salient feature of "new historicist" writing. Ideally, one comes away from a "new historicist" treatment of a text with a new sense of the location of that text, or certain features of it, in its culture, and a new sense of the culture as a whole.

The problems with this approach flow directly from its strengths. The Geertzian approach implies that at any given historical moment, a culture is remarkably and totally unified and, in some deep structural sense, homogeneous. Only this assumption allows for the striking juxtapositions and the freedom of movement in the new historicist text. The trouble with this conception of "reading" a culture, however, is that it seems to rely on a very old-fashioned thematizing and totalizing conception of reading. The literary poetics of "cultural poetics," in other words, is New Critical. Are cultures (or works of art) this unified? Is every point or practice in a culture really a microcosm of the whole? Are certain moments or practices privileged, and if so, how do we account for this? These are questions that arise naturally from new historical practice, but that are not normally addressed in it.

I am afraid that the propagandists for "new historicism"—much more than the major practitioners—have promulgated a certain amount of cant. There is a great deal of talk around about literature doing "cultural work." I find this notion extremely intriguing and appealing. I am sure that there is some sense in which it is true. What I have not seen is any clear account of what this "cultural work" is supposed to be, either in general or in relation to specific cases. Without this sort of specification, the term remains mere cant, an intellectual uncashed check, a flag. If the purpose of "according literature real power"[4] is merely to raise the stock of literature and literary critics, I am deeply suspicious of this claim, or at least of how it is being deployed.

Perhaps the most important thing to say about the "new historicism" is that it is not a method or a theory but a set of particular practices. The idea of praxis is central to it, and the demand that is constantly put on it to theorize itself and its

3. "Art as a Cultural System," *MLN* 91 (1976): 1475.
4. See Jean Howard in *English Literary Renaissance* 16 (1986): 25.

relation to other practices is a bogus one, a conception of what a critical movement is that is based on the model of deconstruction. Deconstruction was theorized into being; "new historicism" was not. I am afraid that new historicism at the moment is in danger of being theorized out of existence, or of existing only in theory. What seems important to me is not that "new historicism" theorize its practice, or define itself clearly against its "competitors," but that the people who do it get on with their practice. It is the actual work of the new historicists—not their statements about their work—that has, rightfully, intrigued us all.

James G. Turner

Rather than trying to define "new historicism" or arguing for and against it, we should ask what are the conditions that make this evocation of historical specificity so exciting? Why should it seem like a movement, a rediscovery? The brilliance of the writing, the resonance of the anecdotes, the ingenious stage-lighting of neglected cultural artifacts, the sheer intellectual curiosity and delight in research—these are qualities shared by the best literary "new historicists" and the most interesting new social historians, who are clearly doing things (cat-massacres, charivaris, etc.) that strike a chord with us. The excellence of the work alone is not enough to explain the trend toward new historicism, however; it is created by a tumult within the history profession coinciding with an intolerable vacuum within ours. History is turning itself inside out and upside down, investing new value in despicable (or at least subordinate) issues such as magic, theatricality, subjectivity, local semantics, rituals, metaphors, riots, modes of reading—issues closer to traditional "literary" concerns. Meanwhile literary theory is turning into a hermetic and airless orthodoxy. Some "deconstructionists," like de Man, may have had good reasons for attacking the appeal to evidence from the past, but their disciples transform evasiveness into dogmatic assertions that their own theory should forbid them to make: "The moment 'history' is recognized as 'discourse-specific,' as having no location outside language, i.e. as neither past nor present nor even the presence of a past, but as a *myth* of presence, a *mediation,* it ceases to be a reliable *ground* for literary criticism." In such an arid landscape, the hungry sheep look up to different pastors.

It is now possible to imagine a nonreductive fusion of the disciplines of literary history and "real" history, as they group together into a common front against non-evidential (e.g., psychoanalytic) and anti-evidential (e.g., deconstructive) doctrines. Such a fusion can only happen, however, if literary studies borrow the evidential skills that are still a necessary (though one hopes not a sufficient) condition for membership of the history profession. Historians, on the other hand, have to break out of an expository, literal, monovocal understanding of the text. I stress *professional* criteria because, whatever the theoretical statements of affinity, few historians could get a job in an English Department and few literary critics, however "historicist," could make it past the History Department interview. Like Lilliputians and Blefuscans, historians and literary scholars are close enough to be rivals; each is an amateur in the field the other has chosen as a profession, a fairy at the bottom of the other's garden.

   ✻   ✻   ✻

  One of the underlying dilemmas of literary studies is whether to read texts in isolation, referent only to each other, or whether to read them as *connected* to some external world. The general current of American English studies pulls strongly toward the former, toward etherealization and disconnection, but new historicism reverses this trend. The problem is that most of the hermeneutic assumptions of the latter approach—connectedness—have been (quite rightly) brought into question. In particular, we can no longer assume a simple reflectionist relation between text and reality, and we can no longer assume a simple and inert foreground/background relation between literature and history. "Recontextualization," a recurrent theme of this conference, is not enough; the whole text-context model has to be overhauled and revitalized.

  This I take to be the premise of American new historicism, with its focus on *representations,* powerful public fictions, as the place where art and politics overlap. Hence its concentration on those periods where political life seems more than usually drenched in illusion and spectacle—especially the late Renaissance—and hence too its emergence in another such period, that of the Reagan Administration (circa 1980–1988). New historicism is healthy to the extent that it remains true to its roots in the hermeneutics of suspicion and the politics of opposition. It retains, in muted form, some notion of social criticism and some of the political resistance, the unmasking urge, that distinguished its semiotic ancestors in 1950s France. (Doubtless there is also a trace of 1960s Berkeley radicalism; Marcuse's notion of "repressive tolerance" seems to underlie, though silently, much "New-Historicist" analysis of power.) It is also oppositional to the extent that it resists the depoliticized "Theory" that has run through the power structure of North American universities like cocaine through the entertainment industry or born-again religion through the Republican right. But if the term *new historicism* can designate a heroic resistance movement, it can also point to the danger of being co-opted by the "power" that fascinates it so much. Wlad Godzich suggests, in a recent essay, that an ostensibly critical movement like semiotics actually fits very nicely into the current consumer culture, in which more and more value is invested in the marketing of images and meanings, the manipulative play of signs. Likewise new historicism could run the danger implied in its oxymoronic name: unless it maintains some critical distance from the "new" label, it could feed the current tendency to fetishize up-to-dateness, to flatten and trivialize academic discourse by reducing its own history to a sequence of ready-made and rapidly discarded fashions.

My point here is not to stick up for the old and belabor the new, not to take sides in a pantomime battle between Old Fogeys and Young Turks, but to call into question the whole process of labeling critics old-fashioned or new-fangled, which in practice redefines the academy as a consumer outlet and subordinates its criteria to those of novelty, marketability and product recognition. It would be genuinely innovative, even subversive, to cut the designer labels *off* our discourse.

* * *

The examples I brought up at Dearborn—suppressed in this volume for reasons of space—concern the problem of historicizing sexuality. I suggested that it is, in practice, reduced to the following question: by what means, what device, is sexuality opened up to historicity? The typical answer is to show sex interlaced with "Power"—a generic, all-embracing and all-explaining Power. It may no longer be true that all philosophy is a footnote to Plato, but it is tempting to see all new historicism as a footnote to Hobbes, a postscript to those masterly passages in *Leviathan* and *Humane Nature* where everything is revealed as a sign of Power—secular litanies that transform reductiveness into high art. But this Hobbesian-political model may actually subtract sexuality from history: it may assume the separateness and timelessness of the sexual in the very act of asking what agency breaks into it from the world of power.

* * *

Since the Dearborn conference, panel discussions and polemic articles on new historicism have flourished. It has been attacked (by Edward Pechter) for being too Marxist-determinist and (by James Holstun) for not being Marxist enough. History has not vanished overnight at the fiat of deconstruction, but the danger that deconstruction addressed remains a real one: the naive invocation of History as a kind of magic savior, a self-evident ground of truth or foundation of reference. It is clearly absurd to assume, like my straw theorist, that the "discourse-specific" must necessarily and absolutely exclude any grounding outside language. But can we point to any actual writings that solve this problem, that steer between over-sophisticated solipsism and crude reflectionism, that manage to be satisfyingly empirical yet not blindly empiricist, and that forge genuine bonds between the historian and the literary analyst?

Notes on the Contributors

DIANA BENET teaches at Georgia State University. She is the author of *Secretary of Praise: The Poetic Vocation of George Herbert* and *Something to Love: The Novels of Barbara Pym,* as well as numerous essays.

MEG LOTA BROWN, who recently completed her Ph.D. at the University of California, Berkeley, is Assistant Professor of English at the University of Arizona. She has published on Donne's *Biathanatos* and is a staff writer for *Seventeenth-Century News.* Her current project is a book-length study of Donne.

M. L. DONNELLY is Associate Professor of English at Kansas State University. A contributor to *The Milton Encyclopedia* and *The Spenser Encyclopedia,* he has presented papers on a wide variety of Renaissance figures and topics. He is currently engaged in further work on panegyric modes and political mythology in the seventeenth century and on the cultural and psychological tensions in Milton's early work.

ROBERT C. EVANS, Associate Professor of English at Auburn University at Montgomery, is the author of *Ben Jonson and the Poetics of Patronage.* His articles on Jonson and others have appeared in *Philological Quarterly, English Literary Renaissance, Shakespeare Quarterly, Texas Studies in Literature and Language, Renaissance and Reformation,* and *Renaissance Papers.*

DONALD M. FRIEDMAN is Professor of English at the University of California, Berkeley. He is author of *Marvell's Pastoral Art* and of essays on Shakespeare, Wyatt, Milton, Donne, and Spenser. His current projects include a book on the representation of sense experience in seventeenth-century poetry and a study of Shakespearean "playing."

SIDNEY GOTTLIEB is Associate Professor of English at Sacred Heart University. Founder and editor of the *George Herbert Journal,* he has published on emblem books, Donne, Herbert, Milton, Swift, and Sterne, as well as on a variety of classic and contemporary films. Most recently, he edited the MLA volume *Approaches to Teaching the Metaphysical Poets.*

MARSHALL GROSSMAN teaches English and Comparative Literature at Fordham University (Lincoln Center). His publications include *"Authors to Themselves": Milton and the Revelation of History* and numerous articles on literary criticism and Renaissance literature.

ACHSAH GUIBBORY is a member of the English Department at the University of Illinois at Urbana-Champaign and the author of *The Map of Time: Seventeenth-Century English Literature and Ideas of Pattern in History.* She has published articles in such journals as *Clio, John Donne Journal, Journal of English and Germanic Philology,* and *Philological Quarterly.*

RICHARD HELGERSON is Professor of English at the University of California, Santa Barbara, and author of numerous studies of Renaissance literature, including *The Elizabethan Prodigals* and *Self-Crowned Laureates: Spenser, Jonson, Milton and the Literary System*.

LEAH MARCUS, Professor of English at the University of Texas, is author of numerous essays on seventeenth-century literature. Her books include *Childhood and Cultural Despair, The Politics of Mirth,* and *Puzzling Shakespeare.*

MICHAEL P. PARKER, Associate Professor of English at the United States Naval Academy, has published essays on Carew, Suckling, Waller, and Davenant and is co-author of an architectural guide to Annapolis. He is currently working on a biography of the early twentieth-century writer and painter William Oliver Stevens.

PAUL A. PARRISH is Professor of English at Texas A&M University. He has published frequently on Renaissance and contemporary literature and is the author of *Richard Crashaw.* He serves on the Advisory Board and as a commentary editor of the *The Variorum Edition of the Poetry of John Donne.*

ANNABEL PATTERSON teaches in the English Department and the Graduate Program in Literature at Duke University. Her numerous publications include several essays on Milton and the following books: *Hermogenes and the Renaissance; Marvell and the Civic Crown; Censorship and Interpretation;* and *Pastoral and Ideology: Virgil to Valéry.*

TED-LARRY PEBWORTH is Professor of English at the University of Michigan–Dearborn. He is author of *Owen Felltham;* co-author of *Ben Jonson;* and co-editor of *The Poems of Owen Felltham* and of collections of essays on Herbert, on Jonson and the Sons of Ben, on Donne, and on the seventeenth-century religious lyric. He is author or co-author of numerous critical and bibliographical studies of seventeenth-century literature and serves as a member of the Advisory Board and as a textual editor of *The Variorum Edition of the Poetry of John Donne.*

STELLA P. REVARD is Professor of English at Southern Illinois University, Edwardsville, where she teaches courses in both English literature and Greek. Her book *The War in Heaven: "Paradise Lost" and the Tradition of Satan's Rebellion* received the James Holly Hanford Award of the Milton Society of America. She is currently completing a book on the influence of Pindar on sixteenth- and seventeenth-century English poetry.

MICHAEL C. SCHOENFELDT is Assistant Professor of English at the University of Michigan–Ann Arbor. He has published on Herbert and is currently completing a book entitled *"The Distance of the Meek": George Herbert and His God.*

RICHARD STRIER, Professor of English and the Humanities at the University of Chicago, is the author of *Love Known: Theology and Experience in George Herbert's Poetry* and of essays and reviews on Renaissance poetry and critical theory. He is co-editor of *The Historical Renaissance: New Essays on Tudor and Stuart Literature and Culture* and is currently at work on Shakespeare's critique of decorum.

CLAUDE J. SUMMERS is Professor of English at the University of Michigan–Dearborn. He is author of books on Christopher Marlowe, Christopher Isherwood, and E. M. Forster; co-author of *Ben Jonson;* and co-editor of *The Poems of Owen Felltham* and of collections of essays on Herbert, on Jonson and the Sons of Ben, on Donne, and on the seventeenth-century religious lyric. His essays include studies of Marlowe, Shakespeare, Donne, Herbert, Herrick, Vaughan, Forster, Auden, Isherwood, and others.

JAMES GRANTHAM TURNER, Associate Professor of English at the University of Michigan–Ann Arbor, is author of *The Politics of Landscape: Rural Scenery and Society in English Poetry, 1630–1660* and of *One Flesh: Paradisal Marriage and Sexual Relations in the Age of Milton.*

ROBERT WILTENBURG is Assistant Professor of English at Washington University in St. Louis, where he teaches courses in Renaissance literature and directs the writing program. He has published essays on Shakespeare, Jonson, and Milton.

Index to Works Cited

This index includes only primary works. Lengthy titles are abbreviated, and anonymous works are alphabetized by title.